Tumbuka/Tonga – English
and
English – Tumbuka/Tonga
Dictionary

Compiled by
Wm. Y. Turner
M.A., M.B., CH.B., D.T.M. & H.

(formerly of the Livingstonia Mission, Nyasaland)

With a new foreword
by
Alex B. Chima
B.D., M.A.(London), DIP. ETHN.(Oxon)

CENTRAL AFRICANA LIMITED,
P.O.Box 631,
Blantyre, Malawi
1996

First published 1952 Blantyre, Nyasaland

Reissued 1996 Blantyre, Malawi
in an edition of 1000 copies

© Central Africana Limited 1996

ISBN 99908 14 14 7

Typesetting and reproduction by
Cape Imaging Bureau
Printed by
Hansa Reproprint,
Cape Town, South Africa

New Preface

by Alex B Chima

B. D., M. A. (London), Dip Ethn.(Oxon)

T IS a great pleasure to contribute to the reissue of the Tumbuka/Tonga
English dictionary by way of this foreword. As both bearer and
researcher into the subject of African culture and societies with an
interest going back almost thirty years, I have always welcomed cooperative
work with those involved in the task of promoting culture and language.
Publishers are to my mind among the most important of such people in so far
as they make available to society a tool that is, in Africa, becoming ever more
effective for the task.

Within the same thirty year period I have harboured fears that Tumbuka,
together with many other Malawian languages, was doomed to vanish,
driven into final extinction by a conscious Government policy of nationalising
just one language. While I agree that such a policy may have economic and
other attractions, its rigid enforcement has struck me, with many other
Malawians, as sad, being dangerously monoculturist and ethnocidal. This
could have become a tragic case of induced cultural extinction and the
elimination of a people's right to function in their own language and culture.

To kill a language is indeed to kill a culture because it is language that
allows humans to build cultural models of their world and to transmit them
across generations. Language is what makes culture possible and makes us
unique in Nature. We do well to remember the important anthropological

iii

principle, 'To each his/ her own'. As far back as 500 B.C. Herodotus had the sagacity to say, "If one were to offer men the choice of all the customs in the world they would examine the whole number and end up preferring their own". In other words people function best on their own turf or familiar ground, culturally, epistemologically as well as linguistically.

This question also becomes one of social justice in so far as it tampers with the cultural tapestry that is God's wonderful gift to our society. With lavish generosity God willed to endow our society with a rich assortment of people, each with their own gifts and talents, genius and cultural experience. It therefore gives cause for concern that this society becomes incomplete if each ethnic group fails to add its particular melody to the chorus of Malawian experience.

For twenty-seven years Malawians harboured this grievance without ability to express or verbalise it, under a government that considered itself beyond criticism. Now that the policy has been reversed and opportunity has once again been given to all the constituent peoples of Malawi to function in their own languages, this thanks to a much altered political dispensation, we must welcome and appreciate that development in these years of favour. It is good news, particularly for those who have had no bilingual facility and for whom the discredited policy seemed to hold no consideration whatsoever.

It is now up to each ethnic group to promote their language. To this end gifts and talents, literary and oral must be identified and evoked. Writers, storytellers and other cultural interlocutors should be invited and encouraged to become involved in this work.

The reprinting of this Tumbuka/Tonga/English dictionary certainly signals a desire on the part of the publishers to make a contribution in this regard - and a very important contribution at that, as already pointed out. The publication is reprinted entirely in its original form thus serving both as springboard and stimulus for those interested in fresh analysis of, and critical reflection on, the two languages. It comes as first of the many publications, new as well as reprinted, that the publishers promise to make available to readers in the Tumbuka and Tonga and other languages of Malawi. The tools and resources for developing these languages are thus, *at hand*. It is the publisher's fervent hope, and mine, that these will now be taken *in hand*, starting with this dictionary.

ALEX B CHIMA
Mzuzu, February 1996

Preface to the first edition

THE publication of this vocabulary will, it is hoped, provide a nucleus for further collection and the opportunity for a fuller study of the material presented. It hardly needs to be said that no finality is claimed for the present contribution: indeed the continual emergence of new material, and criticism of that already collected, have been the chief difficulties in the preparation of the manuscript and it became necessary to proceed with collation of the material already in hand and leave additions and emendations to be dealt with later.

It is scarcely to be expected that agreement will be at once attained on all matters of the meaning of words, their spelling, derivation, etc but collaboration in addition, excision or emendation will be welcomed.

In the present form the vocabulary may be useful to beginners, but from the start a critical attitude should be maintained and every opportunity seized for the fuller elucidation of the words which are met with. Owing to the apt use of metaphor by the African, a word is often encountered first in a metonymic sense, and further investigation is needed to discover its real meaning. In the preparation of this collection words have not been accepted as the equivalent of English words or as expressing English ideas, but the effort has been made to trace them back to their natural environment. The method adopted has been to note a word when first heard and later to enquire from other sources as to its real meaning.

Some vernacular words do not admit of translation by any single English word: in such cases a tentative translation is offered; while in others, again, the phrase in which the word was first heard is given, in the hope that the emergence of other uses may give light from a new angle which will provide the clue to the real meaning.

The Tonga column gives the words only when they are different from the Tumbuka - the words being in many cases the same. The Tonga folk, being rapid speakers, 'slur or elide the final syllable of many words e.g. *kulira* becomes *kuliya*, *kukura* becomes *kukuwa*, *kutora* becomes *kuto'* , the accent in the last example remaining on the final syllable, indicating that the terminal *-ra* has been elided. In further inflections of the verb, however, the elided syllable is first restored, then the final *-ra* is again elided so that *kukotera* becomes *kutore'*. It has not been thought necessary to shew these changes in all cases as they quickly become clear to users of chiTonga.

The interesting consonantal variations, such as *tuli, duli, kendero, kendedu*, must be left to have their incidence elucidated at a future date and occasion.

The Tumbuka/Tonga - English section contains such explanations as are here offered of the meaning and the use of the words as listed: the English - Tonga/Tumbuka section makes no pretence of offering a comprehensive vocabulary of English but is merely a list of those meanings or implications which have been appended to the vernacular words as collected. The Tumbuka and the Tonga words are classified under the initial letter of the root (after removal of the detachable prefix). This may present a little difficulty to a beginner but it is really the most convenient plan and, if the experience of the compiler is any guide, it will prove exceedingly interesting and suggestive.

In certain cases, such as *kaboni*, the word is not classified under the initial letter of its root (*kuwona*) because the prefix is not detachable and has become part of the body of the word. This is indicated in the present example in that the concord used with *kaboni* is not *ka-*, but *mu-*, *ʋa-* : it is therefore listed under K. The same practice is followed with a number of words with initial letter M and N, in which there is no change for the plural.

Derivatives frequently differ in form from the root but will usually be found in reasonable alphabetical proximity: where there is a distinct change a reference is given in the appropriate alphabetical order. A cross reference is an indication that fuller detail will be found under the reference. When a word is in brackets it is not a translation of the heading but has some secondary connection and reference must be made to the vernacular section. Where a word is duplicated for emphasis this is not separately noted.

In the English - Tonga/Tumbuka section vernacular equivalents may be given for different connotations of the English word and these should not be used without reference to the Vernacular - English section in order to clarify the real meaning.

Orthography. The ordinary Roman alphabet has proved adequate for the writing of Tumbuka and Tonga: even in the case of the open 'b' for any Tumbuka or Tonga speaking person, the plain 'b' is adequate as the meaning is clear from the context. For the purposes of this dictionary however as the words have to stand by themselves without context, the symbol 'v' is used for the open 'b' sound but in general for writing etc it is suggested the ordinary 'b' should be used.

Ng' is used to denote the sound of 'ng' in singing; but it is hoped that, as in the Sotho group of languages, when the written form of the language has become familiar, the diacritic mark will be dropped.

Numerous questions have had to be decided where spelling has been indeterminate up to the present. One is usually attached to the form of a word first heard, but an attempt has been made to solve difficulties by correlating the various forms of the word in question and by experience gained from Karonga, Livingstonia, Ekwendeni, Loudon and Bandawe. Such decisions are specially difficult in the use of 'l' and 'r' and have sometimes had to be made rather arbitrarily.

The difficult question of the aspirate has been solved on the following lines. Certain combinations of consonants naturally carry a somewhat rough breathing; in such cases, particularly where a definite aspirate does not occur in the root, no indication is given in the spelling and it is left to the pronouncement of the individual. Where a strongly pronounced aspirate gives a differentiation between words having different meanings,this is indicated by the inclusion of the letter 'h'; e.g. *kukumba, kukhumba.* Otherwise it is omitted except where general consent has stereotyped the spelling with 'h' included.

The African is susceptible to new words from other tongues and will readily use such as come naturally to his purpose. A great many Tonga words have obtained currency in chiTumbuka and vice versa. Many words of Ngoni are in use in both languages. Many Henga, Poka and Senga words have also come into general use and these are not differentiated in this collection.

Apparatus. In the Vernacular - English section nouns are followed by the plural prefix which in most cases is sufficient to indicate the class concord; where further information is needed the noun concords are given in brackets or the inflection is given in full. In the English - Vernacular section the noun concords (sing. and plur.) are given - any difficulty as to the plural form etc is to be met by consulting the Vernacular section - in fact this should always be done.

For verbs in the Vernacular - English section the regular inflections are given as replacing the final 'a' e.g. *kukom-a* p. *-wa.* Any further change of stem or irregularity is given in full.

The following contractions are used:-

tr.	transitive	*intr.*	intransitive
p.	passive	*stat.*	stative
caus.	causative	*intens.*	intensive
rev.	reversive	*dir.*	directive or intentional
rec.	reciprocal	*met.*	metaphorical use

Acknowledgement must be made of the valuable assistance given by many helpers – both African and European, who have patiently and eagerly striven to explain and elucidate the meaning and use of words recorded from many fields of activity. In particular grateful recognition is made to Miss G. B. Genner, M.A. for valued typing help and to Rev. W. P. Young O.B.E., M.C., M.A. for the list of birds in the appendix kindly supplied by him.

Wm. Y. Turner

TUMBUKA—TONGA DICTIONARY

A

TUMBUKA	TONGA	ENGLISH
A		vocative particle of address.
AƱA		these (personal concord).
mwAƱI, mi-		good fortune; luck; happiness; blessedness; opportunity: wa mwaʋi, a happy, or blessed, person: nga ndi mwaʋi, by chance; as luck would have it.
AƱO		those (personal concord).
lwAƱO		pa lwaʋo, by themselves; at their (place or home).
	mwADI, (u-)	string game: "cat's cradle".
mWAKA, mi-		year (plur. myaka) : (adv.) long ago.
chAKA, vy-		year: annual sports day.
chAKA, vy-		handle for hoe, axe, &c.
	AKUMBA	perhaps.
chAMBA, vy-		bhang (Cannabis indica).
kwAMBA		to begin, to commence: (tambe or tiyambe): kwamba mwampu— of sudden acute onset of illness: chiyambo, cha, the beginning.
	kwAMBANA	to quarrel.
kwAMBIZGA		(v. tr.) to poison (e.g. meat for a leopard).
mwAMBI, mi-		The Scriptures. (Nyanja).
	chAMBO, vy-	edible fish (in shoals in L. Nyasa).
kwAMBUKA		to cross over; ford a river: jambu-ko, a crossing, a ford: (of disease) to infect, i.e. to cross from one person to another: kwambulizga, to give infection, (also of yawning).
kwAMBURA		to lack, to be without; (kwambura makutu, to be deaf): used as auxiliary to express negation— kwambura kantu, empty: nchambura kuchitika, it hasn't been done: kwambura kuti, unless, except.
kwAMBURA LWAMBO		to protect (a garden) by 'medicine'.

1

TUMBUKA	TONGA	ENGLISH
mwAMPU, (u-)		promptness; quickness; zeal.
	kwAMUKA	to answer.
—ANA		reciprocal suffix to verb (kukomana).
mwANA, ʋANA, (ʋa-)		child—also young of animals.
mwANICHI, ʋ-		little child: also kana, kanichi (tw-), babe, infant: kanayuni, young bird; kanankuku, young fowl: mwana munyake, brother, sister: twana twa mleza, twins (also twana twa muwoli).
wANA, (u-)		infancy, childhood: also wanichi, (u-).
—ANAKAZI		(adj.) female (with prefix appropriate to noun): mwanakazi, ʋ-, woman.
—ANARUMI		(adj.) male (with appropriate prefix): mwanarumi, ʋ-, man.
kANANDA, ʋak-		an only child.
kwANANGA		(v. tr.) to spoil, to destroy: (v. int.) to sin, to err: (noun) kwananga, zakwananga, sin, crime.
mwANANGWA, ʋ-		a free person: wanangwa, (u-), freedom, liberty, grace, favour: chawanangwa, vy-, free gift, present.
mwANASE, ʋ-		neighbour; companion.
mwANASKO, mi-		upper grindstone.
kwANDA		to begin, commence; n. jando, li- beginning.
kwANDANA		to increase, multiply (of family, stock, &c.) caus.—iska, (also used for arithmetical multiplication).
kwANDULA	kwANDUWA	to gain; to profit; to benefit: n. chandulo, vy-, gain; increase; profit: n. wanduzgo, (u-), gain; profit.
kwANDULIRA		to set in order; to explain; to interpret.
kujANDIZGA		to prevent; to hinder. (see jandizga).
chANDI, vy-		a small calabash, with stem for handle, used as a cup, or spoon.
lwANGA, malw-		crate for carrying fowls, &c.
wANGA, (u-)		poison.
kwANGARA		to dance for joy.
lwANGAVYA, malw-		large wide-mouthed pot with neck.

2

TUMBUKA	TONGA	ENGLISH
kwANGUZGA		to avoid because of taboo.
mwANGUZGU, mi-		taboo: (e.g. a menstruating woman must not salt the dendi).
ANI?		interrogative particle, introducing query.
mwANICHI, ʋ-		see mwana.
kwANIKA		to spread out (as clothes, or flour, to dry): kwanula, to gather up again.
	kwANJA	to love: rec. kwanjana.
kwANKA		to catch (as a ball); dir.—ira, to receive a person (or God) with honour; to welcome: kwanka ntura, or kwanka mbaba, game of chuckies.
	mwANO, (u-)	kuchita mwano, to quarrel.
kwANULA		see kwanika.
mwANYA, mi-		gap or cleft (e.g. between two houses, or between teeth when one is missing, or between a pot and its lid); glen; ravine.
APA		here; near at hand.
APO		there; when; where.
chARU, vy-		country; land; the world: mwene-charu, a native (in his own country).
	kwASAMA	to open (the mouth): also kuyasama.
	ASANI	if.
ASI?		interrogative particle, introducing a question expecting the answer yes.
kwATA		to create: to begin a new thing.
mwATI, ʋ-		creator; maker.
mwATI, mi-		jokes; jests; fibs: (kuyowoya myati).
kwAURA mwawu		to yawn; to gape.
mwAVI, mi-		poison used for ordeal (see kuchinga).
chAVU, vy-		the gums (in mouth).
kwAVYA		to pester: malwavyo, trials, temptations.
	AWA	no; not.
mwAWU, mi-		yawn (see kwaura).
mwAYI, mi-		soot.

3

B

TUMBUKA	TONGA	ENGLISH
	BA, (li-)	gruel (for feeding infants or invalids).
	kuBA	to steal.
kuʋA		to be; to exist; to become: kuʋa na, to have: kuʋapo, to be present: kuʋa maso, to be awake: kuʋa pachanya, to be with child; to be pregnant: (noun) kaʋiro, (ka-), nature; habit.
kuBABA		to give birth to young; to beget; to bear: to carry on back: pass.-ika, or -iwa.
mBABA, mi-		the 'ntura' for throwing up at the game of 'kwanka ntura'.
kuʋAʋA		to be bitter; to be painful.
muʋAʋA, mi-		the mahogany tree.
kuBABAFUKA		to be concave; to be hollow.
muʋAʋANI, mi-		tree whose roots and bark are used as medicine for 'sira'.
ʋaBABI, ʋa-		parents (ʋapapi more common).
chiBABIRO, vi-		the womb.
	BAGHA, ma-	a roof.
kuBAGHA		to eructate; to belch out wind.
kuʋAJA		to carve; to plane wood: (noun) mbazi ʋa-, joiner; carpenter.
kuBAKA		to catch, e.g. a fly in the air.
kuʋALA		to shine—as the sun, fire, or a lamp.
mBALI, ʋa-		brother to brother; sister to sister; friend.
uBALI, (u-)		brotherhood; friendship.
chiBALIRO, vi-	chiBALI, vi-	the placenta, or after-birth.
muʋALI, mi-		a tree with red flowers, and cork bark.
chiʋALI, vi-		a palm·with large fronds, the thick central ribs of which are used for rafters, machila poles, doors &c.
chiBAMA, vi-		bread.
kuBAMA		to low (of oxen).
BAMBA, ma-		a wound; a sore.
kuʋAMBA	kuʋAMBISKA	to roast, or dry, over a fire (e.g. clothes, or meat)—hence met. to hunt: to blister: kuʋambiska homwa, to be hot in the fight.

TUMBUKA	TONGA	ENGLISH
chiBAMBARA, vi-		spleen—especially an enlarged spleen.
	kuʋAMBARA	to make a detour (because of danger in the path, or to avoid a hill).
BAMBIRO, (li-)		example.
kuBAMPIKIRA		to add extra: kubampikana, to unite; to press closely together kubampikanya, to join on to; to stick together.
kuBANA		to steal: kubanirizga, to steal openly.
kuʋANA		to nip (as with pincers); to squeeze; to gag; mabano (gha), split bamboos applied, e.g. to the temples, and tightened as a means of torture to extort confession: kubanula mbano, to open, or loosen, the gag: mbano, zi-, blacksmith's 'tongs'.
	chiʋANA, vi-	a trap.
chiʋANDA, vi-		spirit of departed ancestor.
	muʋANDA, va-	slave; servant.
	chiʋANDE, vi-	bread (made from flour, banana &c.).
BANDI, (li-)		tobacco seed (shed).
	kuʋANDIKA	to approach; to draw near.
BANGA, ma-		spot (e.g. on cloth or skin).
	kuʋANGA	to aim at; to strive after.
muʋANGA, mi-		ironwood tree (used for making charcoal).
BANGO, ma-		guitar-like musical instrument.
kuBANGURA		to cry aloud; to roar.
	chiʋANJA, vi-	foundation, or beaten floor of a house.
kuʋANIKA		to notice; to mark; to pay attention to.
liʋANJA, ma-		band (of warriors).
BANO, ma-		gag. (see kuʋana).
kuBANTA		to jump from place to place (a flea); also of seeds scattered by bursting pods; and grains of lupoko germinating: wabantapo, he is limping about—convalescent: kubantiska, to help (one) to limp along, (also kubaska).
kaBANTIRA, (ka-)		the uvula.

Tumbuka	Tonga	English
kuBANTURA		to break away, e.g. a piece of the edge of a pot; to break a chain: pass. kubantuka.
kuBANULA	kuBANUWA	to open. (see kuʋana).
kuBAPA (mwana)		to carry (a child) in a cloth on the back.
kuBAPATIZA		to baptize: pass.—ika: noun ubapatizo, (wa-).
BARA, (li-)		gruel—for infants and invalids.
kuBARA		to beget, or bear, children, or young.
luʋARA, (lwa-)		ʋamuswa luʋara they have broken his skull: (referring to the wound not the skull).
chiʋARAʋARA, vi-		wild cat (spotted like a leopard).
	kuʋARAʋATA	nyoli yakuʋaraʋata, a speckled fowl.
	kuBARAMATIYA	to clasp in arms; to embrace; (as in climbing a tree, clambering into a canoe, &c.).
maʋARASASA, (gha-)		nkuku ya maʋarasasa a speckled fowl (also of dogs and cattle).
	BARAWARA (li-)	a rainless day (during rainy season).
	BARIWARI, ma-	bracken.
chiʋARO, vi-		limb of body. (met. Church member).
kuʋARURA		to split (e.g. wood); to slice.
kuBASKA		to help someone injured, or weak, to limp along. (see kubanta).
kuBATA		to be calm, still (of Lake): noun, bata, (li-).
kuBATA		to stick, as mud thrown on a wall in plastering: kubatika, to stick to; to cling to—with ku or pa.
	kaBATA, tuka-	'cobbler's pegs': seeds (of a weed in gardens) which stick to clothing.
kuBATIKANA na		to adhere to: chibatiko, vi-, a patch.
(li)ʋATA, ma-		duck (domestic).
kuBAULA		to open; to burst through; to break down (a wall): pass.—kubauka, to be pierced.
kuBAULIZGA		to open up; to dig a hole: (met. to explain).
	chiʋAVI, vi-	a caterpillar which causes great irritation if it touches human skin.
	liʋAVU, mali-	the body.

6

TUMBUKA	TONGA	ENGLISH
kuʋAWURA	kuʋAWUWA	to scorch; singe (e.g. feathers of fowl); to cause an eruption— nyama ya sefu yikuʋawura ʋantu. p. kuʋawuka. (kuʋaʋa).
chiʋAWO, vi-		eruption of spots on skin; rash.
kuʋAWULIRA		to burn grass round a village for protection from grass fires.
	kuBAYA	to kill. kubayana, to quarrel, to fight.
chiʋAYA, vi-		cattle kraal (Ngoni).
luʋAZA, malu-		cleared space in front of hut; the 'yard'.
kuʋAZGA		to read.
chiBAZI, vi-		sheath for a knife.
	BE, maʋE	breast; udder.
	maʋE, gha-	small millet; (used for brewing beer).
kuʋEʋEFUKA		to pant (for breath); wa chiʋefu, a hasty, or impatient person.
kuʋEʋERA		to be sharp (pointed); iwe uli kuʋeʋera mlomo, your mouth is too sharp: to squint; jiso likuʋeʋera.
BEFU, li-		panting from exertion; kuchita befu to be breathless; kuchita pa befu to be hasty.
chiʋEGHA, vi-		the shoulder.
	kuʋEJA	to fish with hook (mbeja).
kuBEMA		to snuff (foro). Kubemisa, to give snuff.
kuʋEMBA		to hate. Kuʋembuka, to be worked up into a rage. Chiʋembu, vi-, a plot.
kuʋENA		to uncover (e.g. skin over a jigger in removing it). Kuʋenuka, to go over the top (of a hill). Mwana waʋenuka wiske, the son is taller than his father. Chisoti ʋenu, hat blew off.
kuʋENDA		to bow down and keep still (as in stalking game), met. of one seeking an accusation.
kuBENDAMA		to bow down or bend sideways as in hiding behind something. Kubendamira, to hide behind (a person or a thing). Wakabendamako pa Y. he hid behind Y.
uBENDE, (wa)		ku ubende, in private; in secret.

7

TUMBUKA	TONGA	ENGLISH
kuBENDERA	kuBENDE	int. to be curved, bent, crooked. tr. kubendezga, to bend. ubendezi, ma-, iniquity.
kuBENEKERA		to turn (basket &c.) upside down so as to cover anything. chibenekerero, vi- a cover.
kuBENEKURA		to uncover; to turn right side up.
BENGA, ʋa-		small squirrel-like animal—grey, with darker rings, long furry tail; eats white ants.
kuʋENKA-ʋENKA		to roam about (as beast of prey hunting).
BEPHE, ʋa-		an imbecile.
	chiʋERA, vi-	plantation (of cassava &c.).
	kuʋERAMA	to bow down as in dodging a missile: also of a bird diving in flight.
BERE, maʋERE		breast; udder. Wakatufya maʋere— of a girl approaching puberty. Mwana wa uʋere, the first-born child.
kuʋEREʋETA		to babble. n. viʋereʋesi, delirium (mwanjira viʋereʋesi, he has become delirious).
chiBEREʋEZA, vi-		bead bandeau for head (Ngoni).
uBEREʋEZA, (u-)		folly. (Ngoni).
.kuʋERENGA		to aim gun or arrow; to count; to read. Yumoza watorenge sumu ʋatatu ʋizamʋerenga, (i.e. chorus). (Nyanja).
kuBEREZUKA		to be silly.
kaʋERU-ʋERU, tuka-		swallows.
kuʋETA		to tame or domesticate; to own (cattle or slaves). kuʋeteka to fawn on; to appease in case of fault; to cajole. n. chiʋeto, vi- possessions. chibeta, vi- purse.
kuʋEYA		to ask; entreat; pray; beseech. dir.—erera, to intercede for.
chiʋEYA, vi-		see chiʋegha.
kuʋEZGA		see kuʋenda.
BI !		blackness; darkness; also of clear water.
	luʋI, li-	speed; quickness. as adv. quickly.
kuʋIʋA		to gather up hoed grass and weeds. shake out the earth, and throw away. Kuʋiʋirizga, to gather all together. n. mbiʋi, zi-, hoed grass.

8

TUMBUKA	TONGA	ENGLISH
BIBI, ma-		dung; refuse.
—BIDI		adj. ng'ombe yibidi, a brindled cow.
mBIDU, mi-		leaves of beans, used as dendi.
	kaʋIDU, (ka-)	nature; habit. (kuʋa).
kuBIDWA		to be displeased; resentful; indignant.
kuʋIGHA		to enclose with a fence. n. luʋigho, malu-, fence; stockade.
	BIGHA, ma-	fence or weir across river for fixing fishing creels.
	ʋIGHA	chise ʋigha! basket not quite full!
ʋIGHA-ʋIGHA		half as much again.
	kuBIKA	to cook (boil).
kuʋIKA		to put; place; set. To bury (the dead).
maʋIKA, (gha-)		an omen. mheni wa maʋika a very evil person. Mjira wa maʋika, a very ignorant one. Kujiʋikamo, to be vain, conceited.
kuʋILIKIRA		to crow (cock). Mawoko ghati chiʋilikire, hands are dirty from work.
ʋINA, (li-)		covetousness, envy.
ʋINA-		ʋina-muhamadi, the people of muhamad. &c.
kuʋINDA		to protect, or gain influence over, by use of "medicine". Kuʋinda munda, to prevent theft. Kuʋinda mwanakazi, to prevent adultery. Kuʋinda nyama, to gain success in hunting. Chiʋinda, mu-, ʋa- (also viʋinda, vya, in plur. only,) one who excels. c. wa sumu, a leader in song; c. wa nyama, a successful hunter; c. wa marango, one who knows the law.
chiʋINDI, vi-		the liver. Kuʋa chiʋindi, to be brave mutunge chiʋindi, pluck up courage.
kuʋINDULA		to stir up—e.g. mud in clear water by throwing a stone.
	kuʋINDUKA	to retch.
kuʋINGA		to hunt (as a dog hunts); to chase; to scare away birds. Kuʋinga nyama, to hunt game.
chiʋINGAVULA, vi-		rainbow.
BINGU, ma-		cloud.

9

TUMBUKA	TONGA	ENGLISH
kuʊINIWA		to envy. Chiʊinu, cha, envy; jealousy (ʊina).
kuBINKA		to be black (bi!); to be dirty. caus.—iska.
kuʊINKA		to chase away, or keep away. (kuʊinga).
kuBINYIRA		to hem (cloth).
kuBINYUKA		to stretch (oneself).
kuBIRA		to sink (in water); to bathe; (to be drowned.)
kuʊIRA		int. to boil; to bubble up (as a spring). Kuʊira m'mtima, to be angry; maʊiru-ʊiru ghinu, your boiling rage.
—ʊIRI		two; cha chiʊiri, the second.
chiʊIRI-ʊIRI, vi-		trunk of body.
ʊIRI-ʊIRI-ʊIRI		uteka ʊiri-ʊiri-ʊiri, green grass.
BIRIʊIRI, (li-)		rust; (or verdigris).
luʊIRO, malu-	luʊI, li-	speed; quickness. as adv. (sing. & plur.), quickly, speedily. Kuʊa pa luʊiro, to be in a hurry.
kaʊIRO, (ka-)		nature; habit. (kuʊa).
kuBISA		tr. to hide; int. kubisama, to hide. Kachibisi-bisi, in secret. Vibizi, vi-, sleight of hand.
—ʊISI		adj. new; green; fresh.
luʊISI, (lu-)		milk. (Ngoni).
chiʊIYA, vi-		earthenware pot.
	kaʊIZU-ʊIZU, tu-	small bird (loud-singing).
—ʊO		3rd. pers. pur. poss. pron. waʊo; laʊo; chaʊo &c.
kuBOFYA		to bind the turban cloth on a chief's head at his installation, (to crown).
kuBOKOREKA		to be hollowed out e.g. shallow holes in road). Vibokororo, shallow holes dug for tuli to stand in.
BOMA, (li-)		a walled enclosure; a Govt. station; the Government. (Portuguese).
chiBOMBONI, vi-		large black ants (evil smelling). (Pomboni).
BONDA, ʊa-		babe; infant; little child.
BONDO, ma-		hoof-marks of game; spoor.
	kuBONGO	to shout; cry aloud.

TUMBUKA	TONGA	ENGLISH
BONGORORO, ʋa-	BONGORO, ʋa-	myriapod.
BONGWANI, ma-		young bull. (Ngoni).
	BONGOWONGO, li	fish poison (leaves).
kuBONTORA		to pluck off, (fruit, flowers); p. kubontoka, to fall off, also kumbotoka. (cp. kubantura).
BORI, ʋa-		zebra.
chiBOTELA, vi-		cripple.
kuBOWORA		to break through into a cavity; e.g. foot breaking through into an ant-hill on road.
kuBOWOZGA		to find (by chance); bowo! found!
	BOZA, ma-	lie. (see kunama).
chiBU, vi-		a small basket (for sima).
kuBUCHIZGA		to appear unexpectedly. Mabuchibuchi, suddenly.
kuBUDA		to err; make a mistake.
uBUDI, mau-		error; mistake; fault; sin.
kuBUDUBURA		v. tr. to wreck, (subj. waves). p. kubudubuka, (of the canoe).
BUKA, ma-		cloth.
BUKU, ma-		book.
	BUKUWA, wa	purple cloth.
	BULI, ma-	wheals, (e.g. of mosquito bites).
kuBULIKA		to appear; to be seen; to emerge. Nyalubwe buli! a leopard suddenly appeared.
BULUMUTI, ʋa-		tree lizard.
kuBULUMUTIRA		to be blind; of tool, to be blunt. Wachibulumutira, a blind person (one closed in). Kubulumutizga, to blind; to plaster all over.
	BUMA, ma-	clod, lump of earth.
BUMBA, ma-		flood.
	BUMBA, ma-	boil.
BUMBUZI, zi-		large blue and yellow hornet, which builds large clay nests and deposits its young with a grub for its food, and seals the nest.
BUMBWE, ma-		a company; a crowd of people; flood (cp. bumba).
kuBUMPA		to be blunt (e.g. axe); caus.—iska, to make blunt;—bumpu, adj. blunt.
kuBUMUKA		to rebel.

11

TUMBUKA	TONGA	ENGLISH
kuBUMURA		to knock (e.g. a box; to knock off ants).
BUNDI, ma-		footstep (noise of foot or hoof).
kuBUNDIRA		to enfold, as a mother encloses her child in her bosom with her own cloth for warmth. kujibundirizga, to cover oneself all over with cloth, (e.g. to keep off mosquitoes).
chiBUNGU, vi-		a grub, or caterpillar, which eats the leaves of growing maize.
BUNGWI, ma-		see bumbwe.
kuBUNYURA		to nuzzle, as a calf strikes the udder with its nose—"bunyu mlomo!".
BURAWURA, ʋa-		moth, butterfly.
BURUBUNTU, vi-		scars.
BURUNGA, ma-		a lump, a mass. Mchere wa burunga, coarse salt. (kuwurunga).
kuʋUSA		to rule over; to reign.
BUTO, ma-		a young girl (child).
	kuBUWA	to take (a pot) off the fire, or flour out of the duli.
	BUWA, ma-	the loofah plant. (sponge).
BUWU, ma-		gully. also chibuwu, ʋi-, a large gully.
	kuBUWURA	to moan. mbuwuru, (u-), moaning.
	chiBWAKA, vi-	relish of sweet potato leaves.
	BWALO, ma-	the open space in a village for meeting and talking. (Nyanja).
kuBWANGANDULA		to break down, to overthrow.
BWANGURU, ma-	BWANGATI, ma-	a toy—spinning circular disc on a loop of string.
	kuBWANJUWA	to miss, to be too late for.
kuBWANTIRA		to jump in a crouching position—like a frog.
kuBWANTURA	kuBWANTUWA	to take something lean over, e.g. a tent, letting it lean over.
kuBWANTUKA		to lean over (as a wall), to stoop, crouch. met. to be downcast. (Mk. 10, 22).
kuBWANYA		to beat, pound, crush, (as with pestle in mortar).
chiBWANYU, vi-		molar tooth.
kuBWANYANA		kubwanyana maso ku maso, to meet face to face.
kuBWARANTIKA		to leap in the womb (i.e. the child); quickening.

12

TUMBUKA	TONGA	ENGLISH
kuBWASKA		intensive of kubwanya.
kuBWATA		to bubble up, as water boiling in a pot.
kuBWATALARA		to be flat: as a cushion which has been sat upon. (see kuwatalara).
BWAZA, ma-		skull.
	kuBWEFUWA	to knock (down).
BWEKA		adv. carelessly, purposelessly.
kuBWENGA		to dip (tozi) in the dendi. (bwe!).
kuBWENTA		to bark (like a dog).
kuBWEREKA		to lend, or borrow.
kuBWETURA	kuBWETUWA	to gabble.
BWEZI, ma-		friend. Also mubwezi, ʋa-.
uBWEZI, (u-)		friendship.
chiBWEZI, vi-		betrothed (of man or woman); sweet-heart.
kuBWIBWITUKA		to well up (as water from a spring).
maʋYEʋYE, gha-)		conscience.
kuBYURURIKA		to be striped (as zebra).

C

—CHA—		medial particle denoting continuation; wachali waka, he is still alive.
	—CHA—	as above without kuli: wachachita, he is still doing.
kuCHA		to dawn; to become light. Kwacha, it has dawned; or (after a shower of rain) the rain has stopped, and the clouds have gone. (Met. of the Gospel Day; also of the joy after childbirth, harvest, etc.).
kuCHA		to take pleasure in; to delight in; to favour.
kuCHA		to be ripe.
CHANKURU		chankuru wende chankuru wakhare, whether he goes or stays.
CHANUSI, ʋa-		witch-doctor who smells out the ʋafwiti. (Ngoni ukunuka, to smell). uchanusi, (u-), the process of smelling out.
—CHANYA		above, over; with prefix ku- pa- or mu-, and followed by the same— pachanya pa ng'oma, on top of the drum. Kuwa pachanya, to be with child. Ndiri muchanya kale kuruta, I am ready to go.

TUMBUKA	TONGA	ENGLISH
maCHANYA, (gha-)		the heavens.
kuCHAPA		to wash (clothes).
kuCHAPULA		to trot (as in running with bush-car).
	mCHAPU, mi-	step. michapu yifupi, short steps.
CHARA	CHA	no; not; . In a sentence the verb is preceded by kuti, and followed by chara. Kuti walipo chara, he is not present.
CHATA, va,		creator. (kwata).
	kuCHAYA	to strike. kuchayiwa, to come of age.
CHE!		red. (kuchesama).
	CHE	still. che che waka, it is still (unfinished). (see cha).
uCHEUERE, (u-)		bulrush grain.
kuCHEDWA		to delay; to be late. Caus.—eska, to detain, retard.
kuCHEFYA		see kuchepa.
kuCHEKA		to cut; to saw. (Ngoni euphemism for diarrhoea).
CHEKA, (li-)		euphemism for dysmenorrhoea.
kuCHEKETA		to cut off, trim, pare (finger-nails, edge of thatch &c.).
kuCHEKA-CHEKA		to be busy; hurrying from place to place.
kuCHEKURA		to grow old. n. uchekuru, (u-) age. mchekuru, (mu-), an old person.
CHEMA, (chi-)		odour, smell.
kuCHEMA		to call, invite. p.—eka, to answer, to respond. dir-era. intens. —erezga, to cry aloud; to shout.
CHEMBERE, va-		cockroach.
kuCHEMBERERANA		to grow old together. also kuchemberezgana. (see nchembere).
mCHEMBO, mi-		pit, hole in ground (e.g. lair of animal).
kuCHEMULA		to eat sima without dendi.
mCHENGA, mi-		sand.
CHENJE, va-		cricket (which makes a loud strident sound when rain is near).
mCHENJE, mi-		quiver (for arrows).
kuCHENJERA		to take care; to be wise; crafty; cunning. caus. kuchenjezga, to warn; forbid.
muCHENJEZI, vamu-		cunning person. adj.—chenjezi wise crafty.

14

TUMBUKA	TONGA	ENGLISH
uCHENJEZI, (u-)		cunning; guile.
kamuCHENJEZI, twamu-		crane-fly; "daddy-long-legs".
kuCHENJEREKETA		to be thoroughly well. chenjerekete!
maCHENYA, (gha-)		cracks on soles of feet; chapped hands.
kuCHENYA		to reprove; scold; warn. p.—eka.
kuCHENYUKA		mlomo ukuchenyuka, lips are cracked.
kuCHEPA		to fall short; to fail; to be deficient. caus.—eska (also kuchefya) to diminish; to lessen. (met. to humble).
mCHERE, mi-		salt. (crystals, or ashes of salt plants).
kuCHEREKA		(dendi) to salt the relish (by dripping water through a percolator in which the salt is kept).
kuCHERERA		to rise early. (prob. from kucha). vakachereramo, they are expert because they started early.
kuCHEREUARA		to keep glancing round for danger (kucheva).
kuCHEREZGA		to watch all night; to be sleepless.
maCHERO, (gha-)		morning (dawnings). namachero, in the morning; to-morrow. Sing. also met with—"Kwava nga mbuchero unyake", another day. (also luchero).
kuCHERUKA		to be hot with anger; to boil with rage.
kuCHERUKIRA		to set on (someone) in anger (e.g. to hound him out of the village).
kuCHESA		to weed (a garden).
kuCHESAMA		to be red, scarlet. (tea likuchesama, the tea is strong).
kuCHETA		to taste.
kuCHETAMA		to be quiet, silent: chete! ute chete, keep quiet. caus.—iska, to make quiet.
kuCHEURA		to beckon. n. ucheuzgi, (u-).
	kuCHEWA	to beware. caus.—eska, to warn.
	mCHEYA, (mu-)	ndi mcheya, he is thin, slender.
kuCHEZERA		to work through the day, without resting time.
kuCHEZGA		to visit (esp. a house in one's home village in the evening); to chat with (a friend). (contr. kupempura).

15

TUMBUKA	TONGA	ENGLISH
CHI!		halt! (on seeing a snake).
CHI-		prefix used with noun or adj. to give an adjectival or adverbial meaning. luso lwa chilendo, a strange custom. kuchita chijirijiri, to work with all one's might.
uCHI, (u-)		honey.
chiCHI, vi-		interrogative; what? (also nchichi?)
(m) CHIUINDA, va-		an expert (especially in hunting: kuvinda).
kuCHICHIZGA		to exhort; to urge, to compel (kuchita).
CHIGWERE, va-		hippopotamus.
CHIJITI		mwanakazi wa chijiti, a strong woman, fit for anything, and walking proudly (kujitika).
	maCHIKA, (gha-)	the menstrual period.
CHIKO, va-		a species of snake (poisonous).
mCHIKO, mi-		a beam in the roof of a house.
	twaCHIKONKORO tu-	small red and black birds.
uCHIKOZI, mau-		murder. (Kukoma).
maCHILA, (gha-)		strong canvas hammock for carrying people.
kuCHIMA		to prophesy. (esp. in a trance). (see nchimi).
kuCHIMBIRA		to flee; to run (away). caus. kuchimbizga, to drive away.
CHIMBWE, va-		hyaena. (Those who carry a corpse to the grave are called vachimbwe, and are ceremonially unclean).
kuCHIMWA		to err; do wrong; sin.
kuCHINDA		sexual intercourse. (also kuchindana).
kuCHINDAMA		to be glorious: n. uchindami, (u-) glory. stat.—ika, to glorify. pass. kuchindamikika of (God).
kuCHINDIKA		to praise; to honour (a chief, or some important person). pass. kuchindikika.
kuCHINDIKURA		to shore up (roof, or leaning wall).
	kuCHINDUWA	to lift roof off wallplate, or grain store.
kuCHINGA		to feed (a child) by cupping the hand over the mouth: to shade the eyes with the hand. Kuchinga mwavi, to administer the poison ordeal.

TUMBUKA	TONGA	ENGLISH
muCHINGA, mi-		lopped branches to be burnt, on ground already broken up, as manure. (see ntevere).
	liCHINGA, mali-	fence of lopped branches.
	CHINGANA	although.
kuCHINJA		to circumcise: p.—ika.
kuCHINTA		to stand firm. caus.—iska, to set up firmly. rev.—ura, to pull up (e.g. tent-pegs). (also kujinta).
CHINTURU, va-		a blind person.
CHINUNGU, va-		porcupine.
kuCHINYA		to gather up and tie (one's cloth) firmly (to keep it on).
kuCHINYIRA	kuCHINYIYA	to admonish, e.g. to bind one to secrecy.
kuCHINYINTA		to counsel; to charge. also kuchinyintizga.
CHIPEMBERE, va-		rhinoceros.
CHIPIRI, va-	CHIPI, va-	puff adder.
kaCHIPYOROPYORO, twa-		chicken.
kuCHIRA		to be well; to be healed. Kuchizga, to heal; to cure.
mCHIRA, mi-		tail.
CHIREMBWE, va-		roan antelope.
CHIRI		ku chiri ku—, at the side of; beside.
kuCHIRIFUWA		to startle. kuchirifuka, to start; to jump (e.g. when pricked).
kuCHIRIGHA		to cook (gruel).
kuCHIRIKITA		to tickle.
kuCHIRIKIZGA	kuCHIRIKIRIYA	to set up firmly; to prop. up. rec. —ana, to face in hot discussion; to stand up to one another.
CHIRORO, va-		a man empowered by the chief to use the authority of the chief in the village; a man of note.
	CHIRU DU, va-	love philtre.
kuCHIRUKA		to be startled; kuchiruska, to startle kuchirukizga, to come suddenly upon.
CHISANGA, va		a species of poisonous snake. (khaki colour).
kuCHISKA		to exhort; to urge on in work. (kuchita).

17   B

TUMBUKA	TONGA	ENGLISH
kuCHITA		to do; to make. dir.—ira, to serve. caus. see kuchiska, kuchichizga.
CHITI		deformed; cripple (see chi-ti).
	CHITIPI-CHITIPI	sound of donkey or mule trotting.
CHIUTA, va-		God.
	CHIWA, ma-	breezes blowing off the hills to the Lake.
	mCHIYA, mi-	tail.
mCHIZA, mi-		a staff; a walking-stick.
uCHIZI, (u-)		grace. (kuchira).
	mCHIZI, va-	same as mzichi; brother to sister, and vice versa.
CHIZIRE		lest.
kuCHIZUKA		to shrink; to recoil: (from fear or horror).
—CHOKO		adj. little; small; few; young. adv. kachoko-kachoko, slowly; gently.
kuCHOKONYA		to probe a hole with a stick. (in surgery—to probe a sinus with a probe).
kuCHOKORA		to break up maize in a tuli, and husk it.
kuCHOMBOLA		to reveal a matter; to denounce; to accuse. (opposite of kuvinda).
CHOMENE		very; much; greatly.
CHONA, va-		cat.
kuCHONA		to settle down (e.g. at Harali); lichona, one who has stayed a long time away from home.
kuCHONGA		to mark (e.g. correcting exercises in school).
kuCHONJORA		to bring to light, or reveal, a matter; to put to scorn. Kuchonjokwa, to be put to shame by being found out in a fault after denial; to be implicated in a wrong. kujichonjora, to bring shame on oneself.
kuCHONTA		to stab; to pierce. (also of words piercing the heart in preaching).
CHOPWA, (li-)		the inner bark of a bush used for making string, nets, &c.; the bush itself.
kuCHOVA		kuchova juga, to deal playing cards kuchova njinga, to pedal a cycle.

18

TUMBUKA	TONGA	ENGLISH
CHOWA, ma-		the tuft of hair on tail of ox or eland. fly-switch—such a tail mounted on stick.
kuCHUCHA		to rain in fine mist. (cp. jumi likuwa).
	kuCHUCHA	to leak, as water from a cracked pot.
	kuCHUJUKA	to fade (colour of cloth); to be worn done.
CHULI, va-		frog or toad.
kuCHUMBURA		to water down (thick gruel, to make it thin). Kuchumburuka, to be fluid;—ruska, to make fluid.
	CHUMI, ma-	ten, machumi ghaviri twenty.
kuCHUNKA		to scatter, as game being hunted, or people after a meeting. caus. —iska.
kuCHUPURA		v. int. to disperse, scatter (people, ashes).
kuCHUTUSKA		v. tr. to dismiss (pupils in school, &c.).
	CHUWA, va-	frog or toad.
CHUZU, va-		waterbuck.
chiCHWAPI, vi-		rubbish: things of no value. (met. of men).
kuCHWETA		to chirp; to twitter. (of birds, or infants).

D

kuDAVIRA		to gaze at; to admire.
DADA, va-	aDA, va-	my (our) father. (see uso & wiske).
	kuDA	to pour. Kudamo, to pour into: kudiya, to pour out.
kuDADAMPURA		to draw out in a sticky string (glue, mucus, boiled arrowroot). p. kudadampuka.
	kuDADAUWA	to unravel (e.g. tangled string).
kuDAFYANA		to argue. (as opposite sides in a mrandu).
kuDAGHA		to moan; complain. (as in pain, or illness).
DAKA, (li-)		apathy. Muli kufwa daka, you don't care.
	DAKAMA (li-) MA-TAMA, gha	the cheek (of face).

TUMBUKA	TONGA	ENGLISH
DALI, MATALI		large mushroom. (comes with first rains).
kuDALIKA		to dawdle; procrastinate. (dara).
DAMA		(of water) to be still, clear. Maji ghakudama, still waters.
DAMBO, ma-		plain, flat land by stream.
kuDAMULA		to separate, e.g. a body of men. p. kudamuka, the lifting and dissolving of darkness by the dawn.
	kuDANA	to call. p.—ika, to answer.
chiDANDANI, vi-		handmaid. (Ngoni intandane, fatherless child).
kuDANDAULA		to set forth in order; to explain; to complain.
kuDANGA		to go before in time; to begin by doing something previous to doing something else. Tidange tirye ndipo tiwuke, let us eat first, then we'll start. Udange uchite, do it first; or danga wachita, or chita danga. Pakudanga, at first.
kuDANGIRA		to precede; to go in front; to come first.
DANGALIRA, (li-)		glow (of a fire). (kulangara).
	DANGARA, ʋa-	fishing-net, anchored in lake.
	DANGAZI, ma-	hole (through which light shines—kulangara); met. window.
DANGO, MARANGO		law; commandment.
kuDAPIRA		to defend a case in court; to deny; to make excuses. Dapi ndake, the onus is on him to clear himself (the implication being that he is guilty). Dapi lake kuti lawoneka chara, his defence is not clear.
kuDAPIRIRA		to support someone's defence (advocate). Utorengepo dapi (of someone talking the part of an accused person) you'll be implicated in the matter.
kuDAPIZGA		to clear the accused: kujidapizga, to clear oneself: kudapizgika, to be cleared, or acquitted.
DARA		carelessly.
mDAUKO, mi-		custom; tradition.
DAZGO, (li-)		purpose. (kurata).

TUMBUKA	TONGA	ENGLISH
DAZI, ma-		the sun; day. Madazi ghose, every day; always. Dazi liri uli? what time is it? Dazi lafuma, the sun has risen. Dazi lanjira, the sun has set.
	kuDEUA NKUNI	to fetch firewood (in a bundle).
	kuDEUUWA	to undo the bundle of sticks.
	kuDEUEYEKA	to be loose—of the binding of the bundle.
	kuDEUEYEZGA	to loosen—the binding.
kuDEKA		to settle down quietly; to be quiet, at ease; (e.g. game feeding). Kudekana mandeka mandeka, to take aside privately, (as in teaching a child to pray).
kuDEKANYA		to be absorbed in something. Kudekanya nagho makani, to give close attention.
kuDEMERERA		to stick; to cling (as a gummed label). kudemerezga, to attach.
kuDEMWERA na-		to take pleasure in; to rejoice in. udemwera ukuru, great delight.
DENDI, (li-)		relish (for sima). Tumadendi twa nkhuli, delicious relish.
DENGA, ma-		rags; bits of cloth. (Henga; woman's sanitary towel).
kuDENGENDUKA		to faint from shock. Kudengendula, to cause such prostration.
DENGERE, ma-		potsherd; piece of broken pot. "Ndamranda kadengere, chandi vakutunga", broken pots can't be mended, but a gourd can be sewn.
	DENKU, ma-	acne; pimples on face.
	kuDENKUWA	to compress (as anklets confining tendons of leg).
DERA, (li-)	DE	position; Kudera nku?, whereabouts? Ku dera kumaryero at the right side. Mu dera, in the air, in the heavens. Kwiba nako kuli dera, stealing is a different thing.
uDESI, (u-)		ku udesi, in secret; in private. (kudeka).
viDERESI, vi-		dawdling.
chiDERU, vi-		disease of fowls; famine.
	DETE, MATETE	reed—grows in marshy soil; used for mats, building houses &c.

21

Tumbuka	Tonga	English
	kuDEZUWA	"nyifwa yidezuwa vanandi ku chivwano", a death loosens many from faith.
kuDEWERA		to swing (as a pendulum). kandewa, a swing.
DI!		pressing hard; sound of footstep. Kantu kakuti di! a thing that falls with some body—a real thing.
DIUA ma,-		stone trap (for rats &c.).
kuDIDIMIZGA		to press firmly upon. (met, to seal).
	chiDIDIRIZI, vi-	earthquake.
chiDIKA, vi-		a flat level place.
kuDIKA		to cover oneself; to wrap oneself in a blanket. Kudikiska, to cover up e.g. a child.
kuDIKISKA		to pursue; to chase.
kuDIKIZGA		to press downwards; to lower.
	mDIKO, mi-	wooden spirtle—for stirring sima.
mDIMA, (u-)		darkness. (also mdimwa).
DIMBA, ma-		dry season gardens in moist meadow land.
kuDIMBA		to grow well, to thrive (boys and girls in mphara or ntanganene). Kuchita vidimbo, to make pretend (children playing at shop, &c.).
DIMI, ma-		flame (of fire).
kuDINA		to beat, or crush, with stone, &c. To stone. p.—wa, to be tired out, "dead beat".
DINDI, ma-		grave, tomb.
	chiDINDIRI, vi-	plant whose root is used as fish poison.
kuDINDIUARA		to be surfeited (especially with fat food).
kuDINGANYA		to hide behind (someone or something for protection); met. to trust in.
chiDING'INDI, vi-		musical instrument of strings stretched over a gourd—like banjo. (harp).
kuDINGINYIKA		to grumble; to complain.
kuDINYA		to crush, e.g. by beating between stones, or a brick falling on the foot. (kudina).

22

Tumbuka	Tonga	English
kuDIRIMURA		to knock over, e.g. a pile of books, or of bricks, or a wall. p. kudirimuka.
DIRA, va-		small pot for dendi. (kadira).
kuDIRIRA		to borrow; to be in debt; to owe.
	kuDIYA	see kuda.
kuDIZGA		to speak softly: kudizgirana, to tell secrets.
chiDO, vi-		danger: Do! beware. (long, broad o).
kuDOUA		to select (from a number of things); to be spotted.
DOUA, ma-		spot (of leopard or on cloth); freckles.
kuDOUERA		to be captivated by interest in place or occupation.
DOUERAMPUNO, ma-		large fleshy caterpillar; (not eaten)
	DOCHI, MATOCHI	Banana (tree or fruit).
DODOLI		kulauiska dodoli to gaze fixedly, to stare. kudodoliska, to stare.
kuDODOMA		to doubt.
kuDODWA		mazgu ghadodwa ku singu, to be hoarse.
DODA, ma-		old man; an elder. (ngoni).
kuDOKA		to wish for; to covet. also kudokera, to covet. udokezi, u-, covetousness, greed.
—DOKO		adj. small; little; few; young.
chiDOKONI, vi-		folk songs; fables or 'nursery rhymes' sung together in the evening; fibs. Also chidokonyo, vi-.
kuDOKOTA		to be scorched. Sima yadokotera, the sima is scorched. "Yinunka chidokotera", it smells scorched.
	DOKOTU, ma-	young fish.
kuDOMPEKA		to fit in temporarily—as an axe not driven home in handle.
	kuDOMO	to snap or burst; e.g. string, or binding. p. kudomoka.
kuDONDA		to be unwilling, or reluctant, to do something; to linger, or dawdle; to fail in a purpose. Kudonda m'mtima, to be faint-hearted.
	DONDO, (li-)	the bush. Mwana wa mu dondo, a bastard.
	DONDO, ma-	the menses; Kutore dondo, to menstruate.

23

TUMBUKA	TONGA	ENGLISH
DONGO, ma-		earth; mud; clay; soil. Dongo la katondo, red soil. Dongo la nkandasi, deep, black, alluvial soil.
DONGOLOLO, ma-		superstitious taboos.
—DONO		adj. small; little; few; young.
	kuDOROMO	to stretch. Kudoromoka, to be elastic.
kuDORORA		to bore a hole; to perforate; to pierce. Kudoroka, to be perforated.
DOTAROTA, ma-		ashes from burning heap of rubbish.
DOWOKO, ma-		beach; landing-place. (kurowoka).
	DOZI, ma-	lump of sima (as taken in hand); bolus.
DOZO, (li-)		dribbles of saliva from an infant's mouth.
kuDUƲA		to reject (e.g wages; because insufficient).
DUƲIYUƲI, (li-)		spider, and/or its web.
kuDUDUMIZGA		to thunder. (subj. vula or chindindindi).
kuDUKA		to jump; to fly; to flit; to leap.
chiDUKURUKU, vi-		goitre.
	DUKUTIRA, ma-	perspiration; sweat. (with exercise). "Samba tukuta", bathe in sweat.
kuDULA MAKUNGWA		to cast lots. (lit. to cut the bark—long and short pieces—of which one has to be chosen). (also kudumula, kuzunula).
	DULI, ma-	mortar for pounding flour, &c.
kuDUMA		to thunder (vula or chindindindi).
kuDUMBA		to speak; converse (kudumba makani). kudumbira, to speak about; kudumbirana, to discuss. Chidumbirano, conference.
DUMBI, (li-)		tremor (of illness).
mDUMBU, ƲA-		sister to brother; brother to sister.
kuDUMIRA		to rush at; to assault (e.g. attack of impi).
kuDUMULA	kuDUMUWA	to cut off; to decide a case—kudumulana lowa, to finish a case. p. kudumuka or kudumulika.
DUNA, ma-		keloids (skin tumours).
kuDUNDA		to have a grievance against. (with na).

TUMBUKA	TONGA	ENGLISH
DUNGULIRA, (li-)		pyrosis; water-brash.
	DUNGURUNGU, (li-)	heat of mid-day sun.
kuDUPULA		to thrash; to beat; (with a stick).
DURU, (li-)		short grass, with head like lupoko.
	viDYA, vi-	arms; weapons.
kuDYAKA		to tread; to step on; to stamp the foot.
kuDYAMPUKA		to fall (as the stone of a diva when its prop is pulled away).
DYEKA, ma-		coloured spots or stripes on a cloth.
kuDYEREMPURA		to draw out in sticky strings (as glue, mucus, arrowroot pudding) p. kudyerempuka.
kuDYEREWURA		same as above. p. kudyerewuka.
DYONKO!		when grass is heavy with dew.

E

kwEGHA		to thatch. Kwewula to unroof. (kweghula).
kwEGHAMA		to lean. dir.—ira, to lean on.
EHE EHENA!		look! behold!.
—EKA		alone; only. Ndeka, I by myself. Teka, we only.
EKLEZIYA, ma-		the Church. (not the building).
mwEMBE, mi-		beard.
lwEMBE, malw-		razor.
kwENDA		to walk; to travel; met. to be alive; to be well. Intens.—eska, (tr. &c. int.) to hurry. Kwenderana na, to be friendly with.
kwENDENDEKA		to go about; to wander about.
mENDERO (gha-)		behaviour; character; life; walk; ways.
wENDEZGANI (u-)		fellowship.
—ENE		real; true; the same; self. Ine ndamwene, I myself; imwe mwavene, you yourselves. &c. Taveneise, we who.
		n. wene na wene (u-) true kin; fellowship.
		adj. Mkristu mwene-mwene, a true Christian. kantu ka kalimo kenekene, a thing of real value.
		adv. kwene-kwene, really; truly. Penepano, at this very spot. Makora ghene, very nicely, gently.
		conj. mwene, in that; when. Na kwenenako, also; moreover.

TUMBUKA	TONGA	ENGLISH
—ENECHO	—ENEKO	real; self. Uanarumi uenecho, real men. n. mwenecho, uenecho, owner; possessor; himself. (often 'the Chief').
chENE, vy-		the forehead.
kwENERA	kwENERE	to be fitting; to suit; ought; to be worthy; to be bound (to do). Wakwenera kwiza, he who is to come. Wakwenera kulangika, he deserves to be punished. "Viri mu kwenera", these (things) are privileged (e.g. for the chief only). Mba kwenera, they are people of privilege (e.g. sons of the Chief).
kwENGA		to melt; kwenga tali, to smelt iron ore: kwenga mafuta, to boil down oil seed for oil. Kwengura, to skim (cream from milk, oil from water, &c.). p. kwengeka and kwengetuka.
kwENJAMA		to float.
chENJE, vy-		torch.
kwENJERWA		to be concerned; to be anxious. dir.—era, to take thought for; to care for.
kwERA		to winnow (e.g. lupoko) (by pouring it from a basket in a wind so that the chaff is blown away).
mwERA, (u-)		the East (or South-east); east wind.
lwERE, malwere		gossip; secrets; mockery.
mwERE, mi-		woman's sanitary towel.
kwERURA		to mock; to deride (e.g. a deformed person). to blaspheme. Here! Here!, railing cry in chorus.
	kwERUKA	to be worn away. Skapato yeruka, the shoe has worn thin. (kweruka).
kwERUZGA		to judge. Mweruzgi, ueruzgi, a judge.
chERUZGO, vy-		judgement. Also chiyeruzgo, vi-, and cheruzgiro, vy-, parable; image.
	kwESA	to try; to taste; to copy.
kwEURA		to take thatch off; to unroof a building. (rev. of kwegha).
EWE! EMWE!		you! my friends! (form of address to those with whom one is familiar).
chEYA, vy-		human hair (of body and limbs).

TUMBUKA	TONGA	ENGLISH
chEYU, vy-		brush; broom. (fibrous root of a rock lily growing on rocky hills).
mwEZA, mi-		current (in river or lake).
mwEZI, mi-		moon; month.
wEZI, (u-)		grace; kindness.

F

FIGHA, ma-		vikura &c. used as stands for pots on the fire. (suggested by native builders for 'foundation').
	FIGHA, ma-	clots of blood.
kuFIGHIRIRA		to support (as pillars of house); to prop (as mafigha prop a pot on fire).
kuFIKA		to arrive; to come to; to reach. Kufiska, to complete; to finish; to perfect. kufikira kuno ku lero, until to-day. nkufiska nkanira, I assert. ndafikapo, I am sure, I am certain. kupataula fikepo, to set forth completely.
	kuFIKINYA	to pick the nose.
kuFINGA		to threaten. rec.—ana.
luFINGO, malu-		a threat.
chiFINGA, vi-		a bundle (esp. of firewood).
	FINGIZA, va-	Scavenger beetle.
kuFINYA		to squeeze.
—FINYI		adj. narrow.
kuFINYINKIRIRA		to shrink; to contract; to shrivel up.
kuFINYISKA		to press; intens. kufinyirizga. rec. kufinyirizgana, to crowd together as in pressing through a doorway.
—FIPA		adj. black; dark.
kuFIPA		to be black; to be dark. Kufipa mtima, to be afraid; to be sorry; to despond.
kuFIPIRWA		to be dirty (blackened).
uFIRA, ma-		pus; discharge.
maFITA, (gha-)		a well-known place; (home).
	FODIA, (mu- or li-)	tobacco or snuff.
FOLIRO, va-		flute.
kuFOMA		to sweat.
FORO, (li-)		tobacco or snuff (Ngoni).
kuFOTA		to wither; to fade; to decay.

27

TUMBUKA	TONGA	ENGLISH
kuFOTOPOKA		to slip out (as a banana slips out of skin).
chiFU, vi-		the stomach. (also rufu).
uFU, (u-)		flour.
muFU, va-		captives; strangers; foreigners.
kuFUCHIZGA		to press (gifts) on one; to overdo; to exaggerate. Reka kundifuchizgira vinandi, ndakhumba ivi pera, dont't pile on a lot, this is all I wish. Ùantu fuchi! people coming in crowds.
kuFUFURWA		to be worm-eaten, e.g. a plank by borers—active voice, kufufutura.
FUFUZI, zi-		weevils; borers; grubs (eating plants).
kuFUKA		to make concave, or hollow, as a hoe.
kuFUKULIKA		to be hollow or concave, as a plate or a bowl. Kufukuliska, to cup one's hands, as in receiving a gift.
kuFUKA		to fold together, as in packing up a tent; to wrap closely together, as a bundle of salt; or as a corpse for burial.
kuFUKATIRA		to enfold in the arms; to hug.
luFUKA, malu-		verandah (esp. behind the house).
kuFUKAFUKA		to be busy about something; e.g. housewife preparing for strangers.
FUKO, ma-		tribe; family; people; nation.
FUKO, zi-		snuff-box. (ng'ombe ya fuko, in Ngoni custom the first gift in betrothal).
chiFUKU, vi-		the rainy season (Dec. to Mar.).
FUKUNYIRA, yi-		heat radiated from a fire, or the hearth.
kuFUKUNYURA		to distribute (goods).
kuFUKUTUKA		to be broken up and loose (sandy soil): kufukutura, to make loose.
maFUKUZI, (gha-)		the dust which gathers and smoulders in making fire with sticks. (kupuka).
chiFUKWA, vi-		reason; cause; a charge in court (i.e. the cause of being accused). With cha, because, on behalf of. Pa vifukwa ivi, on these grounds. Chifukwa nchichi? for what reason? why? Often chifukwa by itself means 'why?'.

28

Tumbuka	Tonga	English
kuFULUKA		to be full to overflowing. Kuzurafuru to be full.
muFUMA, mi-		calabash (for oil).
kuFUMA		to go out, or come out; to emerge caus.—iska and kufumya, to take out; to put out; to eject; to drive out; mafumiro gha dazi, sunrise; the East.
kuFUMBA		to ask; to enquire. rec.—ana, to discuss; to consider together.
FUMBO, ma-		question.
kuFUMBATA		to clasp (in hand). (kuvumbata).
	mFUMBI (u-)	mfumbi wa maji, sediment in water.
chiFUMBU, vi-		a hump on the back; hunch-back.
FUMPHA, (yi-)		abundance; plenty (usually of food).
kuFUMPIRA		to be cloudy. Kwafumpira lero, met. of a crowd e.g. at a "Chaka" Mafumpizi, of clouds; darkness.
FUMU, (yi-)		chief; (plur. mafumu). Fumu, Lord (of God). mfumu, ʋa- husband. Ufumu, mau- chiefship; rule; kingdom. Fumukazi, (yi), chieftainess; queen. Fumu, the first of twins, if male. "Fumu za pasi", chief of the viʋanda, (from Bemba "Imfumu sha mipashi").
kuFUMYA		see kufuma.
FUNDA, zi-		source (of stream).
	kuFUNDA	to be hot. caus.—iska, to heat (air, water, etc.). n̩ chifundizi, vi-, heat, warmth.
chiFUNDU, vi-		mercy; loving-kindness. (kufunda m'mtima).
FUNDI, ʋa-		expert; skilled person.
FUNDO, zi-		an idea—when expressed it becomes—a point in argument; an opinion; suggestion; counsel; advice; accepted conclusion.
FUNDO, ma-		knot (in string or wood); knuckle. Fundo la chovyo, a slip knot.
mFUNDUKUTU, (u-)		restlessness; tumult.
kuFUNDUMUKA		to cast skin. (as snake &c.). also kufundurwa and kufundudwa.
kuFUNDUMURA	kuFUNDUMUWA	to flype; to turn inside out.
chiFUNDUDWE, vi-	chiFUNDURWIYA, vi-	a cast. (skin of snake, lizard, &c.).
	kuFUNGA	to fast.

TUMBUKA	TONGA	ENGLISH
kuFUNGIRA		to prepare a body for burial.
FUNGU, (li-)		smell; odour; scent.
	FUNGU, zi-	a wild fruit like a damson.
	FUNGWE, zi-	wild cat (black and white).
kuFUNKA		to emerge; (as mushroom out of the earth, or discharge from the eyes).
kuFUNTA		to be mad.
kuFUNYA		to spit out (mata, sima &c.); kufunyira mata, to spit at.
kuFUNYUKA		to be blunted, e.g. point of a tool when struck on a hard surface.
—FUPI		adj. short. Pafupi pa (or na), near.
kuFUPISKA		to shorten; to abbreviate.
kuFURA		to scrape out—as earth from a hole being dug, or powder from a bottle.
luFURA, malu-		trench dug for posts of a house: foundation).
kuFURA		to work in iron. (as blacksmith, mfuzi, ʋa-).
FURU, ʋa-		tortoise.
kuFURUKA		to be full overflowing; kufurukira, to be cloudy (met. of a crowd, e.g. at a 'chaka').
kaFURUKUTU, twa-		corn on sole of foot.
mFURUKUTU, mi-		tree used for making ngwembe &c.
	FUSI, zi-	maggot.
chiFUSI, vi-		madness. Wa na vifusi, he is mad.
	FUWU, ʋa-	tortoise.
kuFUTA		to pay, e.g. a debt, or a penalty.
kuFUTA		to pulsate; to breathe. (kututa).
maFUTA (gha-)		oil; fat; grease. Mafuta gha mono, castor oil.
FUTI, zi-		gun. Futi ya fataki, muzzle-loader with percussion hammer for firing cap.
kuFUTWA		to be worm-eaten, or weevilly (grain or plank).
	liFUVI, mali-	haze; (usually heat-haze).
FUVU, ma-		dust.
kuFUVYA		to interfere with; to prevent—as thoughts prevent sleep.
kuFUWA		to flay; to skin (an animal): to be hard (of undercooked vegetables).

30

TUMBUKA	TONGA	ENGLISH
chiFUWA, vi-		the chest; the breast: also a cold on the chest; a cough.
chiFUWU, vi-		wild plum.
kuFUZA		to boil over (in cooking); to effervesce.
FUZI (yi-)		bad advice; bad influence; kupanga fuzi, to give bad advice.
mFUZI, va-		blacksmith (kufura).
FWA!		full. Kuzura fwa, to be quite full.
kuFWA		to die. (met. to be worth—muntu wafwanga gora, a man's value was two fathoms of cloth).
	uFWA, (u-)	flour.
chiFWAFWA, vi-		a weakly person; a weakling.
kuFWAMBURA		to scratch (as thorns in the bush).
kuFWANA na		to be equal to; to be like. (kufwa).
FWANTU		open; free. Yowoya fwantu! speak openly.
kuFWANTAMUKA		to slip out of one's grasp; to escape. Ndajitema, chimayi chikafwantamuka, I have cut myself, the knife slipped (from my hand).
	kuFWARAPUKA	to be loosed (e.g. a knot badly tied).
kuFWASA		to be at ease; quiet; untroubled. Zafwasa—of game feeding quietly, unaware of the hunter.
	kuFWATAPUWA	to snatch.
kuFWATURA	kuFWATUWA	to open up a bundle. Fwantu! open!
	chiFWENI	mortal. Livavu la chifweni, the mortal body. Te ndi chifweni, we are mortal. (kufwa).
	kuFWEFWEMBUWA	to tear (as a crocodile tears a body).
muFWERENJE, mi-		furrow (e.g. for irrigation, or between plant beds).
kuFWIFWINTA		to sob (as one in pain or in sorrow).
muFWIRI, mi-		shade (from heat of sun).
kuFWIRIRIRA	kuFWIRIRIYA	to be eager, earnest; to set one's heart upon. Fwiriranipo! work with all your might! (kufwa). Mpa mfwiro, (it is something I like) till death.
	—FYA	adj. new; ready; cooked.
	kuFYA	to be cooked, ready; to be burnt.
	chiFYA, vi-	high grass lands on mountains (burnt spaces).

31

TUMBUKA	TONGA	ENGLISH
kuFYADULIRA		to tread on, to press down.
	kuFYAFYARA	to be crafty, sly. caus.—izga, to slip away a thing slyly.
FYAKANYA, zi-		notch; fork of tree; spaces between fingers, an angle.
kuFYAKANYURA		to walk, lifting the feet high, as in treading through mud.
	kuFYAPUWA	to work hard.
kuFYATIKA		to stick in a notch.
kuFYENYA		to press upon; to squeeze.
	chiFYEFYE, vi-	the thin part of a fish's tail.
	kuFYO	to break off, or across.
kuFYONORA	kuFYONO	to peel. (to retract the foreskin).
kuFYONTA		to lick food off fingers.
kuFYOFYONTA		to kiss.
	kuFYONYA FYONYO	to make an insulting noise with the lips.
kuFYOPORA	kuFYOPO	to rub off (e.g. skin of a blister). met. to tell lies (to avoid censure for a fault). Kufyopoka, to be skinned (e.g. after a burn). Fyopo! a clean sweep; entirely bare.
mFYOROFYONTO, mi-		the handle of a sikwa (which see).
kuFYORONGARA		to be choked, as plant with weeds· caus.—iska, to choke (plant).
kuFYOROWOKA		to escape—especially if one has spoken a mrandu well, and got off.
kuFYOTA		to be disappointed. (mtima wa-fyota).
	kuFYUUARA	to be yellow (or pink?) also kufyuuira. Fyu!
	FYUKU	kufya fyuku, to be excoriated between thighs (with sweat).
kuFYURA		to wipe. Kufyura soni, to remove disgrace.

G

	GA	goza paku Marta ga, gave Marta a bracelet. chisi ga (on taking off spectacles).
kuGAUA, vi-		to divide. dir. kugauira, to divide into portions or shares.
chiGAUA, vi-		a portion; a share; a division.
	maGAUAGAUA (gha)	an infectious disease (probably yaws).

TUMBUKA	TONGA	ENGLISH
	kuGABUKA	to shine.
kuGADABURA		to turn over, or roll over, e.g. a large stone. kugadabuka, to be upset; to be overturned.
kuGADAMA		to lie on the back (supine).
maGADI, (gha-)		clods. Kulima magadi to break up new ground for a garden. (Ngoni).
kuGADIMA		to shine; to glitter. gadi-gadi!
GAGA, (li-)		chaff (of grain, esp. maize).
chiGAMBA		patch, e.g. on cloth.
kuGAMBIKA		to patch.
kuGAMPA		to hoe deeply with cutting stroke so as to cut grass &c. p.—ika. Kugampura, to open up new ground for planting.
	kuGANAMPUWA	to heave away clods of earth, as in digging down an anthill.
kuGANDIRWA		to be dirty, as the roof of a hut with sooty cobwebs hanging from it.
	mGANDO, mi-	a bed of earth heaped up (for planting sweet potatoes &c.).
kuGANGA		to be bold. Chiganga, boldness, courage; rudeness, insolence. (kungangamika).
	kuGANUKA	to lean over (e.g. wall of house).
kuGARA		to ride (e.g. on an ox, or an ass).
GARETA, ma-		a wheeled vehicle (ox wagon, bush car, &c. probably from Portuguese).
GARIMOTO, ma-		motor car.
	GARU, va-	dog.
kuGARUKA		to rebel.
kuGATA nkonto kwa		to turn the back on (someone).
GAWU, ma-		the cleft (space) of a cloven hoof.
	kuGAWUWA	to separate. p. kugawuka.
chiGAWO, vi-		cassava.
kuGAYA		to grind grain with a badly fitting stone which doesn't grind fine flour. Mgayiwa, yi-, the meal so ground. Now refers to whole maize ground in a mill.
kuGAZAMUKA		to call out aloud (in fear).

TUMBUKA	TONGA	ENGLISH

kuGEZA — to wash (oneself). Kugeza maji, to wash with water.

chiGHA, vi- — thigh; hind-leg (of an animal).

kuGHANAGHANA — to think.

GHANOGHANO, ma- — thought; idea.

kuGHANDA — to be thin, lean; to pine away. Ughavu, (u-) leanness.

GHARA — maji ghara-ghara mu maraya, clothes soaking (after plunging into water).

kuGHARAGHANDUKA — to rise up (from sleep, or to speak in a meeting).

kuGHARAGHANJIZGA — to force oneself to get up (e.g. when ill, and get up to do some work).

kuGHUMA — see kuwuma.

kuGIYA — to dance for joy; to exult.

kuGOUA — to bend. p.—eka. To spend some time at a camp (ugoui, mau-).

kuGODA — to overcome; to defeat; to subdue; to control.

mGODI, mi- — ant bear. Also its hole. (Mine).

kuGODOBOKA — to tilt, or heel, over; to fall over. caus. kugodoboska.

chiGODORO, vi- — disease of cattle (staring coat, swelling &c.).

GOGO, va- — grandparent. (used as a term of respect).

muGOGO, mi- — bars for wedging a door (inside hut).

kuGOLERA — to shine (lamp, or flame of fire). (the flame catches—kukora). Ku golezga, to light, to kindle. Golezga nyali-kozga nyali. Nkorezezgo, zi, a thing for lighting, the wick, a taper.

kuGOLONTIKA — to hop.

kuGOMA — to turn up sod with hoe for planting maize.

kuGOMBETARA — to be curved, e.g. ribs.

kuGOMERA — to cross over (the Lake &c.).

kuGOMEZGA — to hope; to trust; to believe; (to promise).

chiGOMEZGO, (chi-) — hope; trust; faith. intens. kugomekezga.

kuGOMORA — to dig down (e.g. an ant-hill); to adze (a log). Mgomora, mi-, adze.

TUMBUKA	TONGA	ENGLISH
kuGOMPORA	kuGOMPO	to be drowsy, sleepy.
kuGONA		to lie down; (to sleep). Kugona pasi, to lie down; kugona tulo, to be asleep. Kugona chitutu, to sleep without fire in the hut.
kuGONEKA		to lay down, e.g. a child. Mgoneko, mi-, a soporific, a potion to cause deep sleep. Ngwa mgoneko, he has a drug to stupefy.
kuGONEREZGA		to oversleep oneself.
	GONASE, ma-	a kind of mushroom (very large).
mGONDA, mi-		a man's lion-cloth—brought between the legs, and hanging back and front from a belt, or string. (not round the waist).
mGONEZI, mi-		times of long ago; former times. (used to denote former generations).
kuGONG'A		to sing aloud (as when hoeing).
	chiGONG'O, vi-	small fish, with a spiky fin on the back.
GONG'ONTA, ʋa-		the woodpecker bird.
kuGONG'ONTA		to knock (e.g. on door). caus. kugong'oska. (cf. kukong'oska, kukungunta).
kuGONGOWA		to be spiritless, listless, dejected, depressed; to despair.
kuGONKA		to peck (of poultry).
kuGONTA		to limp. caus.—iska, to cause to limp.
	GONTO, li-	back of head.
GORA, ma-		eight yards of cloth.
GORIWORI, ma-		slave-stick; fetters; yoke.
chiGORO, (chi-)		selfishness. ngwa chigoro, he is selfish (denying another a share of food).
mGOROBEDI, mi-		beam of roof-ridge of hut, or horizontal beams in forks of a chitantali.
chiGOROʋEZI, vi-		shallow hole in ground for steadying the tuli when pounding.
kuGOROLERA	kuGOLORE	to triumph over; to overcome a difficulty. Mwagorolera maji—of swimming a swollen river.
chiGOROMIRO, vi-		trachea; windpipe; (see m'mizo).
muGORONGA, mi-		channel (e.g. cut by flood water).
mGORORO, mi-		same as mgorobedi.

Tumbuka	Tonga	English
kuGOSKA		to help along a cripple, or maimed person: also to maltreat a prisoner.
kuGOTA		to come to a stop; to arrive at (a place, or a conclusion).
kuGOWOKA		to be loosed: met. to cease from anger. dir.—era, to forgive, to pardon. intens. kugowozga, to loosen.
	GOZA, ma-	ivory bracelet.
kuGUDUBURA		to overturn, e.g. a pot, to empty it.
chiGUDULU, vi-		sacking.
GUGU, ma-		degenerate mapira, self-sewn (not eaten).
kuGULA		to exchange—anything for anything else; to buy or sell. caus.—iska & —izga. rec.—ana, to trade, barter.
kuGULIZGA		to tell lies; to make false pretences; to malinger. dir.—ira, to accuse falsely; to give false witness. n. chigulizgo, vi-, an excuse.
GULI, ʋa-		a dance. Kuvina guli, to dance the guli.
GULINGA, ʋa-		maggots which move by rolling over and over.
	chiGUMBULI, vi-	a broadish fish with black spots (edible).
kuGUMURA		to wash away, or dig away (plaster of house, bank of stream, &c.). p. kugumuka, to be washed away; seme yagumuka, a landslide. n. chigumura, vi-, a flood (which washes away things).
	kuGUMUWA	as above: mkwakwazu kumugumuwa m'liʋavu thorns have scratched his body.
kuGUMUZA		to shell maize from the cob.
kuGUNDA		to knock (reference to noise, e.g. thunder); also the pulling of a fish on a line, the binding of the poles of a house by knocking them while the binding is tightened).
GUNKWE, ʋa-		tree lizard. (Agama atricollis).
	GUNTU, ma-	an open-wove basket used for straining.
chiGUNWE, vi-		thumb, or great toe.

TUMBUKA	TONGA	ENGLISH
kuGUNYA		to hit, but glance off (as a knife in trying to stab).
	kuGUNYUWA	to knock against, jostle. rec. kugunyurana.
	GURU, ma-	a company of men.
kuGURUMURA		to scrub another's back, to wipe off the water. p. kugurumuka, (of the water flowing off). Munkwara wakukurumuka (or wa gurumuro), Eye-wash-covering up some wrong done.
kuGURURA		to launch (canoe). kugururuka, to be down-cast ("Nkongono zamara").
	GURUTU, li-	a dance (of an immoral tendency).
GURWE, ʋa-		a broad, well-beaten path.
	kuGUTA	to be satisfied (with food). "Ndaguta", I am satisfied. Mgutu, (u-), satisfaction. Mgutu ukuru wakuti ngwanji! very great satisfaction.
	chiGUWA, vi-	a stand for a pot (for storing food) in hut (not at the fireplace). A raised plat-form of mud, e.g. part of floor of hut.
kuGUZA		to pull; to draw; to drag.
GWA!		hard; firm.
	kuGWADA	to kneel.
mGWANDARA, mi-		cutlass.
	uGWARA, (u-)	cowardice.
kuGWARAMBURA		to scratch (as a thorn).
	GWARANGWA, ma-	a kind of palm.
kuGWAZA		to pierce (directly in); to stab. Kugwaza lulimi, to interrupt. "Reka ndigwaze lulimi"—"let me break in."
kuGWAZAMBURA		to pierce the skin and tear it (thorn).
chiGWE, vi-		a plaited string (not twisted); a cloth with fringes.
kuGWEUERA		to go aside privately.
kuGWEDERA		to be loose (as horns on an animal's skull after decay).
maGWEDI, (gha-)		fetters (ankle stocks, slave-stick, chains).
kuGWEDURA		to dislocate; to displace. p. kugweduka.

TUMBUKA	TONGA	ENGLISH
kuGWENTA		to absent oneself; to play truant from school: to pretend to go somewhere, and not go; to avoid an accusation by trying to cover up with something else, i.e. to hedge.
	kuGWERERUKA	to be dislocated.
	chiGWEWU, (chi-)	diarrhoea: dysentery.
	GWI!	blocked! "Ndithaʋiya gwi! ndiweko nju!" "I can't move either way."
chiGWININI, (cha-)		stinginess, (reluctance to contribute—mtima wakana).
kuGWINDA		to shorten; to shrink. (also to be stout).
kujiGWINJIRIRA		to hang oneself (suicide). also kujigwinjirizga.
mGWIRIʋINDI, (u-)		a crowd; a mass.
kuGWITIKA		to be deficient; to come short of a mark: to set poles of a house close together.

H

uHAʋI, (u-)		witchcraft (connected with cannibalism). muhaʋi, ʋa-, witch doctor.
HAMBA, ma-		leaf. ʋantu mahamba—innumerable people.
chiHAMI, vi-		deserted site of a village. also mahami.
muHANYA, (u-)		daytime; sunshine; heat of sun; Muhanya uno, to-day: na muhanya, by day.
chiHANYA, vi-		dry season (May to December), especially the HOT months.
kuHARA		to inherit.
maHARA, (gha-)		wisdom; sense (ghanandi, not ghakuru).
luHARI, malu-		young green grass in dambo; pasture.
kuHARURA		to hoe a garden. (first hoeing of weeds from growing maize—ngarura, yi).
HEMA, ma-		tent.
kuHEMBA		to cut. Ndihemberako, cut me off a piece.
HENA!		ehena! look! behold!

TUMBUKA	TONGA	ENGLISH
kuHENERA		to rejoice; to welcome with joy. Henera!
luHENGO, malu-		large flat basket for sifting.
—HENI		adj. bad; evil. n. uheni, (mau-), badness, evil; sin. Viheni, (vi-), sins. kuva muntu muheni, to be pregnant. muheni wa mavika, a very evil person.
	kuHEREWUKA	to be imbecile; to be an idiot.
kuHETA		to slash, or slice off (as with cutlass).
	kuHIHITA	to hum. Mhihi, (u-) hum of conversation at a distance, not properly heard.
kuHIWA		to nourish (with food and care).
HIYA, ma-		cloth. chihiya, vi-, a big cloth, e.g. a curtain for dividing a room. (The Veil of the Tabernacle).
mHLATI, mi-		the lower jaw.
chiHOVE, vi-		crow; raven. (plur. also vachihove).
HOMWA, ma-		arms; weapons (especially a large spear). Kupota homwa, to make war; to fight.
HONA, (li-)		tobacco; snuff.
HONYO, ma-		hump of an ox (cattle). (also met. for hump of a deformed back).
	chaHORE, vya-	crow. (plur. also vachahore).
kuHOYERA		to rail at; to mock.
HUVA, zi-		lightning.
HUNGWA, ma-		feather. (also luhungwa).
uHURWA, (u-)		puberty (male). Muhurwa, va-, adolescent, boy.

I

IAI		no. (Nyanja). Kuti...........iai, negative. Inya iai, a strong affirmative.
kwIBA		to steal.
IVO		they. (3rd. pers. pron. plur.).
ICHI, ICHO		this, that. (chi—concord).
	—IDU	our. (poss. pron. 1st. pers. plur.—with appropriate concord).
	IFWE	we. (1st. pers. pron. plur.).
	—IJA	self; alone (ifwe tija, we alone.)
lwIJI, malw-		door.

39

kwIKHA		to descend; to come, or go, down. caus. kwikiska, to lower.
ILI, ILO		this, that. (li—concord).
kwIMA		to stand. Kwimirira, to stand up. caus. kwimiska, to encourage. stat. kwimika, to cause to stand; to set up. (used for 'ordination' of elders, &c.); (also in a technical sense, to cause conception).
kwIMA		to be greedy, selfish; stingy. wandima, he hasn't offered me any (sima, &c.). Chiuta wandima vula, God has refused me rain. n. mwimi, vimi, selfish person. wimi, (u-), selfishness.
kwIMBA		to sing.
IMWE		you; ye. (2nd. pers. pron. plur.)
INE		I; me. (1st. pers. pron. sing.).
kwINIKA		see kwanika.
—INU		your. (poss. pron. 2nd. pers. plur.—with appropriate concord.).
kwINUKA		to raise the head; to look up; to bend backwards. caus. kwinuska.
INYA		yes. Inya iai, yes-why not? i.e. yes of course.
kwIPA		to cut, gather and bring (e.g. grass in bundles for thatching; or mushrooms).
IPO		there; then; therefore; wherefore
IPWE!		see kupwa.
ISE		we; us. (1st. pers. pron. plur.).
kwITA		to pour out; to throw away (esp. water).
—ITU		our. (poss. pron. 1st. pers. plur.—with appropriate concord).
IVANGELI, la-		the Gospel.
IWE		thou; thee. (2nd. pers. pron. sing.). Ndiwe wamwene we we iwe tikalindanga, it was you yourself we were waiting for.
IYE		he; she; him; her. (3rd. pers. pron. sing.).
IYO		as above: also demonstrative, nkuku iyo.
	wIYU, (u-)	filth.

kwIZA		to come: kwiza na, to bring: n. kiziro, (ka-) maziro, (gha-), comings, e.g. attendance at school &c.
mwIZA, ʋamw-		first of twins if male (Henga): child born after death of father.
lwIZGA, (lu-)		economy; selfishness; stinginess. (kwima).

J

	kuJA	to sit; to stay. Kuja songa, to sit up. Ujazi wa muyaya, everlasting life.
JAMANDA, ma-		large basket with close-fitting one as cover.
JAMBUKO, ma-		crossing; ford (of a river). (see kwambuka).
JANCHA, ma-		a kind of rat: bushy-tailed; in house; not eaten.
kuJANDIZGA		to be too previous; to anticipate; to hinder; to prevent. (combines the meanings of going before and preventing; e.g. to forestall another in speaking) (kwanda).
JANDO, ma-		beginning, commencement. Wambura jando, without beginning (of God). (kwanda).
	JANI, MANI	leaf. Kura pa mani, a mourning custom (lying on leaves).
	JANJA, MANJA	hand; arm.
kuJARA		to shut; to close. intens.—izga, to shut close; to bar (a door). Kujijara thupi, to protect (body) from danger.
chiJARO, vi-		door.
luJARO, malu-		prohibition (rule or law).
JARAMAKUTU, ma-		flying ants (come out at night).
JARAWE, ma-		large rock.
JAVI, ma-		mat (made from palm leaf).
—JE		negative particle, suffix to verb (walije).
—JEDU		innocent. Mwana mujedu, an infant; mujedu, infancy; innocence.
kuJEDUKA		to be pure. (Rev. 22, 1, Clear).
JEKA		Gona pa jeka, lie on your side.

TUMBUKA	TONGA	ENGLISH
JEMBE, maYEMBE		hoe. (also the iron butt end of a spear shaft for sticking in the ground).
kuJENDERA		to take one's own way; to be self-willed. (ji kwenda).
	JEREKA, ʋa-	green centipede.
—JI-		reflexive medial pronoun—wajitimba, he has struck himself.
maJI, (gha-)		water.
luJI, (lu-)		deep water of the Lake.
	luJI, (lu-)	the red discharge after childbirth.
JIGHA, maYIGHA		waves (on Lake &c.). Mayigha gha ndopa, clots of blood.
kuJIKAMA		to kneel (see kukama).
kuJIMA		to dig. intens. kujimizga. (jembe).
	kuJIMPUWA	to uproot. p. kujimpuka. (kujintuwa).
JINO (MINO)	JINO (MINYO),	(li-, gha-) : tooth.
kuJINTA		to set up firmly; to stick firmly in ground. rev.-ura to pull up; to uproot.
muJIRA, ʋa-		an ignorant person. adj.—jira. n. ujira. (u-), ignorance.
chiJIRIJIRI		kuchita chijirijiri, to work with all one's might.
JISO (MASO) (li- gha-)		eye. kuʋa maso, to be awake.
kuJITIKA		to descend; to jog downhill: jiti ! jiti ! the jerking gait of one going down a steep hill. Vula ya chijiti, real rain.
JIUTA		see Chiuta.
˙JIYAWO, maYAWO		see chigawo, cassava.
JO !		stop ! i.e. come to a stop !
JOCHERO, ma-		altar. (place for burning—kocha).
JOMERA, ma-		woven beer cup: adopted for cup in general.
JOSI, ma-		smoke.
kuJOWA		to hide oneself. Ku jowa, in private, secretly.
kuJOWORA	kuJOWO	to throw away; to cast off; to forsake; to neglect. p. kujoworeka.
JUGA, zi-		playing cards; gambling.
JUMI, ma-		dew. Jumi likuwa, it is drizzling.

42

TUMBUKA	TONGA	ENGLISH
kuJUMPA		tr. to pass beyond; to transgress (a law). int. to elapse; to pass (of time).
JUNGU, ma-		pumpkin, or vegetable marrow.
kuJUNGATA		to sit apart (from grief; or fear—as children); to look sad.
kuJURA		to open (rev. of kujara). p. kujuka, kujurika. caus. kujurizga to knock at (a door), (i.e. to cause to open).
JURU, ma-		a platform, e.g. on posts above the fire in a hut.
kuJURUKA		to step up, or spring up.
muJUWA, mi-		sugar-cane; or sweet maize stalks.
kuJUVYA		to err, to transgress: majuvyo, gha, transgressions.
JUZI		before yesterday: mwenejuzi, in the future.
	JWA !	ku maji jwa! cast into the water!
kuJWANTIRA		to hop. (kugolontika more common).

K

KA-		prefixed to imperative of verb, meaning "Go and......" (kuka, to go).
KA, KASI, ASI		interrogative particles introducing a question. (asi presupposes the answer—yes).
	uKA, (u-)	the Penis.
	kuKA	to go. Njani wakapo? Who goes there ?
kuKAƲA		to be slow, delay in doing something.
KAƲALE, ʋa-		roof for nkokwe.
KAƲANDWE, ʋa-		small hawk.
KAƲAƲA, ʋa-		large lizard. (iguana).
KAƲENDE, ʋa-		the lip of an earthenware pot. Zuzga na pa kaʋende wuwo, fill it to the brim.
KAƲERE, ʋa-		beads. (plur. also tukaʋere).
	KABINƳO, ʋa-	a species of cassava (can be eaten raw).
KABONI, ʋa-		a witness; ukaboni, (u-), evidence; testimony; witness. (kuwona).

43

TUMBUKA	TONGA	ENGLISH
	KABU, ʋa-	a fleshy weed; found in the lake, especially after spate in rivers. (It is gathered and burnt, and the ashes used as salt).
KACHERE, ʋa-		a parasite climber on trees. Wakujibatika nga nkachere—a man depending on another.
KACHEƱERE, ʋa-		a small cat-like animal living in holes.
KAFURIFURI, ʋa-		whitlow of finger (blistering the skin).
KAJILANGI, ʋa-		a self-willed, obstinate, person (kulanga).
kuKAKA		to bind; to tie. p.—ika.
mKAKA, mi-		milk.
	kuKA KAMUKA	to retch (or 'press down' in defaecation or in labour of childbirth).
chiKAKAYO, vi-		the front of an animal's skull. (Ngoni).
KALE		already, before, formerly, long ago. mwenekale, afterwards, by and by.
uKALI, mau-		anger, wrath, fierceness. (kukaripa) adj.—kali, fierce.
KALIGU, ʋa-		a string instrument played with a bow. (violin).
KALIKWIKWITI, ʋa-		a harmless snake.
KALIMBA, ʋa-		an instrument of iron keys on a flat board, usually with a gourd below: played with both thumbs.
KALIMO		value. kuʋa na kalimo na......to need, to have use for. Ndiri nacho na kalimo, I need it.
KALINGUMBWA, ʋa-		a banded snake.
KALIRA (mu-)		cow-pox, chicken-pox.
KALIRI-LIRI, ʋa-		cry-baby. (kulira).
KALIZGA, ʋa-		scorpion.
KALULU, ʋa-		rabbit.
KALUVI, tu-		whistle. (kulizga kaluvi).
mKAMA, mi-		a kind of palm. makama, (gha) the fruit.
kuKAMA		to squeeze, e.g. to wring a cloth; to milk a cow. Kujikama pasi, to kneel. lukama (lwa), milk.

TUMBUKA	TONGA	ENGLISH
KAMBA (wa-)		thumba la kamba, food provision for a journey.
	kuKAMBA	to speak, to talk.
KAMBWE, va-		fox.
kuKAMPA		to take a bite out of (as lion from a carcase); to eat greedily.
KAMBAMBI, va-		head-band. (garland).
	KAMPANGA, va-	a species of fish. (small mbuvu).
	KAMPUPUPU, va-	a species of bird. (? hoopoe).
kuKAMUKA		to dry up, (of stream, pot, or the water in them).
mKAMWANA, va-		daughter-in-law.
kuKANA		to refuse, to deny. caus.—izga, to prevent, to hinder, to forbid. kukanirira, to stick to.
KANCHEVERE, va-		a small kind of millet. (Marambo).
kuKANCHIZGA		to push, jostle, force, compel.
kuKANDA		to step; to tramp on. Kanda apa nane ndikandepo, implies agreement; or e.g. affection between husband and wife.
mKANDA, mi-		beads.
chiKANGA (chi-)		courage; forwardness. (chiganga).
	kuKANGA	to spread out (as Christ on the cross).
kuKANGALIZGA		to persist, to set one's mind on. kujikangalizga, to embolden oneself, to dare. chikangalizga, (chi-), bravery.
kuKANGANYA		to doubt.
KANGOTI, va-		earthenware pot with narrow neck.
maKANI, (gha-)		news; report. (an accusation).
	liKANJA, ma-	a nest for a fowl to lay, and hatch eggs, in.
KANJO, ma-		a long robe reaching to feet. (surplice).
kuKANKAMIKA		to hurry, to hasten.
	kuKANKHAVIYA	to be pleased with, to delight in.
KANTA, ma-		husk; covering of maize cob, bark, &c. makanta nchembere, striae gravidarum.
	KANTHENGA, va-	waterspout (on lake).
	KANYUMBO	a kind of grass useful for thatching
	kuKAPA	to empty (a vessel); to bail (a boat): to lap, as a dog drinking.

45

Tumbuka	Tonga	English
KAPALI, υa-		a kind of tree; the wood is white and soft, and is used for making plates, spoons, &c. also a kind of caterpillar used for dendi, which takes its name from the tree which it favours.
	KAPAMBA, (ka-)	sweetbread; (the Pancreas).
KAPITAO, υa-		foreman; overseer. (Portuguese).
KAPUCHI, υa-		grubs which infest maize (die with rain).
KAPUKU, υa-		a kind of bush mouse. (edible).
maKARA (gha-)	maKA (gha-)	charcoal; cinders. kara la moto, a live ember.
maKARANG'ANJO (gha-)		slag from smelting furnace.
mKARA		ndamkara or ndamkarani, I on my part. Iyo mkara, ise takara, imwe mwakara, iυo υakara. Iwe utiti ndiyani wamkarani iwe, who do you say it is (said to one who has been silent).
	kuKARA	to be annoyed.
kuKARAUA		to wash (one's hands). kukaravya, to wash (another person).
	KARABWE, υa-	otter.
muKARAKATI, (wa)		a tree used for making charcoal.
—KARAMBA		adj. aged. υakaramba, old people.
kuKARAMBA		to be old. Nkaramba, zi-, honoured elders. (ambassador).
kuKARAMURA		to be hoarse. p.—muka (pa singo). (compare kukaratuwa).
	KARANDI, υa-	a kind of white ant.
KARANI, ma-		grass tick—infesting animals or men.
	mKARASONGA, mi-	a species of bean (purple).
KARATA, υa-		paper, letter. (plur. sometimes zi-). Probably from the Portuguese.
	kuKARATUWA	to clear the throat (bringing up phlegm).
kuKARIPA		to be angry. caus.—iska, to enrage also (kukarifya). (see—kali).
KARIRORI, υa-		looking-glass.
KARONGA, υa-		chief; prince; king. (Nyanja).
kuKASA		to mix, e.g. flour and water (with hands or a spirtle). Reka kukasa-kasa, don't touch, (to a child fingering things).

46

TUMBUKA	TONGA	ENGLISH
KASANGAZINJE, ʋa-		a wild creeper used to tie round a finger (as medicine for a whitlow).
KASARASARA, ʋa-		stretcher, hammock. Also the ebony tree.
KASI		interrogative at beginning of sentence (but may follow).
uKASI, mau-		cowhage, a creeper bearing a pod with irritating hairs.
KASKEMBE, ʋa-		biting fly. (Tsetse, and other species).
KASU (li-)		unwillingness to part with anything; meanness; stinginess.
	chiKASU, vi-	ginger.
KASUSA, ʋa-		the small bat. (also kasuska).
	KASWENDI	syphilis (includes also other diseases).
—KATA		lazy. ukata, (wa), laziness: mukata, ʋa,- a lazy person.
kuKATA		vula yakata, it has stopped raining: it has cleared.
	chiKATA, vi-	a bundle of grass roughly twisted round, for carrying usipa, &c. or a bundle of leaves for baby's toilet—vikata vya mavi gha ʋana.
	KATAWA, ʋa-	hammer-headed stork.
—KATI		within; in the midst. (with pa—, ku—, mu—).
muKATI, mi-		pot for cooking dendi.
KATIMO, ʋa-		needle.
KATONDO		dongo la katondo, hard red soil.
KATUBWE, ʋa-	KATUMBWE, ʋa-	otter.
KATUKUTU (mu-)		mumps (swelling below the ear).
KATUKUʋALA, ʋa-		a large lizard. (? salamander).
KATUNDU, ʋa-		load; burden.
KATUNGU, ʋa-		whitlow of finger.
	KATUNGURU, ʋa-	the young of vyambo (in shoals in lake).
kuKATURA		to wipe out, e.g. sima, while soft, from a pot, or to lick it off the fingers.
KAUZI, (mu-)		an exanthem shewing a fine papular eruption with catarrh. (Measles).
KAVALO, ʋa-		horse. (prob. from Portuguese).
KAVUʋA, ʋa-		spirit hut. (shrine, altar). Tunyumba twa kavuwa, spirit houses.

47

TUMBUKA	TONGA	ENGLISH
kuKAVUKA		to lack, to need, to want, to be poor. caus. kukavuska. ukavu (u-), poverty. mkavu, ʋa-, a poor man.
KAVURU-VURU-, ʋa-		whirlwind or waterspout.
kuKAWURA		to dig (a ditch).
KAYA, (la, za)		village. (also chikaya, vi-). Ku kaya, at home.
KAYIDI, ma-		prison. mkayidi, ʋa-, prisoner. (probably a corruption of 'guard').
kuKAYIKA		to doubt, to hesitate. Kaya, I don't know.
KAZA, ʋa-		a small grass, whose seed may be eaten in time of famine.
—KAZI		female. Mwanakazi, ʋa- a woman. Chikazi chane, my mother's family.
kuKAZINGA		to roast (as maize on a shard).
KAZUMBI, ʋa-		shrine, altar.
kuKAZURA	kuKAZUWA	to be dirty; to be filthy. Kukazu-zga, to soil, to defile: p. kukazu-zgika.
uKAZUZI (u-)		filth, defilement, abomination. (also as adjective.)
—KE		poss. pron. 3rd. pers. sing. his, her, its—with prefixes wa- la- cha- &c.
	KE !	sound of tearing cloth, &c.
mKEKA, mi-		a sleeping mat (woven of palm fronds).
KENDERO (ka-)	KENDEDU	walk, custom, conduct. (plur. mendero) (see kwenda).
kuKENYA		to file (a groove). (e.g. filing teeth, or threads on a bolt).
	liKEZO, mali-	a wooden spoon.
	KHA !	sound of knocking. (nkhama).
	kuKHABWIYA	to spill over (water from a full pot being· carried). Khabu-khabu! the oscillation of the water in the pot. Mtima khabu, of Peter when Jesus looked on him after his denial.
	KHAKO, ʋa-	black mamba snake.
	KHANDA, ma-	bag woven of palm fronds.
kuKHARA		to sit, to stay, to remain. Khara ukharo, sit up. Khara paweme, good-bye. Wakhara pa singo pera, he is nearly dead.

TUMBUKA	TONGA	ENGLISH
kaKHALIRO, ma-		habits; character.
kuKHARIKA		to set.
kuKHARISKA		to sit down properly; to settle.
kuKHARIRIRA		to continue, to remain.
muKHARIZGI, ʋa-		a lier in wait; a warrior.
kuKHATA		to cut down maize and stack it (on the stalk).
	maKHATI, (gha-)	leprosy.
chiKHAYO-KHAYO, vi-		the noise of lighting. (kusweka kwa leza).
kuKHAZGA		to wait for; to ambush.
chiKHAZI (cha-)		a condition of settled peaceful life.
kuKHAZIKA		to set down; to set firmly (pot on mafigha).
kuKHOMA	kuKHO	to be firm; to be solid; to be thick: to be strong (of a man). Khoma mtima, be brave. Kukhomeska, to strengthen, encourage.
	KHOMO, ma-	door, or doorway.
chiKHOMO, vi-		a firm peg or post, e.g. a tent-peg.
KHONO, ma-		a pit trap.
KHORA, ma-		cattle-kraal.
kuKHORA		to be firm, strong (e.g. a building). caus. kukhozga, to make firm. Ntowa yakhora, the path is overgrown.
kuKHORWA		to have abundance, to be content. caus. kukhorweska.
—KHOVU		pure. Ukhovu, wa, cleanliness.
kuKHOZA		to offer allegiance to a new chief (as on leaving one village to live in another).
kuKHUƲARA		to stumble. caus.—iska. Chikhuʋazgo, vi-a stumbling-block.
kuKHUMBA		to wish, desire, want, be in need of. intens.—iska, to crave.
KHUMBO, ma-		wish, desire, will. Makhumbiro, (gha-) lusts.
KHUMI, maKUMI		ten. Ʋantu khumi, ten people; ʋantu makumi ghaʋiri, twenty people; Cha khumi, a tenth.
kuKHURA		to draw, or pull, out (e.g. an axe or a hoe from the handle; or a tooth). (the axe head may be dislodged by knocking the handle on a stone).

TUMBUKA	TONGA	ENGLISH
	kuKHURURUKIYA	to forgive. pass. kukhururukika.
kuKHUTA		to be full, to be satisfied. caus. kukhuska. mkhuto, (u-), satisfaction.
kuKHUTULA	kuKHUTUWA	to empty (something out of a vessel). kukhutuliya, to empty out of one vessel into another.
KHUTU, maKUTU		ear. Makutu ngachoko, I don't hear. Kudoroka makutu, 'in at one ear and out at the other'.
KHUTUPULIKA (mu)		one who sits silent amid talk.
	KHWA !	finish to the end! Kufika penepo khwa!
kuKHWEMA		to thrash (as in driving cattle); to thrash grain—rice, millet &c.
kuKHWIMA		to be stedfast, resolute. Khwima mtima! courage!
	(kuKIRA)	to descend. Kukizga, to lower. kukizga mtima, to sigh. (Kwika),
—KO		poss. pron. 2nd. pers. sing, thy. (wako, chako, lako &c).
—KO		suffix) a little, rather. Ndachirako, I am rather better.
kuKOƲAMA		to bend, or bow, to be flabby or flaccid; to nod (as a sleepy person trying to sit up); to bow the head. (kugoʋa).
	kuKOƲERA	to sing in responses (e.g. at a dance).
	KOBWE, ʋa-	a creeper bean (long pods with small beans).
	KOUYO, ʋa-	moss (growing on stones in streams).
kuKOCHERA		to gather together, to congregate (as a crowd gathering to see something). Mukukochera na matenda (of patients gathering at hospital).
maKOCHEZI (gha-)		driftwood (on banks of streams after a flood).
KOCHI, ma-		a fibre like tow, got at the lake.
chiKOCHI-KOCHI		a mark, e.g. a knot tied in grass, to lay claim to a site for a garden, &c.
kuKOCHORA		to question a witness with success in getting evidence; (to cross examine): nkocho, zi—, one skilled in questioning: wakochoreka, or wakochokwa, he is convicted.

TUMBUKA	TONGA	ENGLISH
luKOJO (lu-)	liKOJO (li-)	haematuria (Schistosomiasis).
kuKOKA		to drag, to draw (as oxen drag a cart). Also used of gathering maize at harvest.
chiKOKO, vi-		a wild beast.
mKOKO, mi-		big trees felled, lopped, and left lying in the garden. The chief men of a village.
kuKOKOƲARA		to be bent with age.
kuKOKOƲALIKA		to crow (cock). Tambala kokoliko! Cock-crow.
kuKOKOMERA		to be leaning over as a loose post, or the wall of a house about to fall. Kukokomera na tulo, to be falling over with sleep.
kuKOKOMEZGA		to emphasize, to insist.
kuKOKOTORA		to scrape, e.g. remains of sima in a pot (nkokota), or nkhama off surface of water.
kuKOKONYARA		to be bent with age.
chiKOLI, vi-		a pledge. (kukora).
mKOLI, ʋa-		prisoner; hostage.
uKOLI, (u-)		bondage. (also umikori).
miKOLI, (yi-)		veins.
chiKOLO, (vi-)		a cow given as 'bride-price' but returned after it has had one or two calves.
KOMA, ʋa-		small flat basket. koma wakurunga, one with bands round the edge.
kuKOMA		to kill; to murder. pass.—eka. kukomwa, to suffer tribulation (e.g. excessive hunger, thirst or fatigue.) kukomana, to quarrel, to fight.
	KOMAKACHOKA, ʋa	stork.
kuKOMARIRA		to have a good feed in preparation for work, or a journey; to be refreshed. nkomaliro (yi-), the meal (as above).
kuKOMBA		to scrape (the last scraps of sima, or dendi, from a pot. with the index finger). makombo (gha-) the remains—kukomba makombo.
kuKOMBORA	kuKOMBO	to hand over or deliver (as when a chief sets free a new crop for use). (compare Ngoni, isikombisa: the index finger; the chief points with the finger in delivering judgement). kukombora makombo, to hand over a portion of food to children, or servants.

51

TUMBUKA	TONGA	ENGLISH
chiKOMBOLI, vi-		brick mould.
kuKOMORA	kuKOMO	to take the outer bark off a tree (e.g. to get the inner bark for making bark-cloth). met. to refuse food or drink when asked for.
kuKONDA		to please; to take effect. Mazgu gha Chiuta ghakamukonda, the words of God touched him: dazi lakonda, moto wakonda—when the heat is felt: munkwara wakonda, when it is observed to be acting on the disease: sima yakonda, the sima is satisfying: zakonda kwitu, (the rumour) has spread at home.
KONDE, ma-		verandah; the space under the eaves of a hut—outside the wall.
uKONDE, mau-		game-net.
mKONDO, mi-		spear.
chiKONDO, vi-		bond (s). wa vikondo, a prisoner.
kuKONDOUEZGA		to persist.
kuKONDOMWA		to be satisfied.
	KONDOWOLI	cassava flour. sima ya kondowoli, sima made from cassava.
kuKONDWA		to be pleased, glad, happy; to rejoice. caus.—eska. (kukonda).
chiKONGERA, vi-		a stand (often ornamented) for keeping a pot on, with store of food &c.
KONGO, (li-)		part of the female genitals. (the clitoris).
KONGONO, ma-		knee.
kuKONG'ONTA		to knock, or beat. e.g. bark cloth·
kuKONGORA		to be fully developed as full and regular grains on a well-grown maize cob: or a man with full powers and faculties: to be perfect. Mkongorekwa, ʋa-, righteous person.
kuKONGORA		to borrow.
kuKONG'OSKA		to knock, to bang. (kugong'oska).
	KONGWE, ma-	an old person. ukongwe, (u-), old age.
kuKONKA		to moisten; to wet with water, e.g. mud, or ntimpwa.
kuKONKHOMA		to declare; to set forth in order.
kuKONKOSKA		to detail a matter in order. lukonko, (lu-), detail (may be tiresome).

TUMBUKA	TONGA	ENGLISH
kuKONKOMORA		to hatch out of the shell, as a hen hatches chickens. kukonkomoka, to be hatched; met. to explain.
chiKONKONIMBWA, vi-		egg-shell.
maKONO ghano		the present time (also mokono).
mKONO, mi-		forearm; fore-leg. bracelet of wire wound round forearm.
	kuKONONA	to snore. chinkonono, (chi-) snoring.
liKONONGO, ma-		stork.
kuKONORA		to husk, e.g. rice, maize, millet. (also used of retracting the foreskin).
kuKONOZGA		to beckon.
kuKONTORA		to cast up (constant reminder of indebtedness, or inferiority). kukontora wuzga, to taunt one with having been a slave. Kontoro, li-, nagging, reproach.
kuKONYA		to knead, as in making bread: to crush up, as waste paper.
kuKOPA-KOPA		to coax; to persuade. pass. kukopekeka.
kuKOPEKA		(same as above).
kuKOPEZGA		to beckon with the hand.
kuKORA		to take hold of; to seize; to catch. pass.—eka; intens.—eska. caus. kukozga, e.g. to light a lamp (to cause the flame to catch the wick). Ntowa yakozga, the path is open (well-traodden). kukorana ubwezi, to form a friendship. wakatondeka kujikora, he couldn't contain himself.
maKORA		adv. well, properly, gently. makora ghene, very well, very nicely.
luKORI (lu-)		stinginess.
mKORI, uKORI		see koli.
luKORO, malu-		verandah; or stoep.
kuKOROUEKA		(muvwi) to fit an arrow to a bow).
—KOROUERE		old (of clothes &c.).
kuKOROKA		to be satiated (especially with meat) to be satisfied—kukhorwa koroko!
kuKOROKOTA		to scrape out a pot, or snuff out of a snuff-mull: reference to sound of scraping, or e.g. of rats eating ground nuts. nyezi zikukorokotapo pa chironda, flies are feeding on the ulcer.

53

TUMBUKA	TONGA	ENGLISH
viKOROKOTO, vi-		hemp fibre (scraped from sisal leaves).
kuKOROMERA		to be vary dark. mukoromera (wa) great darkness.
kuKOROMOKA		to cry out aloud; to shout.
kuKORORA		to gather (maize); (twisting the cobs off the stalks).
kuKOROROSKA		to interrogate.
chiKORORO, vi-		pipe (for smoking). (also mtete).
kuKOSA		to perist. noun, chikosa, (chi-).
maKOSA, (gha-)		weight (of a living person): ngwa makosa. (uzitu not used of a person).
kuKOSEREZGA		int. to persevere: tr. to force; to compel.
	mKOSANO, ʋa-	son-in-law.
mKOSI, mi-		the neck.
	kuKOSO	to smite (with a club); to kill.
chiKOSOKOSO, vi-		a persistent cough—whooping—cough. also kakoso-koso.
kuKOSOMORA		to cough. chikoso, vi-, a cough.
kuKOTA		to be bowed (e.g. with age).
mKOTA, mi-		medicine.
kuKOTAMA		to bow (from the waist), to bend down.
chiKOTI, vi-		a raw-hide whip. (knout).
kuKOTORA		to cut twigs off a stick; to scrape out, as sima or dendi from a pot: to circumcise.
kuKOVYA		to dip, e.g. a ball of sima into dendi.
	mKOWA, mi-	a rope.
chiKOWA, vi-		skin; belt.
KOZA, ma-		ivory bracelet. (goza).
	kuKOZA	to micturate, to pass water (urine).
	maKOZO, (gha-)	urine.
kuKOZGA nyali		to light a lamp (kukora).
kuKOZGA		to resemble. rec. with na, to be like— wa kukozgana na wiske, he resembles his father. chikozgo, vi-, likeness, resemblance. an image.
chiKOZI, vi-		a murderer. (kukoma).
	kuKOZIYA ba	to prepare gruel.
KU		(kwa before a vowel) prep. to or from, usually denoting motion: kusi ku gome, under the table.

TUMBUKA	TONGA	ENGLISH
—KU—		(medial) 2nd. pers. pron. sing. thou (you).
kuKUƱA		to knock, e.g. with a hammer; kuƲike kuƲike pwanku, knocked to pieces; destruction. kukuƲa mawoko, to clap hands (or kukuƲa nkufi (or mapi)).
kuKUƱIRA,		to applaud. kukuƲirizga, to egg on, to hurry, to encourage.
kuKUƱURA		to knock dust &c. off hands.
mKUƱA, mi-		brass.
mKUƱI, mi-		hiccup.
	kuKUCHUKA	to cast, or moult, hair (weya).
chiKUFI, vi-		the palm of the hand.
	kuKUKA	to encircle, e.g. a hedge, or a crowd of people round a person. Mitambo yikuka kukikuki, the clouds cover the sky.
kuKUKURA		to carry, or sweep, away as rain, of river, sweeps away rubbish. Chikukura nyune, the rains which sweep away the grass seeds.
mKUKWE, mi-		stacks of maize on the stalk heaped together in the garden.
	chiKUKUSA, vi-	a wheal on the body, e.g. from a blow, or a mosquito bite.
	kuKUKUTA	to gnash (the teeth).
KULULU, ma-		hole; pit in the ground.
chiKULUKUTU, vi-		hole in ground, e.g. dug for salt, (a mine).
kuKUMANA		to meet (with na for the object or person met). caus.—iska. Kukumanya, to join. (kukumana na Chiuta, to be pregnant).
kuKUMBA		to dig. ukundikumba wuzga, you dig up my (past) slavery. Kukumba (or kukumbirana) fuko, to seek out ancestry, or genealogy.
kuKUMBIRA		v. tr. to assemble (e.g. soldiers).
chiKUMBA, vi-		skin.
kuKUMBATA		to fold the arms across the breast. (met. denoting sorrow as a mother who has lost her children).
kuKUMBATIRA		to enfold in the arms, e.g. to protect a child from cold.
	KUMBI	interrogative at beginning of sentence.

55

TUMBUKA	TONGA	ENGLISH
chiKUMBI, vi-		a kind of white ant—often in a brick wall.
maKUMBI (gha-)		birth customs: e.g. if a twin birth happens the man leaves the house—it is nyumba ya makumbi; the woman is muntu wa makumbi (unclean).
kuKUMBUKA		to remember. Chinkumbo, vi—, remembrance: kukumbuska to remind; chikumbusko, reminder.
kuKUMPIRA		to oscillate; to shake about, as water being carried in a pot: to spill over.
mKUMWANA, va-		daughter-in-law.
chiKUNDA, vi-		pigeon-loft.
kuKUNGA		to light: kungako njasko, light a light.
kuKUNGA nyumba		to thatch the first row of small bundles of grass round the edge of a roof.
	chiKUNGU, vi-	the finishing bunch of grass on top of a roof.
kuKUNG'UNTA		to shake, v. tr., e.g. to shake a skin to remove dust. To strain—the strainer (kungu) is shaken to hasten percolation.
	kuKUNGUNUKA	to roll off. Vuwa ye pafupi kukungunuka, the clouds will soon roll away.
KUNGWA, ma-		bark (e.g. of a tree). chikungwa, or chikwa, the bark of a large tree used as a basket, or even as canoe. Kudula makungwa, to cast lots (lit. to cut pieces of bark).
KUNI, ma-		a tree, a piece of wood. Firewood, nkhuni, zi.
muKUNKA, mi-		grub (in roots of cabbage, tomatoes &c.
chiKUNKU, vi-		pillow, carved of wood. (cushion).
kuKUNKURA		v. int. to roll over. caus. kukunkuzga, to roll, e.g. a log or a stone. nkunguru, zi—rollers.
KUNO		hither (of place or time).
kuKUNTA		to scrape, to grate, to file: to pluck a fowl. p. —ika, to be frayed. makuntwa, gha- fragments, crumbs. maukasi ghamkunta, cowhage is irritating him,
	maKUNTU, (gha-)	ruins (of a hut vacated after death of its owner).

56

TUMBUKA	TONGA	ENGLISH
kuKUNTIRAPO		to be patient, forbearing, long-suffering. chinkunti, vi-, a patient person. uchinkunti, (u-), patience.
KUNTU, ma-		strainer; sieve.
kuKUNYURA		to pluck (a fowl).
kuKUPIKA		to cover, e.g. to roof a ntamba. Chikupiko, vi-, a helment.
kuKUPIRA	kuKUPIYA	to wink. Kukupizga, to beckon by a wink.
kuKUPURA		to wave, as a flag. p. kukupuka.
KURA		there, yonder (at some distance).
kuKURA		to grow; to increase in size. dir.—ira, to go on growing. makuriro, (gha-), growth. caus. kukuzga, to enlarge, to magnify. kujikuzga, to boast, to be proud.
chiKURA, vi-		small ant-nests of hard clay (in dambo): used as pot-stands at fireplace, and for pointing brick-work.
—KURU		adj. big, large, great. n. ukuru, (u-). mukuru, va-, elder brother or sister (of same sex).
kuKURUMURA		see kugurumura.
kuKURUNGA		to wind, or bind, round and round.
kuKURUNGARA		to harden, as maize roasted over too slow a fire. caus. kukurunga-zga.
	kuKURUNGIYA	to rub (earthenware pots) with a stone in the final hardening an polishing with black lead or red nkhama.
	kuKURUNGUNDA	to rub, or bite, the gums, as an infant biting on a ring to bring teeth through.
chiKURUPATI, vi-		the finishing bunch of grass on top of a house roof (or other orn-ament). (finial).
kuKURURA		to overcome (in argument) by refusing irrelevant matter. p. kukurumika.
kuKURUWA		to spread and smooth mud plaster (on floor or wall).
kuKUSA		to gather together, to heap up. (e.g. in fishing, as the net is drawn to the shore it gathers fish and other things in one heap. Mkwawu nchikusi-kusi, kusora kantu cha). p. kukusika.

TUMBUKA	TONGA	ENGLISH
mKUSA, mi-		rope of twisted bark; cord.
KUSI		below, under; kusi ku gome, under the table. ku sika, lower down (see sika).
kuKUTA		to call out, to cry aloud.
KUTI		conj. that; in order that.
KUTI......chara		negative. Kuti walipo chara, he isn't here.
	mKUTI, mi-	mkuti wa sima, a portion of sima left over.
luKUTU, malu-	liKUTU, mali-	pen, fold, kraal; (roofed especially for sheep and goats, or fowls); also chikutu, vi-. (also refers to the period of seclusion of a woman after childbirth (till the umblilical cord separates)—no man may approach, not even the husband).
	kuKUWA	to grow. kukuska, to cause to grow. kukuskiyako, to add to.
KUWOKO (kwa-)		hand, arm. (plur. mawoko).
chiKUYU, vi-		fig-tree: also mkuyu, mi-. Nkuyu zi-, figs.
kuKUZGA		see kukura.
luKUZI, malu-		bow-string (of hide): reims.
KWA		see ku.
KWA		concord particle for infinitives used as nouns. Ndiko nkwachi? what about it?
chiKWA, vi-		the back of a tortoise (shell): a piece of bark cut from a tree, used as a basket for carrying earth &c., even as a canoe.
wuKWA, (u-)		jealousy (esp. between polygamous wives).
kuKWAUA		to creep, to crawl (as a child does).
muKWAKWA, mi-		a lame, or crippled, person.
uKWAKWA, mau-		lasciviousness.
kuKWAKWARIZGA		to take away slyly; to filch.
chiKWAKURURU, vi-		the cast skin of a snake.
chiKWAKWATA, vi-		sandal (s).
mKWAKWAZU, mi-		a thorny creeper in bush.
luKWAMBA, malu-		belt or cord for fastening the loin-cloth.
	kuKWAMPUWA	to snatch away.

TUMBUKA	TONGA	ENGLISH
kuKWANA		to be adequate for a number of people, or for a purpose. (kuyana).
chiKWANGA (chi-)		dryness. mtima wa chikwanga, a dry heart.
	chiKWANJU, vi-	reaping-hook.
kuKWANTA		to scratch (the body).
KWANYA, ma-		leaves of beans used for dendi. Kuvunga mchere mu kwanya, salt not mixed but left at the bottom—met. the real makani is concealed.
kuKWAPA		to flick away (flies), as cow does with its ears—noise of flapping. nkwapa, the arm-pit. chikwapa, vi-, a defect of the arm—lack of power e.g. to throw a stone.
kuKWAPURA		to snatch away. also kukwampura.
kuKWAPATIRA		to hold (something) in the arm-pit. rec.—ana, to cling together: arm-in-arm.
muKWARA, mi-		game tracks (in bush).
	kuKWARAMUWA	to scratch (as thorns).
kuKWARAPURA		to spring a trap. p. kukwarapuka. chipingo chakwarapuka, the trap has been sprung (without catching anything).
KWARE !		indeed! (expressing surprise); also used to mean perhaps.
kuKWASKA		to touch.
kuKWATA-KWATA		to run from one thing to another, without accomplishing anything.
uKWATI, u-		marriage, wedding.
chiKWATI, vi-		a bundle (of salt &c. wrapped in leaves).
mKWAWU, mi-		large seine net.
	kuKWAYUWA	to eat (cassava) raw.
	kuKWAZUWA	to scratch. mkwakwazu, a thorny creeper.
kuKWEƲA		to inhale; to smoke; to snuff (foro). kukweʋa uta, to draw a bow.
kuKWEƲEKA		to be troubled. kukweʋeska, to cause trouble.
	kuKWECHUWA	to thrash (with a switch).
kuKWENDULA		to pull open the eyelid with a finger.
na KWENENAKO		and moreover.

TUMBUKA	TONGA	ENGLISH
KWENI		but; yet. Ndipo kweni (ndikweni) nevertheless.
mKWENI, va-		son-in-law.
kuKWENTA		to scrape, to file. (kukunta). rec. —ana, to rub against one another, as branches of trees.
luKWEPO, malu-		stripes (with chikoti).
kuKWERA		to climb, to ascend. caus. kukwezga, to raise, to exalt, to promote. Kuvwara vikwezga, to tie up one's cloth for working, or running.
KWERENJE, va-		sparrow.
mKWERI, vam-		baboon.
uKWERU, u-		openness (not hidden): light. pa kweru, openly. (kungweruka).
	chiKWETA, vi-	a plantation (of cassava); a garden.
kuKWETURA		to draw out (as a knife from its sheath).
muKWEVU, mi-		trail, or track, left by something crawling. (kukwava).
kuKWEWUKA		to be valuable. ukwewu, mau-, something valuable; treasure.
kuKWEZGA		to raise. (kukwera).
chiKWI, vi-		a thousand; a great many.
	chiKWIKWI, (chi-)	an impediment in speech; stutter.
	kuKWIKWINA	to rub against—as tree branches rubbing against one another, making a squeaky noise. (chikwikwi).
kuKWININIKA		to grumble or complain.
kuKWINJA		to draw up' taut (e.g. batten of tent rope).
kuKWINYATA		to be bent, or crooked (e.g. of a withered arm or leg). kukwinyatiska, to bend (arm or leg). Mtima ukukwinyata chomene pa icho, to be highly displeased, to disagree. Chisko chakwinyata. face is downcast.
kuKWINYANA		to shrink (of cloth).
kuKWINYIMBUKA		to be disappointed. chimkwinyimbo, (chi-), disappointment.
kuKWINYIRIRA		to be crinkled, drawn together; to frown.
kuKWINYIRIZGA		to sulk.
kuKWIRA		to choke. Yo wakwira mata waryenge vyamampha, who chockes with spittle will eat good things.

60

TUMBUKA	TONGA	ENGLISH
kuKWIYA		to be disappointed; to be angry. n. kwiya, (li-), resentment. kakwiya, (ka-), an objection.
kuKWIZA		to hitch up, or roll up, e.g. sleeves for work, or cloth from legs in crossing a stream.

L

uLA, maula		witchcraft; sorcery. Kuwukwa maula, to practise divination by use of bones &c.
	kuLAUA	to taste. kulaua usipa, to beg for some usipa.
kuLAUIRA		to watch for; to hope for. (cp. kudauira). Kulauiska, to look at; to see. Kulauirira, to gaze at something going on—e.g. a dance.
kuLAKALAKA		to desire greatly; to lust.
	kuLAKWA	to err; to sin. ulakwi (u-), sin.
kuLALISKA		to bid farewell to.
LAMBA, ma-		belt.
	mLAMBA, mi-	a large fish.
	kuLAMBA	to borrow.
kuLAMBA		to do obeisance before (a person), to bow down (really of rolling on the back). dir.—ira, same meaning.
mLAMBA, mi-		old stale beer; dregs of beer (drunk the following day, after cooking with water).
	kuLAMBA	to roam; to wander (see kulambarara).
kuLAMBARARA		to make a detour; to go round a hill, instead of over it; to avoid (fire, or fallen tree).
	kuLAMBURA	to pay, e.g. wages.
	mLAMBAGOMBE, u-,	the milky way (stars).
mLAMU, uamlamu		brother-in-law, sister-in-law.
LAMYA, (li-)		telegram. (general term for telegraph).
kuLANGA		to instruct; to warn; to charge; to rebuke; to forbid; to punish (discipline): to initiate (of "intiation ceremonies"). nchikuru chilanga, the punishment is severe. Dango, marango, law; order. Msungwana wakulangwa, a girl who has heard the moral instructions of the women; an untouched virgin. Kajilangi uaka-, an obstinate, self-willed person.

61

kuLANGULA		to command; to enjoin; to ordain. Langulo, ma-, a decree; an order.
kuLANGA		to split (as wood under the heat of the sun).
kuLANGARA		to allow light to shine through, as a roof with holes, or thin translucent cloth.
mLANGA, mi-		a break in the rains.
chiLANGA-LANGA, cha-	liLANGA, ma-	drought during rainy season. (also refers to glare of the sun).
	kuLANKASA	to wander about.
uLANKASI, mau-		playing unnecessary pranks; naughtiness. mischief: lasciviousness (kulakalaka). (Kulankasika).
kuLAYIRA		to bid farewell. rec.—ana.
	maRAYI (gha-)	farewell instructions (e.g. of one dying). (a will).
kuLAYIZGA		to command. dir.—ira, to charge. Kulayizgana (with na) to promise; n. chilayizgano.
	LE	msana wa le, to-day. (lero).
kuLEƲA		to commit adultery. uleʋe, mau-, adultery. (kuleʋana may mean coitus without an immoral connotation). (Maleʋe, gha-, the female labia majora when elongated—word of Ngoni origin).
mLEƲEZI, mi-		a tree of softish wood useful for planks.
kuLEMA		to be heavy, slow, tired, weary; (to stick to an opinion). Vyalema, (limbs &c.) are heavy—i.e. the speaker is tired. Ngoma zalema, the maize seed has failed to germinate (because of drought). Vula yalema, rain has failed for some days in the rainy season, caus.—iska, to tire. muhanya ukulemiska ʋantu, the heat tires people.
kuLEMERWA		to be burdened.
kuLEMARA		to be deformed or crippled. Chilima, chi-, a cripple. Kulemazga, to cause deformity.
kuLEMBA		to mark: to write. p.—eka. dir.—era, to write names for engagement as workers. mulembi, ʋa-, a scribe. malembo, gha-, marks, The Scriptures.

TUMBUKA	TONGA	ENGLISH
chiLEMBA, vi-		crown.
	mLEMBA, mi-	a kind of tree used for torches.
	kuLEMBE	to seek. intens. kulembeze.
uLEMBI, (u-)		poison for arrow-head.
muLEMBI, mi-		trunk of elephant.
mLEMBERWA, mi-		a swarm of bees.
uLEMU, (u-)		favour; kindness; grace; honour.
—LEMWA		adj. ignorant. ulemwa (u-), ignorance.
kuLENDA		to be viscous, glutinous, slimy. (as birdlime).
kuLENDERA		to hang (as a bat from its perch): kulendera m'kuni m'chanya.
kuLENDEMUKA		to drop off, e.g. bricks falling; to sag, as a branch hanging over a stream.
uLENDO, mau-		a journey. (kwenda). Ulendo wapya, ready to start.
mLENDO, ʋa-		stranger.
kuLENDURA		to draw out in sticky strings e.g. glue, mucus, arrowroot pudding, &c. p. kulenduka.
kuLENGA		to make; to create. Mlengi (mu-), The Creator. Vilengiwa, vi-, created things; the creation. Mlenga-lenga, mi- the heavens; the firmament. Kulengera lusungu, to pity. (Vipyo vyane vyandilenga chitima, my troubles have caused me sorrow. Ndamulengera chitima chifukwa cha vipyo vyake, I am sorry for him because of his troubles). Kulenga (soni) to shame; kulengeska to shame. Lulengo (lu-) a shameful thing.
kuLENGAMA		to be clear, as still water, or the atmosphere. (see mlenga-lenga above).
	muLENJI, mi-	morning. Ndi mlenji, in the morning.
kuLEPURA		to slash across.
kuLERA		to nourish; to feed; to nurse; to rear, or bring up a child. Chileraʋaranda ʋachi-, a rearer of orphans (met. of rain). Charu cha mlere, fertile country.
	mLERE, (u-)	quietness, peace, content.

63

TUMBUKA	TONGA	ENGLISH
	kuLERESKA	to look; to see.
LERO		to-day; the present time. Muhanya wa lero, to-day. Sabata la lero, this week.
	uLESI, mau-	laziness.
	kuLESKA	to wipe.
LEZA, ʋa-		lightning; God. May be used in the sense of Fate—"kasi ukuseka leza?"—to one mocking a lame man.
mLEZA		twana twa mleza, twins.
uLEZI, maLEZI		small millet. (used for making beer).
mLEZI, ʋa-		a nurse (kulera). ulezi (u-), nurture.
mLEZI, mi-		hind leg (of animal: the thigh (of man).
kaLEZU, ka-		the chin.
kuLI		to be. dir. kuliri. Umo waliri, the state in which he is.
chiLIUA, vi-		wattle wall, plastered.
LIBWE, ma-		stone; rock. (plur. also mawe).
kuLIKITA		to beat (with hand or whip); to thrash.
muLIKO, mi-		light; lamp.
LIKO, ma-		dirt, esp. of body. (generally in plural).
LIKOTI, ʋa-		stoat or weasel.
kuLILIMA		to flame (the flickering of flames of fire).
kuLIMA		to hoe; to work. Mupe kulima, work hard—(get a move on). Ndimi zake, the portion hoed by someone. Chilimira a hoeing of a garden by a party (usually with beer).
	chiLIMIRA cha	somba, net fishing in deep water.
mLIMA, mi-		shore of lake; river bank.
muLIMBA, mi-		a truss (of calico).
	kuLIMBA	to be firm; to be strong. Chilimbi, vi-, a strong man. Vilimbi vya kwimba, expert singers. Kuli-mba-limba, to try hard; to strive strenuously.
	kuLIMBIKA	to brace oneself firmly; to hold fast. Limbikani, pateremuka, steady, it's slippery. Also, to be laid up in store—sisi lakulimbika, hair that has grown strong and thick.

TUMBUKA	TONGA	ENGLISH
	kuLIMBANA (na)	to contend; contest; strive; fight. mlimbano (u-), strife.
	uLIMBO (u-)	birdlime. Kulimbika muti, to smear birdlime on tree; kayuni kalimbikika, bird is caught; kayuni kalimbuka, bird has escaped.
luLIMI, malu-		tongue. lilimi lakudapo mche, a flattering tongue.
kaLIMO, tu-		a small piece of work; work. Kuva na kalimo na, to have need of, to have business with. Chiri na kalimo, it is valuable.
mLIMO, mi-		work. (kulima).
	LIMU	adv. completely; very; altogether.
kuLINDA		to wait; to await; to watch; to linger; to tarry. Linda danga, wait a little. Ukandilinde ku nyumba, come and accompany me to the house.
mLINDI, va-		watchman.
chiLINDO, vi-		watch hut (e.g. in garden).
kuLINDIRIRA		to await; to expect; to hope for.
kuLINDIZGA		to await; to expect.
LINGA, ma-		stockade; fence; paling, (refuge).
mLINGA, mi-		blind-worm.
kuLINGA		to peep over; to appear (a small part only seen): to aim: lingu! peeping up! intens.—izga, to peep; to face; to be opposite to.
kuLINGANA (na)		to be like; to be equal to; to agree with. kwakulingana na, according to. caus.—izga, to make equal, level, like.
mLINGI, va-		mlingi-David, the late David; valingi-David na Yobe, the late David and Job.
kuLINGULIRA		to peer.
kuLIPA		to pay. dir.—ira, to pay wages.
maLIPIRO, (gha-)		wages.
kuLIPITIKA		to flow in freely (as oil into a vessel; cattle into kraal; crowd into house; snake entering hole). li-piri-piri-piri.
kuLIPUKA		to leap (as e.g. flames of fire); to start (be startled). Mtima ukalipuka, heart leapt for joy.

65

E

TUMBUKA	TONGA	ENGLISH
kuLIPWITIKA		to be relaxed; to be soft, flabby, pliable; Ute waka lipwiti, let your muscles relax. caus. kulipwitiska.
kuLIRA		to cry; to weep; to mourn: to crow &c. (of animals). caus. kulizga, to make to sound; to ring (bell); to beat (drum) &c.
LIROMWAKA		adv. from long ago (and still continuing).
LISAWA, ma-	LISAWO, ma-	gunshot (for muzzle-loader).
kuLISKA		to feed; to herd; to tend (cattle). (kurya). mliska, ʋa-, herd-boy; (met. Pastor).
	kuLITA	to be supple (as a thin bamboo or board).
LITEMA, ma-		an infant; a babe.
mLIWO, mi-		ankle bells (tied on children's ankles). yikuti, were-were-were.
	kuLIYA	to weep; to cry.
maLO, (gha-)		place.
kuLOUERA		to be drunk. Uloʋevu (u-), drunkenness. Mloʋevu, ʋa-, drunkard. Nkuloʋera kwa ndopa when a wounded animal separates from herd (due to internal haemorrhage).
kuLOLA		to care about (something); to pay attention to (e.g. some task).
kuLOLOTERA		to be languid; to die down (of fire).
mLOMBWA, mi-		a kind of tree (like mahogany).
muLOMO, mi-		mouth.
kuLONGA		to lay up in store—see kuronga.
kuLOSKA		to prophesy; to foretell. Losko, ma-, prophecy. (kulowa).
mLOSKO, mi-		rust (on iron).
kuLOTA		to dream. Loto, ma-, dream.
kuLOWA		to practise witchcraft; to bewitch; to poison food.
LUUA, ma-		flower.
	kuLULUTIYA	to sing praises to. (ululation).
LUMBURWE, ma-		a fibre plant growing wild (used for stringing beads).
muLUNGU, ʋa-		God (Nyanja).
LUSI-LUSI		adv. often.
	LUZI, ma-	inner bark of tree (used for rope).

66

TUMBUKA	TONGA	ENGLISH
LWARARA, ma-		an open space. pa lwarara, openly.
maLWAVYO (gha-)		trials. (kwavya).
	LWENDA, ʋa-	chameleon.
LWIVI, ʋa-		chameleon.
chiLYOKO, (cha)		greed.

M

	aMA	mother (voc. of address).
	kuMA	to stand.
	uMAƲONGO (u-)	enmity. ʋamaʋongo, ʋa- enemies.
MACHEZA, ʋa-		long axe—carried as an ornament, not for work.
MADGHA, (gha-)		cats' cradle (string game).
MAKINA (gha-)		machine (esp. sewing machine) (English).
	MALISECHI	kuʋa malisechi, to be naked.
MAMA, ʋa-		my (our) mother (1st. pers. only). Mama-vyara, ʋa-, mother-in-law.
	chiMAMA (chi-)	stammer; impediment in speech.
luMAMBA, malu-		a broad-leaved grass, with sharp edge, growing in moist places on vipya.
	—MAMPHA	adj. good. Umampha, (u-), goodness. Muntu wamampha, a good man.
kuMAMUKA		to learn by experience.
	—MANA	adj. small, little; few. Kamana-kamana, gently, slowly.
kuMANCHA		used with verb to intensify its meaning—timanche kumute-mweska, let us love him much. Kumancha tanja, to love us greatly (Tonga). Uheni wama-nchandana mu charu, sin has greatly increased in the land.
	kuMANGA	to bind; to tie up.
chiMANGO, vi-		peace.
kuMANYA		to know; to be able; (I) can, intens.—iska, to know thorough-ly; to know for certain; to under-stand. Manyi, I don't know; perhaps. Umanyi (u-), know-ledge. p. kumanyikwa, to be known.
chiMANYIKWIRO, vi-		a sign; a token.
	MANYAMI, ʋa-	small red mushroom.

TUMBUKA	TONGA	ENGLISH
kuMARA		to be finished. Kumarizga, to finish, to destroy. Kumazga, to impoverish. Zombe watimazga —nchunga kulije, when locusts have eaten the young bean shoots.
chiMARO, vi-		bride-price. (lobola).
MARUZU		kutimba maruzu, to shoot in flight.
chiMASA, vi-		eczema.
kuMATA		to stick dongo on wall; to plaster. Chimati, vi-, wall; i.e. the thing plastered. p. kumatwa.
vaMATANJE, va-		hill dwellers.
kuMATIKANA		to stick close together (as maize on cob).
	kaMATOUERO, tu-	a small bird with a squeaky chirp.
	MAWA	to-morrow.
chiMAYI, vi-		knife.
kuMAZGA		to impoverish. (kumara).
maMBA, (gha-)		scales (fish).
viMBA, vi-		a disease causing swelling.
	kuMBA	to sing. kumbiriya kampundu, to welcome with ululation.
	MBAGHARA, zi-	rib.
MBALI, zi-		plate; dish.
MBALI, (yi-)		side (Nyanja). Zuva lero chipita mbali, the sun is to the North in the cold season.
MBAMBO, zi-		ribs.
MBAMBAVU, zi-		ribs; side of chest.
MBANDA, va-		one who kidnaps or kills people; murderer. zimbanda, zi-, murders.
MBANO, zi-		green sapling used by blacksmith for holding hot iron on anvil: tongs. (kuvana).
chiMBARA, vi-		sima left over (e.g. for an early start next morning on a journey).
	MBARARA, zi-	ground nuts.
MBATA, zi-		horn; bugle; trumpet. Kulizga mbata, to sound the horn.
MBATATA, zi-		potato.
MBAVI, zi-		axe.
MBAVU, zi-		rib.
MBAYA WE !		alas! (a despairing wail).

MBEUA, zi-		rat.
MBEJA, zi-		hook. (esp. fish-hook).
MBEMBE, zi-		anger; wrath; rage.
	MBERA, zi-	small top made of calabash. Kuponya mbera, to play the game of spinning tops to goals. (see sikwa). Mbera za mu maso, spectacles.
MBERE		already; before. pa mbere pa, in front of. (used of thing done on the same day). Mwenembere afterwards; later on (same day). Vya ku mbere, former things.
MBERERE, zi-		sheep.
MBEU, zi-		seed; seedling; young plant.
MBEYEKA		ndakharanga ku mbeyeka, I was sitting aside, or round a corner (e.g. behind a pillar in church).
MBI !		clear! Na maso wuwo mbi e nkanira! (on recovering from dropsy). (kumbininika).
	MBIKU, zi-	store; treasure. (kuvika).
	kuMBININIKA	to be scattered.
MBINTI, ma-		lumps in sima.
	MBIRI, zi-	rust.
MBIRI, zi-		news; report (may be bad report).
luMBIRI, malu-		report (no bad implication); reputation; fame.
MBIRIUIRI, zi-		big drum.
MBIRIGHA, va- or zi-		second wife from same family (e.g. if first wife dies without issue; but may be given while first is alive).
	maMBIZA, (gha-)	sap (exuding from e.g. broken stems of plants of rubber, cassava, potato, &c.).
MBOHOLI, zi-		potato.
viMBOKORI, (vya-)		discharge from eyes (inflammatory).
chiMBOMBOMBO, vi-		a kind of termite. (ant).
kuMBOMBONTA		to run. (esp. of children).
MBOMI, (mu- or yi-)		a (sexually) impotent man. ndi mbomi.
MBONDO, zi-		pound (English).
chiMBONDO, vi-		a payment, e.g. bride-price; or fine.
MBONI, zi-		the pupil of the eye, mboni ya jiso.

TUMBUKA	TONGA	ENGLISH
MBONI, zi-		witness. (kuwona).
MBONIWONI, zi-		a vision; a dream.
kuMBONYA		to cover (something) e.g. by turning a basket over it; to blot out. Vula yambonya mapiri para, the rain has covered the hills yonder. (Ngoni).
kuMBONTYA		to plaster over, e.g. with mud, (stick, tree, or person).
	MBORO, zi-	the penis. (kuyuka, erection).
kuMBOTOKA		to fall off. (see kubontora).
	MBOWUWOWO, zi-	wax in ear.
MBU ?		what? how? when? Ukristu ngẃakuti mbu? what is Christianity? Fundo njakuti mbu? what is the point? Uti urute pa mbu? when will you go?
MBUꞴA		dry stalks of lupoko.
MBUHA, zi-		grey hairs. Mbuha zamera—a sign of age.
MBULIKA, zi-		flying ants (edible).
MBUMBA, zi-		family. ꞴA mbumba, relatives; brothers &c.
chiBUMBULI, vi-		a small calabash, pot, or parcel: also a musical instrument.
	MBUMU, zi-	stripes, e.g. with chikoti. (kupuma).
MBUNA, zi-		game-pit.
MBUNDA, zi-		ass; donkey.
	chiMBUNDI-MBUNDI	kwenda c..., to walk blindly.
chiMBUNDI, vi-		bribe.
MBUNGU, zi-		caterpillar.
luMBUNI, malu-		torch; light.
	MBUNU, zi-	covetousness; envy.
MBURU, ma-		lumps in sima.
MBURU, yi-		dropsy.
MBURUMA		a mass,.a lump; wholeness.. Sembe zakocha za mburuma, whole burnt offerings.
luMBURWE, (lu-)		fibre used for stringing beads (grows wild).
MBUTO, zi-		seed; seedlings; (esp. food plants).
	uMBUUYA (u-)	worthlessness; vanity.
	MBUVU, zi-	a large fish.
waMBUWU, ꞴA-		a dumb person: (also mbuwu, yi-, zi-).

	MBUYA, va-	grandparent; master; Lord. (term of respect).
	MBUYAU, va-	cat.
viMBUZA, vi-		a disease of possession. Patient and ng'anga both called vimbuza, or mbuza. Kuvina vimbuza, to exercise the spirits.
MBUZI, zi-		goat.
chiMBUZI, vi-		latrine.
kuMBWAMBWANTA		to shiver; to tremble.
chiMBWAMBWA, vi-		trembling palsy (usually in plural).
MBWANI, zi-		the deep sea; the ocean.
kuMBWATA		to go often needlessly to a place.
	MBWENO	enough. Wachitenge mbweno, he has made up his mind to do it.
MBWERA, mi-		the navel; the umbilical cord.
	kuMBWITA	to miss, e.g. in shooting.
MBWIWI, zi-		spring (of water). (kubwibwituka). Maji gha mbwiwi, water from a spring—cold, used for cooling beer &c.
MBYURURU, zi-		stripes (zebra).
MDENGWENDE		Chiuta wa mdengwende, the Most High God.
kaMDONI, twa-		a small biting fly.
chiMEHE, vi-		white ant.
kuMEKA-MEKA		to drizzle.
MEMBE, zi-		house fly. (general term including several species).
kuMEMENA		to grind (or gnash) the teeth (mino).
kuMEMERA	kuMEME	to drizzle (gentle rain). (kumera-mera).
kuMENYA		to take off a tozi from the sima in the basket; to break bread, &c.
kuMERA		to sprout (seed); to grow.
muMERA, mi-		the sprouting (early shoots) of grain.
chiMERA, (chi-)		leaven; ferment (esp. sprouting millet for fermenting beer).
kuMETA		to shave; to cut (hair). chimeta, vi-, razor.
	kuMEZA	to swallow.
kuMIJA		to sprinkle; to sow by casting (as millet).

	kuMIMITA	to strain.
	kuMINA mamphina	to blow the nose (wiping away mucus with fingers).
kuMIRA		to swallow: p. kumirwa. Kumiririra (mata), to insist (or kumiziriya—Presbytery wandimiziriya kuno, presbytery has insist—on my coming here). Ku-mu miririra, to long for, (or year over) him. Wamiririrwa, he is longed for.
MISE, (gha- or yi-)		afternoon or evening. na mise, in the afternoon. Mise ghano, this evening.
kuMITA		to be pregnant (of domestic animals) (Ngoni). chimizi, vi-, the large udder of pregnant, or suckling, animal.
—MIZO		adj. dry. (komira). dongo ndomizo, the mud is dry. nkhuni zomizo, dry firewood.
muMIZO, mi-		gullet.
MKWARA-MKWARA		kwenda mk... to hurry on without stopping.
MLEMA, va-		large bat.
	MNG'ONA, zi-	crocodile.
	vyaMNKHWIRO, vi-	sugar ants.
—MO		see —moza.
—MO		affix with sense of mu, in. (kunjiramo).
MONO, zi-		castor oil plant. mafuta gha mono, castor oil.
kuMOTOKA		to gather together; to assemble. kumotoke nkhungu, to run together after nkhungu fly.
uMOYO, (u-)		life. kuva moyo, to be alive. pa moyo, pain in the abdomen; diarrhoea. adj. wamoyo, alive, living.
—MOZA		one. (often in short from -mo). Kamoza, once. Kamo-kamo, rarely; seldom. Pamoza na, beside; together with. Mozimozi, the same, like. Vose pamoza, all together.
MPA ?		(ndi pa?). where? Pakuvinya mpa? where is the pain?
MPAVA		flat. (see kupavama).
MPACHI, zi-		spy (kupachira).

TUMBUKA	TONGA	ENGLISH
MPAFWA, zi-		liver.
MPAKA, zi-		boundary; limit. Also as conj., until. (kupakana).
MPAKO, zi-		bag of flour as provision for a journey.
MPALA, zi-		impala antelope.
MPALI, zi-		broken maize (ready for pounding into flour).
MPALIKA, zi-		tributaries of a river.
MPAMBA, zi-		a kind of tree. Kukong'onterana mpamba, or kumwerana mpamba, a sign of reconciliation.
	MPAMPA, zi-	tree ants (biting).
MPANDA, zi-		branch of a tree; forked stem used as a support.
	MPANDO, zi-	young cassava plant (kupanda).
MPANDO-MPANDO, zi-		fire-flies: borers in wood.
MPANGO, zi-		property; possessions; goods; chattels.
MPANGWE, zi-		leaves and flowers of pumpkins (and of mustard) used as dendi.
chiMPANI, vi-		large earthenware pot.
MPANJI, zi-		cave; lair; den.
MPANJIZGO, zi-		door-posts, inside house. (kupanjira).
MPANTI, zi-		flea.
MPAPU, zi-		offspring; seed; generation. (kupapa).
MPARATA, zi-		flying-ants.
MPASA, zi-		reed mat.
chiMPATA, vi-		callosities (e.g. on hands, caused by the pounding stick); corns.
MPATU, zi-		bush buck. Kuzgoka mpatu, to be sent to coventry.
MPAVU, zi-		strength; power; might.
MPAZI, zi-		grasshopper, (mpazi zanguwa).
	MPEKESA, zi-	witchcraft. (kupekesa).
	MPEMERE, zi-	rumour. (see kupemere).
MPENDAMA		pa dazi mpendama, when the sun declines. (see kupendama).
MPENDUZGA, zi-		the lot (see kupenduzga).
MPEPO, zi- ·		wind; air; atmosphere; cold.
MPEPESKA, zi-		propitiation (kupepeska).

TUMBUKA	TONGA	ENGLISH
MPEPETE, zi-		side; edge; rim; margin; bank; shore. Ku mpepete, aside.
MPEREMBE, zi-		koodoo.
MPEREREKEZGO, zi-		the ends (of the earth). (kuperera).
MPERO, zi-		grindstone (nether).
MPESKA, zi-		the fruit of a wild vine bearing small fruit. (used for vine and grapes in N.T.—see mupeska).
kaMPETA, tu-		sparrow.
MPETAMANI, zi-		green tree snake.
MPETE, zi-		ring; or lip ornament.
	liMPEZI, mali-	lightning. Malimpezi ghasweka.
	uMPHAUI, (u-)	poverty.
MPHAKO, zi-		hole (e.g. in tree, or tooth).
uMPHANDA, (u-)		kuvina umphanda, to exercise spirits. (see vimbuza).
MPHANDI, zi-		flat pieces of white shell worn on string round neck: the knee-cap.
chiMPHANGA, vi-		large brown hawk.
MPHANYI		conjunction introducing conditional clause, meaning would, or should Mphanyiko, a little better (of a patient recovering).
MPHARA, zi-		place for speaking (kuphara): house for boys. wa mphara, a bachelor.
chiMPHARA, (chi-)		dawning light (before the sun is up). (chimphara chafuma).
	MPHAZI, zi-	grasshopper.
	MPHE, zi-	nether grindstone.
	MPHEKA, yi-	fire-stick—hard and pointed, twirled by hands in notch of the chisiku.
	MPHEKEZI, zi-	a hole.
MPHENKERO, zi-		the nostril (see kupenka).
MPHERE, zi-		itch.
MPHEREBUNGU, zi-		caterpillars, pale green, found in grass, used whole as dendi.
	MPHERESKA, zi-	a wild vine.
	MPHINDA, zi-	bundle (e.g. of salt).
	MPHINDU, zi-	tracks where grass has been laid by something going (or being dragged) over it.
MPHINGU, zi-		burden; load.

TUMBUKA	TONGA	ENGLISH
MPHIRI, zi-		bolus (of sima).
MPHIRIWOKO		kuva mphiriwoko, to be ambidextrous.
MPHIYI, zi-		charms. e.g. 'medicine' in two sections of reed tied together and worn at the neck for "maso".
	MPHOMPO, zi-	an ornamental aze.
	MPHORO, zi-	sima left over (kupo).
	MPHUMPU, (yi-)	wholeness. ncha mphumpu, it is whole.
	chiMPHUNGA, vi-	storm; tempest.
MPHUPUTURU, zi-		cartilage.
MPHURURUNGWA		kukhara mphururungwa, to be left destitute.
MPHUTI, zi-		labia majora (female genitals).
MPHWAYI, zi-		slackness; unwillingness; idleness; dawdling; neglect.
MPIKURO, zi-		opposition; an objection (kupika).
MPINDAMSORO, zi-		hindrance, obstacle.
chiMPINDIKWA, vi-		enemy, or enmity. (also mpindikwa, zi-).
MPINGA, zi-		bar for door (outside).
MPINJIKA, zi-		cross (kupinjika).
MPINJIRIZGO, zi-		cross bar for inner door-posts.
maMPIZIRA, gha-		sap (exuding from broken stems of rubber, potato, euphorbia, &c.).
	MPOFWA, zi-	a yellow mushroom.
MPOMO, zi-		noise (e.g. of a waterfall).
MPOMPWE, zi-		a special axe, with long curved iron, carried by the mbuza.
MPONJE, zi-		the tuft at the end of a maize cob; ear of corn; tassel.
MPONKE, zi-		discharge from eyes (catarrhal).
	MPOROKOTO,	mavi gha mp.... scybala (faeces).
MPOROZI, zi-		maggot; worm.
MPOTO (yi-)		the north (from local geographical reference).
MPOTO, zi-		reward; wages. (nyanja mphoto).
MPOVU, zi-		bubbles; foam; froth.
MPOYO, zi-		reed buck.
MPOZWA, zi-		half-grown (cassava) plant.
chiMPULI, vi-		large pot with wide neck.
chiMPUMBA, vi-		ticks on fowls' eyes.

TUMBUKA	TONGA	ENGLISH
MPUMPI, zi-		wild dogs.
MPUMPU, zi-		cloth bound on head as sign of chief. Kuvwarika mpumpu, to appoint as chief.
kaMPUNDU, (ka-)		ululation. (Tonga—kumbiriya kampundu).
MPUNDWE, zi-		bundle of grass.
chiMPUNGO, vi-		a precipitous place (e.g. after a land-slide).
MPUNGO, zi-		a sort of porch roof over the door of a chilindo to shed off rain: a small booth, e.g. at a graveyard.
MPUNO, zi-		nose. Mpuno zitari? Are the ends long enough (to tie), (e.g. of broken string of ankle bells).
chiMPUPURU, vi-		strong wind; storm.
MPUSU, zi-		arrow with big wooden head (for birds).
MPUVYA		misleading (see kupuvya).
MPUWU, zi-		hollow in bamboo or bone; hole in tooth; cavity.
MPUZI, zi-		grains of maize. (also lumpuzi).
MPWAFWA, zi-		lungs.
kuMPWENENEKA (m'mtima)		to be disappointed.
MPYEMPYEMU		kupyera mpyempyemu, to sweep thoroughly. mtima mpyempyemu, heart thoroughly clean.
MSARA		kufwa msara, to die of want (e.g. on a journey).
MSUMA		wholeness; health. sopo wa msuma, a whole piece of soap. Kuva msuma, to be healthy ("every whit whole"). Tiri va msuma, we are well.
	MSURU, va-	maungoose.
MTEKITEKI		vula ya mtekiteki, a soft drizzling rain.
chiMTUNGA, vi-		storm.
MU, MWA, M!		prep. in; into; among. musi mu kuni, at the foot of the tree.
—MU—		medial in verb, accus. 3rd. pers. pron. sing.
—MU—		medial in verb followed by -ni, accus. 2nd. pers. pron. plur.

TUMBUKA	TONGA	ENGLISH
luMULI, malu-		light; lantern.
kuMULIKA		to shine (upon). Muliko wakumulika mafuko, a light to lighten the gentiles.
MULUNGU, (mu-)		God (nyanja).
MUMO		conj. as; since; in that. Mumo waliri, in the condition in which he is.
MUNA (wa-)		eczema.
MUNJIRE, vamu-		wart hog.
MUNYE, tu-		small black flies.
MUSI		below; under.
	MVEKA	first row of thatch; eaves (mu mveka).
	MVIMBA	see kuvimba.
MWA		see mu (mu a).
kuMWA		to drink.
MWAKUTI		since; because; as; inasmuch as.
MWALI, va-		girl; maiden.
uMWALI, wa-		puberty (female). 1st. mo. wakura umwali; 2nd. mo. wawerezga; 3rd. mo. wageza.
	chiMWAMAFUTA, vi-	small ground lizard.
MWAPU, (u-)		zeal.
MWANCHI, va-		model; doll (of clay, grass, mazayi &c.); image.
	MWANKHU	hollow. liri mwankhu, of a tooth with hole.
kuMWANTA		to throb with pain.
kuMWARARIKA		to be scattered and lost—as fowls in bush.
	kuMWARIKA	to faint; to die. Mtima mwa! faint.
MWAZI		open; empty. Chitete chiri mwazi, the basket is empty.
kuMWEMWETERA		to smile with pleasure. Chimwemwe, vi- joy; delight.
	MWENGA	other place or state. (sometimes pamwe). pamwenga, otherwise; perhaps. Muntu wamwenga, another person, or a certain man.
MWENYI, va-		Indian (often the storekeeper).
kuMWERERA		to exude, as a porous pot exudes moisture.

TUMBUKA	TONGA	ENGLISH
kuMWETUKA		to flash (as lightning—mwetu, mwetu); also used of throbbing pain.
MWIKO		ndi mwiko, it is taboo, or unlawful.
MYA!		completely finished! Nyengo mya, a long time has passed.
kuMYANGA		to lick (with tongue). Kumyanguta, to devour.
kuMYATIKA		to tell fibs (kwata). Wandimyatika waka, he has told lies about me. Myati kuti yikwenerera mrara chara, fibs don't become an elder. (see mw-ati).
—MZIRA		adv. of negation. Umoyo wamzira kumara, life unending. Ng'ombe zamzira kumanyikwa, unknown oxen.
MZIRE		lest (with dir. form of verb).
MZIRO		ndi mziro, it is taboo. (see kuzira).
MZUMI, ʋa-		mole.

N

N—		see ndi.
NA		conj. and; with. prep., by; with; about; concerning. Na yumo, na kamo, none at all.
muNA, (wa-)		eczema.
NADI		truly; indeed; really; surely; verily.
	—NAI	four. Chintu cha chinai, the fourth thing.
	mNAKA, ʋa-	eel.
	kuNAMA	to lie (untruth).
kuNANA		to requite; to recompense.
kuNANAMPURA		to draw out in sticky strings (as glue, mucus, arrowroot pudding, &c.). p.—puka. Nanampu!
—NANDI		much; many. unandi, (wa) amount; number.
kuNANGA		to damage; to destroy; to injure; to spoil; to sin. (kwananga).
NANGA		although; even; in the meantime, or first. Linda nanga, wait a little. Ndichitepo nanga, first let me do it. Nanga followed by nanga, pakunji or nesi, whether —or.

TUMBUKA	TONGA	ENGLISH
kuNATA		to be sticky, or tacky. Chankaramo chindanate, the nkaramo grass hasn't become tacky (which is a sign that rains are over). Masungu ghake ghanata, its smell sticks (e.g. to hands).
—NAYI		four. Chintu cha chinayi, the fourth thing.
kuNCHANCHAMIRA		to be bitter, or sour (as lemon).
NCHANKURU	NCHINKURU	but because. Mphanyi wakafwa nchankuru ng'anga yafika, he would have died but because the doctor arrived (he recovered). mphanyi nchito yanditonda ncha nkuru munyane wafika, the job would have beaten me, but because my fellow arrived (we managed it).
NCHEUE, zi-		dog.
NCHEFU, (yi-)		a small-leafed plant, eaten by sefu, with a purple, sweet-scented flower.
NCHEMBERE, zi-		matron; multipara. Ndiwe nchembere karinga how many children have you had? Makanta nchembere, striae gravidarum—marks on abdomen of childbearing.
NCHEMULI		relish. Sima ya nchemuli, sima with relish.
NCHEMO, zi-		call; cry. (kuchema).
NCHENE		knowingly; wilfully; on purpose. Ngati mchenga wa nchene, many—as sand.
NCHESA, zi-		weed growing among food crop. (kuchesa).
	maNCHESA, (gha-)	bulrush (burnt for salt).
NCHIMA, zi-		large monkey.
NCHIMI, zi-		a "familiar" or "medium"; one who gets in touch with departed spirits. (kuchima).
NCHINDA, zi-		bundle (of grass, reeds, firewood).
	NCHINDAMIRO, zi-	prop, e.g. post for verandah.
NCHINDI, zi-		honour; glory. (kuchindika).
NCHIRI-NCHIRI-NCHIRI		much game standing in the bush.
NCHITO, zi-		work (kuchita).
NCHUNGA, zi-		beans.

TUMBUKA	TONGA	ENGLISH
NDA !		mu kuni nda! up in a tree. Nda-nda steps climbing.
NDA...		nda wakwananga... I, a sinner,...
maNDA (gha-)		tiny mushrooms. Manda ghaku-vunda pa konde, there's many a slip twixt the cup and the lip.
muNDA, mi-		plantation; garden.
NDACHA, zi-		black monkey.
kuNDANDA	kuNDANDAMIKA	to draw up in line; to form a line (people).
NDANDA		kwa ndanda, for ever; to eternity.
luNDANDATI (lwa-)		ring (Ngoni).
NDAUARA		kwenda ndauara, to hurry. Nkiza ndauara, I came quickly.
NDEKANO, zi-		parting of paths. Pa ntowa ndekano, at the fork of the path. (kurekana).
NDEMBERA, zi-		flag.
NDENDENDE		in a crowd of people.
	kuNDENGA-NDENGA	to swing; to sway.
chiNDERE, vi-		foolish person; fool. muntu chinde-re, vantu vindere.
kuNDERERA		to draw near; to move along (a seat).
	kaNDERERE, tu-	small red and black seed.
NDEVULIRA, (yi-)		the "beard" at the end of a maize cob.
	NDEZU, zi-	large mushroom.
NDI		first pers. pron. sing. I; prefixed to verb, n- ni- ndi-: medial in verb, me, wandichema, he has called me. Nda mwene, I myself.
NDI		copula: it is; is. Joined with pronouns—ndine, ndiwe &c. (see grammars). Ndivyo nvya-chi? what about these? (things previously referred to).
wuNDI (u-)		goose-skin (when cold).
maNDIMA (gha-)		lemons.
NDIMBA, zi-		depths (e.g. of lake).
NDIMI, zi-		ndimi zake, the portion of land hoed by a person. (kulima).
NDINDA, zi-		watch hut (in garden). (kulinda).
	NDIFU, zi-	large thick yellow banana.
chiNDINDI, vi-		secret: mystery.
chiNDINDINDI, vi-		earthquake.

80

TUMBUKA	TONGA	ENGLISH
	NDINDIRA, zi-	pledge.
NDIPO		and. Ndipo kweni, nevertheless. Ndipo uli, and yet.
	NDOƲA	muti wakuti ndoʋa pa ntowa, a tree overhanging the path.
maNDOƲA (gha-)		hopper stage of locusts. (one, wa mandoʋa).
NDODO, zi-		stick; staff.
NDOKI, zi-		plantain.
chiNDOKO (chi-)		venereal disease (? syphilis).
NDOMO, zi-		point; promontory, spur of hill; (nipple of breast).
kuNDONDA		to follow in line; to walk in Indian file. kundondomeska to arrange, e.g. a procession.
kuNDONDOROSKA		to follow hard on the way; to seek earnestly.
	NDONDOWA, zi-	heavy stone used as anchor.
NDONGOZI, zi-		a leader.
NDOPA, zi-		blood.
NDOTA, zi-		dryness of the mouth (e.g. in fever) (nyota).
NDOZI, zi-		peas.
NDRAMA, zi-		money.
NDUƲARUƲA, zi-		the lourie (bird). Kuvwara nduʋa—only chiefs may wear the feathers.
NDUƲE, zi-		small-pox.
NDULU, zi-		bile; gall; gall-bladder.
kaNDUNDU (ka-)		anger; wrath.
NDUNDUMBI, zi-		resentment or animosity (between two who have quarrelled). Kwenda ndu-ndu-ndu, to hold aloof.
NDUNGU, (yi-)		ferment; yeast; leaven.
NDUVYO, zi-		report; message. (see kuruvya).
NDUZGA, (yi-)		revenge; vengeance. (e.g. a three-cornered mrandu).
	—NE ?	interrogative. muntu mune? which man? chintu chine? which thing.
—NE		poss. pron. first pers. sing., my (wane, lane, chanc &c.).
kuNEGHA		to take water out of a vessel; to fetch water.
NEMBA-NEMBA, zi-		the white lining of an egg-shell; the tough white membrane of a spider's nest on a wall.

F

Tumbuka	Tonga	English
NENA		with prefix ku-, above, higher (of position or of social status). Tiponye kunena—when in a dispute the matter is referred to the chief.
chiNENA (cha-)		the pubes, or lower part of abdomen.
kuNENA		to tell; to say; to speak. intens. —eska, to affirm; to speak the truth. Unenesko, (u-), truth. Muneni, ʋa-, speaker (evangelist).
kuNENEKERA		to hang on the edge (of something). Kunenekezga, to hold (something) lightly in fingers (not with firm grip).
kuNENG'ENERA		to draw near; to approach. Kuneng'enezga, to put a cork loosely in a bottle, or a lid loosely on a tin, &c.
NESI		interrogative—at end of question; expects negative answer. conj. lest; nor. Panji nesi, nor; not even.
NGA		as; according to; nga ghaʋe mazuʋa, concerning the days... Nga ndi para, as if. Before verb stem, may; mungachita, you can do it. Before and after verb stem, a prohibition, mungachitanga, you must not do it. Nga ndi umo, in the way in which. For conditional sentences see grammars.
chiNG'A, vi-		the pelvis.
muNGA, mi-		thorn.
kuNG'ADA		to put a cap (mng'ado) on the penis (Ngoni custom).
NG'AMBA, zi-		a break in the rains of several days dry weather.
NGANA		so-and-so; a certain (person).
	chiNG'ANDA, vi-	cap for hammer gun.
kuNG'ANAMULA	kuNG'ANAMUWA	to turn; to change; to reply; (to interpret). met. to mean. with mtima, to repent. p. kung'anamuka, to turn (oneself), to repent.
NG'ANGA, zi-		doctor.
kuNGANGAMIKA		to be set; to be determined; to be resolved: to insist. nga-nga-nga, unyielding. (see chiganga).

TUMBUKA	TONGA	ENGLISH
kuNG'ANIMA		to shine (as flames of fire, or fireflies).
NG'ANJO, zi-		smelting furnace. Makarang'anjo, (gha-), the slag from the smelting.
	kuNG'ANUWA	to knock; to strike. Kung'anulirana, to jostle, (of a crowd).
kuNG'ANUZGA		to hustle.
	NGANYA	my friend—familiar address.
kuNG'ANYA		to beat, or mash (e.g. boiled potatoes); to crush; to grind.
kuNG'APULA	kuNG'APUWA	to thrash (with switch). (kunyapula).
chiNGARA, vi-	chiNGA, vi-	woman's sanitary napkin or towel.
NGARAUA, zi-		boat; vessel (larger than wato).
NGARANDI, zi-		ditch; trench.
	chiNG'ARA-NG'ARA,	(chi-) glare (of sun).
uNGARI, mau-		secret.
NGARO, zi-		blue crane. (sts. chingaro: Ngoni, indwa).
NGARURA, (yi-)		the first hoeing (weeding) of growing maize garden. (kuharura).
	kuNG'ATA	to be smooth (e.g. puddled clay).
kuNG'ATUKA		to be smooth (of sima—without lumps).
maNGAWA (gha-)		debt; obligation.
kuNG'AZIMA		to shine.
maNGENJEZA (gha-)		ankle bells.
	NG'O	negative: ng'o kwanja pe, no love at all.
	paNG'O (pa)	the anus.
chiNGODYA, vi-		corner.
kuNGOFIRA		to hurry.
chiNGOMA, vi-		maize. (also ngoma, zi-).
NGOMA, zi-		a competitive dance in the kraal. (Ngoni).
NG'OMA, zi-		drum.
NG'OMBE, zi-		cattle; oxen; cow; bullock.
NG'OMBWA, zi-		a skilled worker (e.g. carpenter).
	kuNG'ONDO	to strike, or beat. Kung'ondoka, to be harassed. Kung'ondoska, to trouble. Mtima ng'ondo! oppressed with troubles!
muNG'ONG'O, mi-		ridge, esp. parallel ridges like marata.

TUMBUKA	TONGA	ENGLISH
muNGONGONDA, mi-		ridge, e.g. the corner of a wall.
	NGONGORI, zi-	debts. (kukongora).
NGOZA, va-		image; doll. (idol).
NGOZI, yi-		accident. Yikava ngozi, it was done accidentally. Also refers to compensation.
	—NGU	poss. pron. first pers. sing. my. (wangu, langu, changu &c.).
	muNGU, mi-	a small edible gourd.
NGULI, zi-		spinning-top (kuvina); plug for hole (e.g. in a tuli); circular block on top of central pillar in a hut, to which the mapasu are nailed.
NGUNDA-NGUNDA-NGUNDA		of many low things clustered together (e.g. graves, houses, wild pig &c.).
kuNGUNGUMA		to be raised in rows. Mingunguma (yi-), corrugations in sand (in stream, or raised by wind); wheals raised by chikoti on skin; cp. corrugated iron. Ngu-ngu-ngu, raised up—also used of ranges of hills. (cp. nkunguru, rollers on lake).
	maNGURONGONDO	(gha) xylophone.
NGURU, zi-		shield.
NGURUVE, zi-		bush pig.
NGUWO, zi-		cloth for carrying child.
NGUYI, zi-		high forest: small woods in vipya glens.
chiNGWA, vi-		bread. (made from banana flour usually).
	NGWANDO, zi-	landing net. Ngwando neghu! net lifts (the fish).
NGWATA, zi-		calf.
NGWAZI, zi-		hero—in war or hunting (lion or leopard). (kugwaza).
chiNGWAZI, vi-		widow's cap—of string bound on head &c. (Ngoni custom).
	kuNGWAZURANA	to quarrel fiercely, or hotly.
NGWE !		light; clear; shining. (kungweru-ka).
chiNGWE, vi-		string; cord (of twisted fibre).
NGWEMBE, zi-		plate; bowl; dish.
kuNGWERUKA		to be light; to be clear (after clouds).

84

TUMBUKA	TONGA	ENGLISH
NGWI !		spring jump!
NG'WINA, zi-		crocodile.
NI—		see ndi.
kuNING'INA		to hang; to dangle. Kujining'inya, to hang oneself.
kuNINKA		to give.
kuNINIZIKA		to beseech. (a whining, grumbling, importunity).
NJANI?		who? ʋa njani? who? muli ʋanjani? who are you? mba njani? who are they?
NJANJI, zi-		train. (railway).
NJARA, (yi-)	NJA, (yi-)	hunger; famine: kufwa njara, to starve.
NJASKO, zi-		a light. (e.g. a piece of grass used as a taper). (kungako njasko, light a light).
NJATI, zi-		buffalo.
	NJAYA, zi-	a big tree bearing a large fleshy fruit.
	NJEGHEYU, zi-	the cheek; the jaw bone.
kuNJENJEMA	kuNJENJEME	to shiver (with cold or fear). Mutipe mitima yakunjenjema yakupokera mazgu ghinu, give us God-fearing hearts to receive thy word.
NJERE, zi-		seed; grain.
viNJERU, vi-		wisdom; cleverness; sense; intelligence.
NJERULIRA, zi-		exaggeration. (kutarulira).
NJERWA, zi-		brick.
	NJEZA, zi-	skill. Ngwa njeza, he does skilled work.
NJI		some; other; a certain—. Zuʋa linji, some day.
NJIƲA, zi-		dove (wild—in bush).
NJINGA, zi-		a wieghted spindle for spinning cotton; bobbin; wheel; bicycle. (kuzinga).
kuNJIRA		to enter; come in; go in. caus. kunjizga, to put in; to bring in; to insert. Dazi lanjira, the sun has set. (see also kupanjira). Umoyo wa ʋantu ukunjirirana nga ndi nyama ya njovu, people's lives are inter-related like elephants' flesh (which at one part tastes like fowl, at another like fish &c.).

Tumbuka	Tonga	English
NJIRE, zi-		convulsions (in infants).
muNJIRI, vamu-		wart hog.
kuNJIRIKIZGA		to instruct.
muNJIRIRA, mi-		garment.
NJIRISI, zi-		charm; amulet.
NJOVE, zi-		claw; talon; finger-nail.
NJOKA, zi-		snake; serpent.
NJOMBE, zi-		pay; reward.
	mNJORWA, va-	small eel.
	NJU !	see gwi!
NJU ?		which? (of persons, or first class).
NJUVI, zi-		conscience.
NJUCHI, zi-		bees. (wuchi, honey).
NJUWURU, zi-		ankle-bells.
	NJUYU, zi-	beans.
NKALI, zi-		a wide open pot.
	NKAMA, zi-	sledge-hammer (blacksmith's; a stone).
NKAMBAKO, zi-		bull.
luNKAMWA, malu-		charu cha lunkamwa, dry country; desert. (also chinkamwa, and uchinkamwa).
maNKANANA, (gha-)		sputum (muco-pus). also mankananimbwa).
	NKANDAMO, yi-	the noose in a trap. (kukanda)·
NKANDASI		dongo la nkandasi, deep, black, alluvial soil.
NKANDWE, zi-		pit (for stamping clay). (kukanda).
NKANGA, zi-		guinea-fowl.
NKANIRA		completely; entirely; absolutely; indeed; especially; altogether.
NKANKU, zi-		champion.
	uNKANKU (u-)	glory.
	NKANO, zi-	crab (water).
NKARAMBA, zi-		an honoured elder; messenger; ambassador.
NKARAMO, zi-		lion.
	NKATA, zi-	pad for head when carrying a load.
NKAZA, (yi-)		hardness; harshness; severity; cruelty.
NKAZI, va-		father's sister; aunt.

TUMBUKA	TONGA	ENGLISH
NKHAUI, zi-		bullock.
	NKHAMA, zi-	red colouring (for pots &c.).
NKHANYA, zi-		astringency; sourness; bitterness. Vi na nkhanya, they are sour (fruit).
NKHARA, zi-	NKHA, zi-	crab.
chiNKHARA, vi-		a strong man; a robust man. (Giant).
uNKHARA, (wa)		full strength. Ku unkhara ndinda-fikepo, I haven't yet reached full strength.
NKHARO, zi-		custom; habit; character; nature. (kukhara).
maNKHARO, gha-		strength; vigour.
	NKHASI, zi-	turtle.
NKHAZI, zi-		euphorbia (planted round stock-ade, or graves).
	NKHOMO, zi-	a large fish.
NKHULI, (ya)		nakedness (also unkhuli). wa nkhu-li, naked.
NKHUNDA, zi-		pigeon (domestic).
	NKHUNGU, zi-	tiny flies (in clouds on Lake Nyasa).
muNKHUNGU, va-		thief; robber. Unkhungu, theft.
NKHUNI, zi-		firewood.
luNKHUWA, (lwa)		loss of strength (due to fasting); famine; hunger. Kufwa lu-nkhuwa, to lose energy (in work, or on a journey).
NKHWEMI, zi-		beaters (beating game).
NKOUEZI, zi-		string for carrying, or tying on, anything: a loop (kugova). Kankovezi, tu-, shoe-lace.
NKOCHO, zi-		one clever in talking a mrandu (kukochora).
NKOKA, zi-		a falling trap (e.g. as set for a leopard).
	NKOKOTA, zi-	remains of sima in a pot. (kukoko-tora).
	NKOKOTO, zi-	a drag for a lost net (made of thorny branches tied together).
NKOKWE, zi-		store (for maize &c.): a barn.
NKOMBO, zi-		small calabash with handle: cup.
NKOMI, zi-		a deadly snake, said to have a comb, and to crow like a cock.

TUMBUKA	TONGA	ENGLISH
NKOMOKAZI, zi-		a cow which has calved (Ngoni).
	NKONDE, (wa)	the north: a north wind.
—NKONDE		five. Wachinkonde, fifth.
NKONDO, zi-		war. Uankondo, ua-, warriors; soldiers.
NKONGONO, zi-		strength; power; might. Great strength, nkongono zikuru. Strength for different kinds of work, nkongono zinandi.
	chiNKONONO, chi-	snoring.
NKONTO, zi-		the back of the head.
NKONYE, zi-		snail.
NKONYORO, zi-		the back of the neck; the nape of the neck.
NKOPI, zi-		eyelids: (sometimes used for face, or front).
maNKORORO, gha-	maNKORO, gha-	mucus or sputum; expectoration.
NKOROMBE, zi-		shell (of snail, &c.).
NKORONGO, zi-		forest; wood (trees with thick undergrowth).
NKOROZI, zi-	NKOROZO, zi-	root.
muNKORWE, (wa)		great darkness. (kukoromera).
NKOSWE, zi-		advocate; intercessor; pleader.
	NKOWA, zi-	full-grown cassava plants.
mNKOZA, mi-		shin (of leg). Also mukozo, mi-.
—NKU ?		interrogative—where? Usually added at end of verb; mukuyanku? where are you going?
nyaNKUUINDA, (wa)		mist.
NKUFI, zi-		the palm of the hand. (see kukuua).
NKUFU, zi-		the tampan bug (ornithodorus moubata).
NKUKU, zi-		fowl; poultry.
NKUMBA, zi-		pig (domestic).
NKUMBARURU, zi-		crested hoopoe.
NKUMBI, zi-		high spirits; excess of joy. Nkumbi zakwera, spirits are high. Nkumbi zawa, spirits have fallen, i.e. to lose heart, to be depressed.
NKUMBI, zi-		moisture in a pipe (tobaccosmoking).
	NKUNGUMKOMA, zi-	ants which build nests in trees.
NKUNGUNI, zi-		bed bug.

NKUNGURA, zi-		wood from a garden (for fence or firewood).
	NKUNGURU, zi-	logs used as rollers (e.g. for canoe). Met. rollers (waves) on lake.
	NKURA, zi-	small ant-heaps (usually in dambo).
NKURANDI, zi-		red ants (biting).
NKUTO, zi-		a cry; crying out aloud. (kukuta).
NKUYU, zi-		figs (wild). Chikuyu, vi-, fig tree.
NKUZI, zi-		bull. (Ngoni).
maNKWANDA, gha-		wrinkles (on body or cloth).
	muNKWANI, mi-	leaves of pumpkin or beans used for dendi.
NKWANTI, zi-		expert (e.g. in singing, in stealing); (may be used of an animal).
NKWAPA, zi-		armpit.
muNKWARA, mi-		medicine; charm. (also mankwara).
chiNKWAWO, vi-		gully; gorge.
NKWAZI, zi-		fish eagle.
NKWENDI, zi-		the menses (fem. monthly discharge). Ndatora nkwendi: nkwendi zafika.
NKWENYU !		bite off! (e.g. sugar-cane).
NKWERU-NKWERU		light or clear (clouds dispersed or lamp lit). (kungweruka).
	NKWEZA, zi-	long green snake—green mamba.
NKWIKWI (ya)		squeaky noise made by two branches of a tree rubbing together. met. of a stiff argument (kulimbana kwa fundo ziviri).
maNKWINYA, gha-		wrinkles on face: mankwinya ghaza, he is scowling.
	NKWIPI	mbavi yasere mu nkwipi, the axe has sunk so far into the handle that the latter strikes the wood.
—NO		this: charu chino, this country: dazi lino, to-day.
maNO, gha-		mind; wisdom; sense.
mNOFU, (u-)		flesh; muscle.
NOMBO, zi-		eagle.
kuNONG'OMERA		to be nice (sweet or salt).
muNONKORO, (u-)		flavour. (kununka).
—NONONO		hard; difficult. unonono, mau-, difficulty; a serious matter (fault); adversity.

TUMBUKA	TONGA	ENGLISH
kuNONOPA		to be hard. (Nyanja, to hurry). caus. kunonopeska and kunonofya, to make hard.
kuNORA		to sharpen.
kuNORA		to withold; to refuse or deny something to somebody (prob. with sense of stinginess).
kuNOWA		to be nice, pleasant; to taste nice (sugar or salt). caus.—eska, to flavour; to make nice or pleasant.
kaNOWERO, (ka)		pleasantness, sweetness (sugar or salt).
kuNOZGA		(caus. of kunowa) to make pleasant; to make right; to make smooth; to arrange. kunozgera, to prepare (e.g. a meal). vula yakana yanozga, it is nice the rain has held off. Mchere ukunozga kurya, salt makes food palatable. Maraya ghakunozga muntu, clothes make one respectable. Chandinozga? an ironical question when something has been unpleasant or hurtful.
NTA		not: (negative particle preceding and separate from verb—chiefly in subordinate, adjectival or relative clauses. Avo, nta vakumanya, vanganena:
maNTA, (gha)		fear; terror.
NTAMBA, zi-		store for grain.
	NTAMBI, zi-	branch (e.g. of a vine).
ziNTAMBO, zi-		strings worn round neck by a widow as mourning.
	NTAMBURA, zi-	fishing net fixed to sticks stuck in sand.
NTANDA, zi-		fabulous enormous fish in lake. Makani ghali na ntanda, the matter is too difficult.
NTANGA, zi-		a group of equal age; a generation.
NTANGANENE, zi-		girl's hut or house.
NTANGARARO, zi-		the fork between the legs: the groin. (kutangarara).
chiNTANGUNI, vi-		proverb; fable; parable.
NTANGWANIKA, zi-		occupation; busy-ness.
NTANO, zi-		fable (told or acted).
	NTANTA, zi-	purlins.
NTANTI, zi-		story; fable.

TUMBUKA	TONGA	ENGLISH
luNTATA, (lwa)		perseverance. (chitatata).
	NTAZI, zi-	strength.
—NTAZI		with pa or ku: in front of; before (time or place)—from the point of view of the person or thing looking forward; (see nyuma).
NTEUERE, zi-		branches cut and laid on new gardens to be burnt—ground not broken up (contrast michinga).
	NTEMA	mwasere ntema, puerperal fever.
NTEMBO, zi-		curse.
	NTEMBWE, zi-	ditch cut round garden.
chiNTEMWE, vi-		a plant (like pineapple) used in the rite of kusinka muzi.
NTENDA, zi-		disease; illness; ailment.
	NTENDERO, zi-	relish (for sima). (kutendera).
NTENKU, zi-		pimples on face; acne.
	NTETE, zi-	the lochia (of women).
NTEURA		so; thus; such; therefore; wherefore. Muntu wa nteura, such a man.
	NTHA, zi-	hole (e.g. in a tree, or a tooth).
NTHABANI, zi-		thread-worms.
	NTHAMBA, zi-	store for maize or beans.
	NTHAMBA, zi-	a species of small bean, grown on a bush.
NTHANDA, (yi-)		the Morning Star.
NTHARIKA, zi-		proverb; parable.
muNTHAVI, mi-		branch (of tree); bough. (kuthaza).
	NTHENDE, zi-	a species of white ant.
	NTHENGO, zi-	hoops of a creel (for trapping fish).
NTHENGWA, zi-		marriage (kutenga).
NTHOMBA, zi-		smallpox. (Nyanja).
NTHONA, zi-		hole in upper lip for mpete.
NTHONDORO, zi-		a castrated goat.
NTHONTO, zi-		filth; refuse (about village); also applied to evil in heart: met. sores on leg (presumably caused by filth).
muNTHOPA, mi-		sweet-sop. (from a wild form in bush).
viNTHULI, (vya)		clots of blood.

TUMBUKA	TONGA	ENGLISH
NTHUMBO, zi-		abdomen; womb. (matumbo, bowels).
NTHUNDU, zi-		load; burden.
NTHUNGULI, zi-		eunuch; a castrated animal.
NTIMBANYA, (ya)		confusion (in a crowd).
NTIMBO, zi-		blows (kutimba).
NTIMBU, zi-		sediment (e.g. in water). (kutimbula).
NTIMPWA (ya)		meal-water (fresh mixed—millet meal and water, sometimes with ground nuts). (may also be made thick, in lumps).
—NTINI		small; little; few. na kantini kose, not even a little; not at all.
NTOKO !		move off! (starting ulendo). Ntokoni, tiyeni. Ntokoniko! forward!
NTOMBOZGO, zi-		reproach; sneer; taunt.
muNTONDWE, mi-		a wonder; a portent. (kutondwa).
NTONGA, zi-		club.
kuNTONYA	kuNTONA	to drop, or drip. Matontera (gha), drops.
NTOROMI, zi-		leopard.
	kaNTOROZI, ka	urethra.
NTOWA, zi-		path; road; track; way. (used of repeated action—ntowa zinayi, four times).
muNTU, va-chi		man; human being; person; people.
chiNTU, vi-		thing. kantu, tu-, a little thing; a trifle.
uNTU, (wa)		being; manhood. (also semen or sexual seed of male). Umoyo wavo kuti mbuntu chara, their life is not real.
NTUMBIRWA, zi-		a child who has been weaned because its mother is pregnant.
	muNTUKAZI, va-	a woman; female.
NTUMI, zi-		one sent; a messenger. (kutuma).
NTUNDUMWE, tu-		hillocks; humps in ground.
NTUNDOROPA, zi-		"the shew" in obstetrics: (mixture of mucus and blood). Nthumbo yalira ntundoropa—a sign of progress.
NTUNDUNG'OMA, zi-		ganglion; swelling.
NTURA, zi-		small, yellow, wild fruit, inedible (used for games).

TUMBUKA	TONGA	ENGLISH
	muNTURUMI, va-	a man; male. Unturumi (wa), manhood, courage.
kuNUNA		to "cup" or bleed (for headache &c.) by cutting the temporal artery and applying suction through a horn (chinunu).
kuNUNA		to be fat (of meat). (suggests sound of sizzling on fire, or of charcoal crackling on fire).
muNUNG'UNA, va-		younger brother or sister (of same sex).
kuNUNKA		to smell (intr.); kunuska, to smell (tr.).
NUSU		a part; (half).
muNWE, mi-		digit; finger; toe.
kuNWEKA		to long for; desire; crave.
NYA—		honorific fem. prefix to chiwongo.
kuNYA		to fall (as rain); to defaecate.
	chiNYAPOMBO	chatuwa—prolapse of the rectum; piles.
maNYAUIRI, (gha)		urticaria; nettle-rash.
kuNYADIRA		to stroll; to walk slowly as in stalking game.
NYAKASI, mau-		uncleanness; mzimu wa unyakasi, an unclean spirit. (kunyanyara).
kuNYAKATA		to crush to powder (e.g. a tablet). p.—ika, to melt (hail stones in sun; green bricks in rain).
NYAKATEMA, va-		(kamoza, kaviri) a matron who has borne children. Nyakatema wa mahara, a wise, experienced woman.
—NYAKE		some; other; each. Imwe mwava-nyake, some of you; ku- or pa-nyake, elsewhere.
kuNYAKUKA		to raise oneself on tip-toe; to arise.
NYAKUTU, va-		fowl which has laid eggs; hen.
NYALI, zi-		lamp; light.
	NYALIBAZA, zi-	the womb.
NYALUBWE, va-		leopard.
NYAMA, zi-		flesh; meat; game.
NYAMAKAZI, zi-		pain, (with or without swelling).
NYAMBO, zi-		bait.
NYANDA, zi-		bark-cloth.

TUMBUKA	TONGA	ENGLISH
	maNYANDA, (gha)	splendour (e.g. at a guli); happiness.
kuNYANG'AMIRA		to be deep (e.g. a well). nyang'a-nyang'a!
NYANGULO, zi-		anchor.
	kuNYAMUWA	to raise; to lift up.
NYANJA, zi-		lake; sea. (occasionally of river).
NYANKARARA	NYANKARA	sisi lakuti nyankarara, hair soft and thin—a sign of ill-health.
NYANKUƲINDA		mist (a proper noun); nyankuʋinda wakorana, a mist is on the ground.
liNYANYA, mali-		yam.
kuNYANYARA		to abhor.
kuNYANYATA		to totter (child learning to walk). Kunyanyaska, to teach to walk.
kuNYAPULA		to thrash (with switch).
viNYARA, (vya)		filthy, abominable things. (kunya-nyara).
NYARURYA, ʋa-		a terrible enemy (undying hatred). (Satan).
kuNYASKA		to heat before a fire (e.g. drying cloth, or re-heating food); to toast.
NYATA, zi-		garden by stream (soil moist and soft).
NYATAZI, ʋa-		fowl which has laid eggs; hen.
NYATUTWE		see tutwe.
chiNYAWO, vi-		masks used in initiation ceremony —also used for the ceremony itself.
kuNYEKA		to burn well; to glow (of fire); to be scorched (of food); met. of ulcer eating away flesh. kunye-ska, to scorch.
kuNYEKETUKA		to melt, or become soft (as butter in sun, or a pot not properly burnt in water). Nyeketu! of laying a cloth with ointment gently on a sore.
kuNYEKEZGA		to press down; to weigh down; to lean upon.
uNYEMBA, (wa)		tamarind tree, or fruit.
kuNYENDERERA		to move closer together (e.g. to make room on a seat).
kuNYENGA		to deceive; p.—eka.
NYENGO, zi-		time.

TUMBUKA	TONGA	ENGLISH
kuNYENKAMA		to press close in behind someone (as a fearsome child).
NYENYE, ma-		edible flying ants.
muNYENYEMBE, va-		a slender person.
kuNYENYENKA		to tickle. Manyenyenko, (gha), itchy sores on paws, or hoofs, of animals.
kuNYENYERA		to itch.
NYENYEZI, zi-		star.
kuNYEREMUKA		to slip away unobserved.
maNYERENYEZA (gha)		moss hanging from old trees.
NYERERA, zi-		small, black, house, ants.
kuNYETA		to slink away.
NYETE		charu chiri waka nyete, the land is flat.
kuNYETUKA		to sparkle, to glitter. (nyetu-nyetu!)
NYEVULIRA, zi-		the tuft, or beard, hanging from a maize cob.
kuNYEVYA		to hide something secretly.
kuKUNYEWA		to be moist, damp or wet. caus. kunyevya, to moisten.
NYEZI, zi-		fly.
NYIFI, zi-		sweet maize stalks, or sugar-cane.
NYIFWA, zi-		death.
kaNYIMBI, tu-		a black and white rodent (?skunk).
NYIMBO, zi-		mosquito. (Nyanja for hymn).
kuNYIMPURA		to uproot. p. kunyimpuka.
NYINA, va-		mother (of 3rd. person). (mama, my mother, nyoko, thy mother); nyinafwe, nyinamwe, nyinavo, our, your their, mother. Nyina-vyara, va-, mother-in-law. Chi-nyina, the queen (of bees or white ants).
NYINARUMI, va-		maternal uncle.
NYINDA, zi-		lice.
NYIRENDA, zi-		small, reddish, caterpillars.
NYISKA, zi-		small antelope; duiker.
NYIVWI, zi-	NYIVU, zi-	grey hair. Nyivu zame, grey hairs have come. (thy) mother.
	NYOLI, zi-	fowl; poultry.
NYONDO, zi-		hammer.
NYONGA, zi-		pelvis, hip bone.

TUMBUKA	TONGA	ENGLISH
kuNYONGORORA	kuNYONGO·	to twist. p. kunyongoroka. Mwachinyongo, you have gone and turned back on the road.
	kuNYONGOZEKA	to twist about (in pain). caus. kunyongozgeska.
uNYORO, (mau-)		chain; fetters; (stitch in wound).
kuNYORORA		to straighten. p. kunyoroka, to be straight; to be upright; to be righteous. caus. kunyoroska, to straighten; to justify.
muNYORORO, mi-		worm.
NYOTA, (ya)		thirst.
kuNYOZA		to sneer at; to deride; to slander.
NYOZI, zi-		string.
kuNYUKA		to soften a hide by rubbing.
kuNYUKUTA		to crush up (as a piece of paper).
NYUMA, zi-		behind. (with pa- or ku-) behind, after. also ku manyuma. Kuwera chifutanyuma, to retreat backwards.
NYUMA, ʋa-		the second of twins.
NYUMBA, zi-		hut; house.
kujiNYUMWA		to betray oneself; to be ashamed; to be conscience-stricken.
NYUNE, zi-		grass seed swept from path by first rains (chikukura nyune).
	NYUNGU, zi-	calabash plant.
kuNYUNG'UMIRA		to suck (as a sweet). intens. kunyung'umizga, to clean the teeth with the tongue after eating.
kuNYUNGURA		to twist: to maltreat or torture (twisting limba, or beating with fists).
kuNYUNKUTURA		to twist off (e.g. twig or fruit). p. kunyunkutuka.
kuNYUNTUKA		to spring; to pounce (e.g. as a leopard).
kuNYUNYA		to sprinkle (as salt, or powder).
kuNYUNYUTA		to grumble; to complain.
	kuNYURURUKA	to stretch (oneself).
	kuNYUTUWA	to stretch (e.g. nyuwa in making bark-cloth). p. kunyutuka. caus. kunyutuska.
	NYUWA. zi-	bark-cloth. (kusara nyuwa, to beat out bark-cloth).

96

O

TUMBUKA	TONGA	ENGLISH
mOA, mi-		beer. (brewed from millet &c.).
kOCHA		to burn; to roast. p.—eka. (see kupya).
	kOCHERE maji	to temper (iron—done with water).
mOFI, ʋ-		a timorous person; coward. wofi (u-), fear.
kOFYA		caus. of kopa.
chOFYO, vi-		something terrifying; fear.
chOKORO, vy-	chOKO, vy-	widow.
OKWE !		expresses disapprobation. (also ekwe!).
chOMBO, vy-		dhow; hookah (gurgling).
kOMIRA		to be dry. p. komirwa, to be thirsty. Dongo ndomizo mu nkandwe, the mud is dry in the pit. (when not moist enough to be worked). caus. komizga, and k'omiriska, to make dry; to dry.
	kONDA	to be thin (of a person).
kONESKA		to give a feast—evening, e.g. to a party which has hoed a garden. used for the Lord's Supper: monesko, mi-, the Lord's Supper.
mONGO, mi-		marrow (e.g. in long bones).
wONGO, mi-		brain.
mu(w)ONGO, mi-		the back; the spinal column.
vyONI, (vya)		leprosy. Ʋa vyoni, lepers.
kONJA		to catch an animal in a trap or net.
	kONJA	to fish with a seine net.
kONJORA		to take from a trap (or net) an animal caught in it. (also kuwonjora).
kONKA		to suck (e.g. child at breast). caus.—eska, to suckle.
	mONKERO, mi-	the nipple. (used of feeding bottle).
mONO, mi-		creel (for trapping fish).
kOPA		to fear; to dread; to be afraid. p.—eka, to be respected. caus. kofya (kofyiska), to frighten; to terrify.
kOPEZA		to borrow; to lend; to buy "on tick".
chORI, vy-		the vagina.

TUMBUKA	TONGA	ENGLISH
	kOROWA	to be soft (e.g. of meat, or cloth); to be gentle; or tender-hearted; to yield. korovya, to soften. kujorovya, to humble oneself. —orowevu, gentle.
—OSE		all; every; the whole. Uantu vose, all the people.
kOTA moto		to warm oneself at a fire.
mOTO, mi-		fire. moto wawa, the fire has caught (in making fire with sticks—kupuka).
chOTO		ashes.
kOVWIRA	kOVYA	to help; to aid; to benefit. Movwiri, v- helper. (Tonga, movyi, v-).
chOVYO, vy-		noose. fundo la chovyo, slip-knot.
	kOWA	to bathe; koweska, to wash.
OWE !		alas!

P

TUMBUKA	TONGA	ENGLISH
PA		at; on; upon. Pa lwavo, by themselves. Pauli? when? Makani agho wakayowoya pa ngana, what he said about somebody.
PA!		full.
kuPA		to give. p.—ika. Upe kulima, hoe diligently.
kuPAUAMA		to lie flat (as of a shallow stream or a plate). Kugona kampava, to lie on back.
kuPACHIRA		to spy (country or enemies). Mpachi, zi-, spy.
	chiPADWA, vi-	chip (of wood). (kupandura).
kuPAFULA		to kick.
kuPAJUKA		to fall away from (as a dead branch from a tree).
kuPAKA		to pack (things into a bag or box). rev.—ura, to unpack.
	kuPAKA	as above; also to wind string on a stick with notches at ends for netting. rev. kupakuwa.
kuPAKARASKA		to rustle things about (as in packing).
kuPAKANA		to adjoin; to border on. vakapaka-nanga minda yavo, they were neighbours. (also kupakizgana).

TUMBUKA	TONGA	ENGLISH
chiPAKARARA, vi-		trouble; hindrance; calamity. Charu cha vipakarara, a difficult country.
	kuPAKASA	to flourish (of growing grass); to set reeds closely together as purlins in roofing a hut.
kuPAKATA		to fold (child) in bosom; to hold closely; to hug. Chipakato, vi-, breast; bosom.
mPAKO, mi-		food provision for a journey (bag of flour &c.).
PAKUNJI		perhaps; or.
PAKUTI		for; as; because; since; inasmuch as.
kuPAMANTA		to strike with palm; to slap. ndamkukupamanta na malupi ghatatu, I'll give you three slaps.
kuPAMBA		used as an auxiliary with a verb to suggest probability—vati vapambe kundichindika, it may be they will honour me.
kuPAMBA		to cluster on (as maize on cob) Kupamba somba, to string fish on a reed. p. kupambika, to bear fruit. chipambi, vi-, fruit. Mpambo, mi-, garland of flowers.
	kuPAMBAWUWA	to separate; kupambawuka, to be separated.
kuPAMBANA		to differ; to be separate. Umo vakupambanirana, how they differ from one another.
kuPAMPUKA		to awake; to get up. caus. kupampuska, to waken; to arouse.
PAMPU, ma-		diligence; zeal; eagerness. also forwardness; interruption; rudeness.
	kuPANA	to sue for payment. chipanira, vi-, an excessive demand; extortion.
kuPANDA		to plant; to sow (one by one, not broadcast—as maize, sweet potato &c.).
PANDA, ma-		a shoal (of fish); a row (of men).
	mPANDA, mi-	a fence.
PANDE, ma-		a part; a share; a division.
kuPANDIRA		to make excuses; to deny. Mpandira, mi-, excuse.
mPANDO, mi-		a seat; stool; chair.
	chiPANDO, vi-	a stump (in path).

TUMBUKA	TONGA	ENGLISH
kuPANDURA		to split; to divide. Chipanduko, vi-, a part split off; chips (chopped from wood).
chiPANGA, vi-		an enclosed yard; porch; trap.
luPANGA, malu-		sword.
kuPANGA		(Nyanja, to do; to make). Kupanga (fundo), to instruct; to give a course of detailed instructions or advice. vipango, vi-, instructions.
	chiPANGO, vi-	a plot.
kuPANGANA		to make a covenant, agreement, or promise. chipangano, vi-, (and pangano, ma-), a promise; an agreement; a covenant.
kuPANGWA		to be aroused, or urged, by instinct. (e.g. migratory birds—not of men). caus.—iska, hunger, or constant hunting, may cause animals to migrate. (p. of kupanga).
kuPANGANDIRA		to grow out of place (e.g. a new tooth).
kuPANGIRA		see kupanjira.
PANGWE, ma-		a musical instrument like a guitar.
kuPANIKIZGA		to bear witness; to testify; to be sure. kuponya kwakupanikizga, to be a sure shot.
PANJI		perhaps. panji...panji, either...or: whether...or. Panji vula yingiza, perhaps the rain may come. Panji nesi, nor; not even.
kuPANJIRA		to fit an axe (or hoe) into its handle.
kuPANJWA		a man may entertain visitors and give up his hut to them saying, "Nkapanjwe kunyake." "I'll fit in elsewhere".
kuPANKURA		to break down and destroy (e.g. a house). pankuro, (li-), destruction.
PANO		here; also penepano and papano.
kuPANTA		to burst—as plant pods, flinging seeds to a distance.
kaPANTI, va-		a weed which bursts as above, often the seed flies into peoples' eyes.
	kaPANTI, va-	cassava and Ceara rubber plants which throw their seeds as above.
PAPA, ma-		wing (e.g. of flying ants).

100

TUMBUKA	TONGA	ENGLISH
	kuPAPA	to give birth; to bear (offspring).
chiPAPA, vi-		skin.
kuPAPANYURA		to tease out (as cotton).
	kuPAPANYUKA	to be tattered) e.g. a book).
kuPAPASKA		to feel about; to grope (as one looking for something in the dark). dir.—ira, to grope for. (used also with jiso as subject).
—PAPATI		adj. thin, flat.
kuPAPATARA		to be thin, or flattened (as a cushion which has been sat on). Kujipapatizga, to contract oneself so as to pass through a narrow opening. Chiuta wakajipapatizga kukhara mwa ise.
muPAPI, va-		parent. (kupapa).
kuPAPIKA		with -po or -ko suffix, to add to: with -mo suffix, (to go) and return (same day).
PAPINDO, ma-	maPAPIKO, (gha)	wings, pinions.
PAPO		there (apo).
PAPU, ma-		lung.
chiPAPURURU, vi-		cast skin (e.g. of snake or lizard).
PARA		there; yonder; away from us both, (of time) when.
kuPARA		to scratch, or scrape; to plane (a board).
	chiPARA, vi-	fireplace in hut.
chiPARAMBA, vi-		desert; bare soil.
kuPARAMIRA		to be caught in a tree, or on a roof (e.g. a stick or a ball): (Senga) to approach; to draw near.
kuPARAMURA		to depreciate; to be little; to disparage; to slight; to run down.
kuPARANA		kuparana ubwezi, to make friends.
chiPARANTA (chi-)		kufwa chiparanta, to be very thirsty. Malo gha chiparanta, a desert place.
kuPARANYA		to destroy; to scatter). p.—ika. Paraniko, ma-, destruction.
kuPARAPATA		to scrape or abrade. Muswa ukuparapata mabuku, white ants deface books.
kuPARAPASKA		to feel about, or grope, with hands (as in seeking something in the dark).

TUMBUKA	TONGA	ENGLISH
kuPARARA		to spread out—as a band of men hunting, or seeking something; to open out flat (of mushroom). Ufumu ungaparara luviro.
kuPARASURA		to brush away.
luPARO, malu-		sifting basket.
kuPARURA		to tear; to split. Kuparura munda, to open up a new garden (also kuparura marongo, or magadi). p. kuparuka.
kuPASA		to roof (a house). rev. kupasula, to pull down; to demolish (house); to destroy.
maPASU, (gha-)		rafters.
kuPASA		to bear fruit. chipasi, vi-, fruit.
PASI		below; under; down. (followed by pa).
	kuPASKA	to give.
kuPATA		to dislike; to hate; to reject; to divorce. p. kupatikika. rec. kupatana, to separate (of husband and wife).
kuPATULA		to separate; to divide; to differentiate. (also kupatuska and kupatulanya).
kuPATULIKA		to be separated—hence to be holy.
kuPATUKA		to divide; to go aside (as forked path). (euphemism for defaecate). Kupatukana, to part from one another: kupatuskana, to cause to part.
chiPATA, vi-		gateway (e.g. through a fence, or stockade); a divorce. (also chipati).
mPATA, mi-		ravine; gorge; valley.
kuPATAULA		to recount; to detail; to explain; to set forth in order.
kuPAURA	kuPAUWA	to take down (one by one) things that have been hanging (as fruit from a tree). (rev. of kupayika).
	PAVWA !	sound of a body falling into water.
PAWEME		good-bye. Murute paweme.
kuPAYIKA		to hang (tr.). (Used of crucifixion).
kuPAYIRA		to wink.
kuPAZA		to escape from bondage.

TUMBUKA	TONGA	ENGLISH
kuPAZGA		to hand over for safe keeping (e.g. a child to grandparents; or money to bank).
	kuPAZGA bwalo	to appeal to court.
	PE	see pera.
chiPEKA, vi-		bracelet of woven grass.
	kuPEKESA mpekesa,	to test by ordeal. Mpekesa zakonda, the test has succeeded.
PEKESI, ma-		dry stalks of maize, millet &c.
kuPEKULA		to joke; to jest.
kuPEMA		to drizzle (rain).
	kuPEMERE	to sprinkle. Vuwa yipemere, it is drizzling. Kumpemere mata, to spit on him. Mpemere ya waka, a rumour.
kuPEMANA		to be reconciled (of two parties) caus. kupemaniska, to reconcile.
kuPEMBA		to kindle a fire (by blowing).
chiPEMBO, vi-		a fireplace.
chiPEMBERE, vi-		rhinoceros.
kuPEMBEREZGA		to persuade; to urge.
kuPEMBUZGA		to soothe; to comfort; to pacify. (as a mother singing a lullaby to a crying child).
kuPEMENTERA		to sprinkle (e.g. water).
kuPEMESKA		to gather up and throw over the shoulder the end of a cloth worn loosely.
	PEMPO, ma-	request; prayer. (Nyanja, kupempera).
kuPEMPURA		to pay a visit of several days to a friend in another village: used of visiting a village to inspect school.
kuPENDA		to count; (arithmetic).
kuPENDAMA		dazi lapendama, the sun has declined (in the sky). Pa dazi mpendama, in the afternoon. (cp. kubendama).
kuPENDERA		to be deformed (kubendera).
kuPENDUZGA		to draw lots; to hide in the hand for one to guess and get. Mpenduzga, zi-, lot.
	kuPENEVYA mazu	to misuse words so as to deceive.
liPENGA, mali-		bugle (Nyanja).
mPENI, mi-		knife.

103

TUMBUKA	TONGA	ENGLISH
kuPENJA		to seek; to look for; to wish; to be about to (do something). intens. kupenjisiska.
kuPENKA mpuno		to blow the nose.
PENTYA-PENTYA		unsteadily (as a drunk man walks).
kuPEPA		to be well disposed; to be gentle. Pepani, "beg pardon". Kupepeka, to flatter; to seek favour with. Kupepeska, to appease with an offering; to propitiate.
	kuPEPETUWA	to turn about.
	maPEPI, (gha-)	a kind of white ant (said to have no queen).
—PEPU		adj. light.
kuPEPULA		to lighten; to make light of.
kuPEPUKA		to be light. caus. kupepuska.
PERA		adv. only; alone. Ndipera, really; enough! finish!
kuPERA		to finish; to come to an end. To be contrite (in the sense of promising not to continue the evil). Wapera wachita... although he has done...
kuPERA		to grind (grain).
mPERE-PERE-PERE !		a crowd of people, or nyama, standing about.
kuPEREKA		to give up; to hand over; (to betray or to deliver).
kuPEREKEZGA		to conduct; to accompany on way.
	kuPEREMERA	to excel. Peremero, (li-), excellence
kuPERERA		to come short.
kuPEREWERA		to come short; to be insufficient.
	kuPESA	to comb (hair). Chipeso, vi-, comb.
PESI, ma-		stalk of maize, or sugar-cane.
PESKA, ma-		necklace of large white stones (Arab).
muPESKA, mi-		a creeper or vine (wild). Mpeska, zi- the fruit. (used for grape vine and grapes).
kuPETA		to winnow; to sift (e.g. husk out of broken maize). Luparo, malu-, the winnowing basket.
	kuPETA	to bend over. Mpete, zi-, a ring.
kuPETEKA		to fold.
uPETI (u-)		grace.

TUMBUKA	TONGA	ENGLISH
	PEWA, ma-	shoulder.
	chiPEWA, vi-	hat. (Nyanja).
	kuPEYA	to sweep.
kuPHAKA		to anoint; to rub (with ointment or liniment). Also kuphakazga.
PHAMPA, ma-		the shoulder-blade (scapula).
luPHANDA, malu-	PHANDA, ma-	forked stick or post (stuck in floor of hut for hanging things on).
kuPHAPA		to grow thin; to atrophy; to be withered (of a limb).
kuPHARA		to tell; to declare. Kuphalira, to tell to; kupharazga, to declare; to preach. Kupharizgana, to run races; to compete (e.g. at a show, or exhibition).
kuPHASKA		to ward off (danger) from oneself. Kuphasizga, to ward off from another (e.g. arrows or spears; but also unseen dangers).
kuPHATA		to strip (leaves from a stem); to knock dust off a cloth; to moult (fowl).
kuPHATIRA		to stick in a narrow space (or in mud).
PHERE, (yi-)		beer. (Nyanja).
kuPHIKA		to boil; to cook in a pot. Mphika, mi-, pot. chiphikiro, vi-, a feast.
kuPHINDA		to walk quickly; to hasten (for a purpose).
mPHINGA, mi-		bar for shutting door.
kuPHINYA		to wink, or shut one eye in focussing an object with the other: to gird up the loins (with belt or other end of cloth). (to bring smoke out from nostrils when smoking).
(lu)PHIRI, mapiri		hill; mountain.
PHODO, ma-		quiver (for arrows).
kuPHOKWA		to be saved (snatched from danger). Mphokwa, (u-), safety.
PHOMPHA		kuchita phompha, to make light of, to trifle. Reka kuchita phompha, stop trifling.
PHONDO, ma-		door (made of planks) of house.
kuPHOTORA		to clean thoroughly; to scrub; to scour. kuphotoka, to look well (as a sick person recovering); to act shyly (as a girl with a lad).

Tumbuka	Tonga	English
kuPHUKWA		to desire; to crave. P̂hukwa, (li-), loneliness.
	PHUMU, ma-	steeped cassava.
	kuPHUMUKA	to burst forth (as a river overflowing its banks).
	PHUZO (li-)	impudence; folly; cruelty.
luPI, ma-		palm of hand. kukuʋa mapi, clap hands.
chiPIJA, vi-		a part partitioned off in a hut; a room.
kuPIKA		to carry a load on a pole between two men.
kuPIKUKA		to move up and down as the load on the pole does with the motion of the men—piku-piku-piku! (technical—of the penis in erection).
kuPIKISA		to rub (grain) in the hands so as to remove husk. Kupikiska, to defame.
kuPIKITA		to cut across; to hack (nyama) in pieces (instead of dividing it in sections).
kuPIKURA		to lever up (e.g. a weight) with a pole; to root up (sprouting maize—as rats do); to oppose a plan, or a proposal.
kuPIMA		to measure; to weigh; to judge.
kuPIMA		to shiver (with cold).
mPIMINTA, mi-		a small bundle (e.g. of split bamboo); a roll of papers.
chiPIMPHIA, vi-		a thing cut off; (a resume of a speech).
kuPINDA		to stretch a string of a bow, kupinda uta; kupinda mawoko, to fold arms across the breast; to set a trap. (used of arching a roof—as the string arches the bow).
chiPINDA, vi-		a partition in a hut; a room. (kupinda).
chiPINDI, vi-		large calabash without handle.
mPINGO, mi-		a company; a flock; (congregation).
kuPINGIRIZGA		to bar (a door).
kuPINDANA		to oppose one another in a quarrel. Mpindano, zi, strife.
	kuPINDIKA	mwapindikakunji kuno? what is your ill-will which prevents you coming to us?

TUMBUKA	TONGA	ENGLISH
kuPINDIKANA		to strive; to quarrel; to fight. Chimpindikwa, vi-, enemy; adversary. Mpindikwa, zi-, enemy (also enmity).
kuPINDIRIZGA		to make difficult; (in a discussion).
kaPINDIZGORI		hung up by the legs; (headlong, Acts 1, 18). also kapingizgori).
kuPINGA		to sing aloud for joy (in a company) to dance for joy.
maPINGA, (gha-)		harm befalling a pregnant woman (supposed to be due to adultery of husband). Munkwara wa mapinga, contraceptive drug.
kuPINGAMA		to lie crosswise (e.g. tree across road).
	kuPINGA	to carry. Mpingwa, zi-, a loop for carrying. Mphingu, zi-, a load; a burden.
chiPINGO, vi-	chiPINGA, vi-	trap; snare.
chiPINI, vi-		nasal ornament.
kuPINJIKA		to lay across (e-g. firewood); mpinjika, zi-, a cross.
kuPINTUKA		to cause stabbing pain (as when a thorn in the flesh is moved), pintu, pintu!
	kuPIPA	to wipe an infant's buttocks when soiled by faeces.
maPIRA, (gha-)		large millet; Kaffir corn.
mPIRA, mi-		rubber; (ball). Kwanka mpira, ball game.
	maPIRINGINDI	mavi gha mapiringindi; hard faeces; scybala.
kuPIRINGIZGA		to bar a door by a pole slung across it. to cause stabbing pain (as pleurisy)—which catches the breath and prevents proper breathing.
kuPIRINGUKA		to stroll to and fro (at market or a fair).
kuPIRIPITA		to struggle; to strive with a difficulty.
chiPIRIRI, vi-	chiPIRI, vi-	scorpion.
kuPISKA		to tie a string criss-cross (round a bundle). Kwendera mpiska, to sneak round trying to find some fault in a supposed friend. (to feel about under a woman's cloth).

TUMBUKA	TONGA	ENGLISH
kuPITA		to pass by; to go (Nyanja). Chipita mbali lero—of the declination of the sun in the cold season.
PITO, ma-		a whistle.
kaPIYU-PIYU, tu-		chicken.
kuPIZGURA		to tip up (as when one sits on the end of a bench). p. kupizguka.
kuPOKA		to take; to seize. (to save; to rescue).
kuPOKERA		to take; to receive; to accept; to get; to welcome (person). Kupokerana, fellowship. Kupokera sumu, response in singing.
luPOKO, (lu-)		small millet (used for making beer or sima).
POKO-POKO		shaky (e.g. as horns loose on a skull).
	chiPOKORO, vi-	thorny, yellow, fruit—used as dendi.
kuPOKOTORA		to describe in detail (e.g. a journey).
kuPOKOZORA		to pluck out; to pick out; to scrape out.
kaPOLO, vaka-		slave (esp. male). (Nyanja).
kuPOMA		to sound aloud (e.g. waterfall; people shouting; or derisive laughter).
kuPOMBA		to wind (as cotton on a reel, or binding a nkata). Kupomborora, or kupombonyora, to unwind. Kupomboroka, to be unwound, loose.
kuPOMBONYEZGA		to untwist, or fray, string. Kupombonyezga makani, to mix up a matter so that it is not clear.
	kuPOMBONYUKA	to be frayed out (as the end of a rope).
chiPOMBO, vi-		a species of tree.
POMBONI, va-		large black ant with an evil smell.
	kuPOMPA	to flow; to pour (as water from a roof, or from rone-pipe into tank); to leak. Chironda chikupompa, the ulcer is discharging (pus). Chiviya chikupompa the pot is leaking (or maji ghakupompa mu chiviya).
kuPONA		to escape; to be safe. Kuponoska to save. Kuponoskeka, to be saved. Chiponosko, (chi-) salvation. Mponoski, va-, saviour.

TUMBUKA	TONGA	ENGLISH
kuPONDA-PONDA		to stamp (with feet). (Nyanja).
kuPONDEREZGA		(pasi) to weigh down; to subject (a person).
	chiPONDI, (chi-)	chipondi cha Uachirwa, the late Chirwa.
chiPONGO, vi-		a he-goat.
kuPONGOLERA		to open a channel (e.g. for water).
mPONGOZI, va-		mother-in-law and her sisters.
kuPONTORA		to pluck fruit from tree by twisting stem. kupontoka, to bend down from the waist—pesu!
kuPONYA		to throw; to cast; to shoot (bow or gun). Kuponya pachanya, to refer (a dispute) to the chief. Kuponyeka ufumu, to be installed, or invested, as chief.
maPOPA (gha-)		desert; wilderness. (malo gha mapopa).
mPOPI, mi-		pipe (e.g. for water).
kuPOPOMA		to roar (as a cataract, or breakers on Lake).
kuPOPOTOKA		to be twisted (of basket, nkokwe, house).
kuPORA		to cool; to be healed (ulcer). caus. kupozga, to cool; to heal. sima yapora, the porridge has cooled. Ndopa zipore, let passions cool down. Marundi pori! legs over-tired with walking.
PORI !		phiri lakuwoneka pori, the hill just peeping over the ridge; something just sticking up.
PORI-PORI !		gently; softly.
kuPOROMOKA		to fall from a height.
kuPORONKANYA		to pierce through and through.
mPORORO, mi-		tattoo marks (e.g. of Bemba—in line on forehead).
kuPOROTA		to pierce. Kuporoska, to perforate.
kuPOROWOTA		to be loose in socket (e.g. axe in handle).
kuPOSA		to twist (e.g. fibre to make string)
POSO, (li-)		rations. (for a journey, or when working away from home).
kuPOTA		kupota homwa, to wage war.
chiPOTI, vi-		bead necklace.
	kuPOZOMOKA	to fall off (e.g. from a bundle being carried). To be saved. Chipozomosko, vi-, salvation.

TUMBUKA	TONGA	ENGLISH
chiPOZWA, vi-		maize plant before the cob appears.
kuPUKA moto		to make fire (by rubbing sticks). Moto wawa, the fire has come (the tow catches).
kuPUKUNYA		(mutu) to shake the head (in doubt, or unwilling to speak about something).
kuPUKURUKA		to be perplexed, or non-plussed. Uali pukuru waka, they are uncertain.
chiPULI, vi-		boundary mark (claim-peg, half cut tree, or knotted grass, &c.).
kuPULIKA		to hear; to perceive (by sight, smell. taste, hearing, touch). Pulikani, listen! Khutupulika, pay attention!
kuPULIKIRA		to obey. Kupulikiska, to listen, to understand. Kupulikikwa, to be heard.
kuPULIKANA		to believe. Chipulikano (chi-), faith.
	kuPUMA	to strike; to beat. Kupuma nkondo, to make a raid.
PUMBA, ma-		a boil.
	luPUMI (lu-)	white ants (flying—eaten).
kuPUMULA		to rest. caus. kupumuzga, to cause to rest.
kuPUNDULA		to maim; to make lame. Waku-pundukwa, a lame person.
	kuPUNGA	to settle a case (of a third party in a "triangular case").
mPUNGA, (u-)		rice.
chiPUNGU, vi-		tail-less eagle.
	mPUNGU, va-	mid-wife (see Nyanja dictionary).
	mPUNGU, (u-)	north wind.
kuPUNGURA		to pour (into).
PUNGWE, va-		youth; young man.
kuPUNTA		to withdraw allegiance (from a chief).
kuPUPA		to cut (e.g. grass, or hair—not shaven).
chiPUPU, vi-		small bundle (e.g. of grass stems for thatching).
kuPUPUTA		to blow; to brush; to dust.
PURA, ma-		bees-wax.
	chiPURA, vi-	cutlass.

TUMBUKA	TONGA	ENGLISH
	chiPURA usiku, wa	an evening planet (? Venus).
kuPURA		to pound (grain—in tuli). p.—ika. Kupuzgana, to pound together in company.
kuPURA		to take from the fire (e.g. a pot, when its contents are cooked).
	PURU, ʋa-	a small duiker. (horn used for medicine).
kuPURUKA		to go astray; to err; to sin. Kupuruska, to lead astray.
chiPURUMBA, vi-		a mass of iron after smelting.
kuPURUNGIZGA		to move stolen cattle from place to place to mislead the owner; to overstate; to overshoot the mark.
kuPURURA		to strip off, or pluck off (fruit or leaves from a tree).
	kuPURUSKA	mpepo yipuruska mani, the wind blows off the leaves.
mPURURUNGWA (u-)		poverty. Ndakhara mpururungwa, I am stripped. (like a tree without even a leaf).
PURURU, ʋa-		owl.
kuPURUTA		to fall (leaves): mahamba ghakupuruta mu makuni na mpepo, the leaves are blown off the trees by the wind.
kuPUSA		to be foolish. Kupusika, to deceive.
uPUSIKIZGI, (u-)		deceit.
PUSI, ʋa-		small monkey.
—PUSU		adj. easy: nchipusu, it is easy.
kuPUSUMPA		to hurry: caus.—iska, to make to hurry. Lupusu, (lu-), haste. Ndiri pa lupusu, I am in a hurry.
kuPUTA		to blow (wind); to puff at (breath).
	chiPUTU, vi-	tuft of grass; clod.
kuPUVYA		to mislead; to deceive: to stultify (instruction, by failing to comply). p. kupuvyika or kupuvyiwa. Kupulika mpuvya, to mis--understand.
	kuPUWA	to pound (grain in mortar).
	kuPUZGA	to perceive. Chipuzga chisungu cha muntu, (game) feels the scent of man.
kuPUZGANA		see kupura.

111

Tumbuka	Tonga	English
kuPUZURA		to smite; to kill (with club, not spear).
muPWA, va-		nephew or niece (man's sister's child).
PWA !		nyengo pwa! a long time (waiting)!
kuPWA		to dry up (water in a vessel, stream &c.). Thupi lose ipwe, ipwe! (of a patient recovering from dropsy).
—PWAFU		flat; soft. Upwafu (u-), worthlessness.
kuPWAFUKA		to be soft (e.g. football; a ripe boil).
kuPWALALIKIRA		to die out (fire in green grass).
kuPWAMULA		v. tr. to burst. Kupwamuka, v. int. to burst (e.g. a pot).
PWANKU !		smash! (see kukuva).
kuPWANYURA		to break up; to smash (e.g. a pot).
kuPWATURA		to burst; to tear apart (e.g. bonds).
kuPWEKA		to be soft, or pulpy; to be thin (of sima).
kuPWEKETUKA		to become soft (of cloth).
kuPWEPWA		to whisper; kupwepwera, to whisper closely.
chiPWEPWE, vi-		cold season. (winter). (dew lying in morning).
kuPWERERA		to be diligent; to care for (e.g. a child); to be troubled about; to take care.
kuPWETEKA		to hurt; to pain. p. kupwetekeka.
PWETEKIRI, va-		tomato.
kuPWIRIPITUKA		to laugh heartily. Kuseka pwiripitu!
	PWITU, va-	small birds. (? sparrows).
	kuPWITUKA	to be broken in (as a pot with water set on bricks is softened and broken in below).
—PYA		adj. new; fresh; ripe.
kuPYA		to be burnt; to be cooked; to be ripe; to be ready. Kupya mpyuku, excoriation between thighs due to sweat in walking.
chiPYA, vi-		high grass lands on mountains (burnt spaces).
chiPYEPYE, vi-		the flat part of a fish's tail. Kumkora chipyepye chara, don't catch him by the tail—he'll slip from your grasp.

kuPYERA		to sweep; to brush. Chipyerero, vi-, brush, broom. Mitima yakupyereka, clean hearts.
chiPYO, vi-		trials; sufferings. (kupokera vipyo).
kuPYORA		to break across, or off. p. kupyoka. (of stick or stone—contr. kuswa).
PYU !		yellow. kana kapyu (of a very young child).
	kuPYURURUKIYA	to be yellow (or pink).
PYUMPYU, (li-)		zeal.

R

—RA		demonstrative, yonder—yura, chira, &c. also prefixed by ku- pa- or mu- denoting distance in space or time from speaker.
	kuRA	to lie down; to stay. Kararidu, ka-, habits, character.
maRAUI (gha-)		the south (local tribal reference).
kuRAGHARA		kut'aka raghali! exhausted!
kuRAKATA		to fall off; to be shed (e.g. leaves from trees, hair of head). (met. of deaths in epidemics). caus. kurakaska, to shake off; to shake down; to break down or crumble.
	kuRAMA	to be tough; to be strong.
chiRAMBA, vi-		small, open, smelting furnace.
kuRAMIRA		to sit on eggs (fowl).
	kuRANDA	to go astray; to wander.
mRANDA, va-		a bereaved person; an orphan. (mother bereft of child or child bereft of mother).
uRANDA, mau-		bereavement; destitution.
kuRANDARA		to lean over (e.g. a post); to bend or bow (from the waist). Kurandalika, to tilt (as in making a tent-peg lean over—kut'aka randali).
mRANDU		a case at law; a charge; a story; a business; matter to be talked over.
maRANGO, (gha)		laws (see dango).
kuRANGURUKA		to think; to meditate.
kuRAPA		to take an oath; to swear; to vow. Kurapizga to cause to take an oath. Chirapo, vi-, oath. (e.g. Tikakumane pa mutu utuva, let me see your skull. Huva yikuparure, the lightning rend thee.).

TUMBUKA	TONGA	ENGLISH
	uRAPASI, (u-)	urapasi wa vantu, a multitude of people.
chiRAPI, vi-		tale; fable (in song with chorus).
—RARA		adj. old; adult. Murara, va-, a senior person; an elder, (respected as such). Urara, (u-), old age.
muRARA, mi-		fibre (for sewing a cracked chandi).
maRARO (gha-)		graves; tombs.
uRARO, mau-		bridge.
kuRASA		to pierce; to wound; to stab. (met. of stabbing pain in pleurisy). Chiraso, (chi-), also karaso, (ka-), stabbing pain; pleurisy.
kuRATA		to aim towards; to lead to; to go to. Warata munwe ku...he has pointed to...Marati, (gha-), aim; goal.
kuRAZGA		to make to aim; to direct towards. Kurazga nkonto ku..., to turn one's back on...
RATA, ma-		corrugated iron.
viRATO, (vi-)		sandals.
kuRAUKA		to take food in preparation for some effort e.g. work, or travel—usually early in the morning).
(li)RAYA, ma-		garment; shirt; jacket; dress.
	maRAYI (gha-)	farewells; parting instructions; (a will). (kulayira).
mRAZA, mi-		signs of mourning; (cloth bound round head; cap made of strings; strings round neck).
mRAZA, (u-)		whey from sour milk. (Ngoni).
liRAZI, ma-		rays (of sun).
kuREKA		to stop, or to leave off (doing something); often used as a negative, reka kuchita, don't do it: used as idiom meaning—'that's why'—wakatituma reka (ni) tiza, he sent us so we have come. caus. kurekeska, to prevent, to cause to stop.
kuREKERERA	kuREKE	to leave alone; to forgive.
	chiREPA, vi-	small fishing net.
viRERE, (vya)		dance with matete and maize stalks.

TUMBUKA	TONGA	ENGLISH
	kuRGHA	to eat. Janja la marghe, the right hand.
kuRIƲA		to mend (as in patching cloth). chiriʋa, vi-, plastered wall.
chiRIMIKA, vi-		a hoeing; a hoeing season; (used for year).
—RINGA !		(with appropriate concord) how many? karinga? how often?
kuROƲA		to fish (with net, or poison): mrovi, ʋa-, a fisherman.
kuROKORA		to express from a narrow opening (bean from shell; pus from abscess): kurokoka, to exude or emerge. caus. kurokoska.
kuROKOTA		to imagine.
kuROKWA		to fall as rain. Vula yikurokwa.
kuROMBA		to ask; to beg; to pray: (lu) rombo, ma-, request; petition; prayer.
	uROMBA (u-)	wealth, riches.
mROMBO, mi-		plant with large leaves (like rhubarb)—(leaves and root used as dendi).
viROMBO, vi-		spirits. Kuvina virombo, to exorcise the spirits causing illness by drumming and dancing.
kuROMBOTORA		to weaken. Kurombotoka to be weak (prob. a transposed form of kutomboroka).
chiRONDA, vi-		sore; ulcer; (wound).
maRONDA (gha-)		goods for barter or sale.
	kuRONDE	to receive; to get.
	liRONDO, ma-	storm.
kuRONDORA		to follow. (also kurondezga).
kuRONGA		to put grain (e.g. maize) into a nkokwe or ntamba; to lay up in store. Kuronga mrandu na ngana, to bring an action against someone. intens. kurongezga, to pack (e.g. snuff into snuff-mull).
mRONGA, mi-		river; stream.
maRONGO (gha-)		clods (on ground newly broken up with hoe).
	uRONGO	ku urongo, in front.

TUMBUKA	TONGA	ENGLISH
kuRONGORA		to set before; to shew; to lead; to point out. Kurongozga, to lead by going in front; to conduct; to guide; to set (e.g. a plank) in front, pointing forward (not cross-wise)—i.e. in an antero-posterior position. Kurongo-zgana na, to accompany; to go along with.
chiRONGOZI, vachi-		leader; guide (also ndongozi, zi-, and mrongozi, va).
chiRONGOLERO, vi-		pattern; example.
	kuRONGORO	to speak; to talk.
kuRONGOSORA		to prepare; to set in order. p. kurongosoreka, to be prepared; to be ready.
uRONGWE, mau-		dung; manure.
kuRONJERANA		to greet; to exchange greetings and news on meeting. Maronje, (gha-), greetings. Ndakumana nayo kweni kuti ndamuronjera chara, I have met him but haven't spoken to him.
kuRONKORA		to disappoint.
	ROPA (mu-)	blood; (purple). Kumwa ropa, to drink blood.
kuROPORA	kuROPO	to overcome the power of witch-craft by the use of an antidote (chiroporo, vi-).
	kuROPWA	to be raw, tasteless, or wersh (e.g. sima cooked with water which hasn't boiled); met. to be weak.
kuROTOKA		to rush (as into battle). Kurotokera, to attack.
kuROWOKA		to cross over (stream or lake): vula zarowoka, the rains have broken (come over). kurowoska, to ferry across.
chiROWOKO, vi-		landing-place; frequented part of shore; beach.
kuROZGA		to test; to try out. Chirozgo, vi-, test; (evidence): wedge to keep axe firm in handle, or plug to fill up a hole (tested) to fit): windfalls or firstfruits (the first taste of the fruit).
kuRUKA		to weave; (to knit): (making nets, baskets, mats—contr. kuwomba).
	maRUKWA (gha-)	rushes (growing in swampy places —burnt for salt).

TUMBUKA	TONGA	ENGLISH
	kuRULIKA	to set in order. kurulikika.
kuRUMA		to bite. Kuruma sayati, to clench the teeth.
kuRUMBA		to praise; to admire. Kajirumbi, (ka-), a conceited person. Rumbo, ma-, praise.
—RUMI		adj. male. Chirumi, (chi-), father's family.
kuRUMURA		to stop suckling (of a child, or a calf). p. kurumurwa (subject the child or calf).
RUMWA,		crack (in pot, or dry soil). (kuruma).
liRUNDA (li-)		hump (of ox).
kuRUNDA		to heap together; to add to; to throw on a heap (e.g. rubbish heap).
RUNDI, ma-		leg; foot.
mRUNDO, mi-		pot with wide neck.
chiRUNDU, vi-		a heap; four yards of cloth.
kuRUNGA		(and kurunganya) to join together; to splice; kurungako, to join on to; to add to; kurunga dendi, to add salt to the dendi, or to mix the dendi: kurungana (pamoza) to be joined, to be at one.
maRUNGA (gha-)		joints. (used also in reference to the muscular twitchings of an animal after death).
RUNGI-RUNGI		smooth.
chiRUNGO, vi-		ferment (e.g. millet moistened till it sprouts, then dried and ground —used for brewing beer); leaven; yeast.
	kuRUNGUCHIZGA	to teach.
kuRUNGURA	kuRUNGUWA	to be hot. Kurunguzga, to heat.
	kuRUNGURUKA	to think; to meditate.
	mRUNGUZI, mi-	an irritating grass.
mRUNGWANA, ʋa-		an Arab.
kuRUNJIKA		to be straight; to be right; (of good aim in shooting, to 'hit the nail'). caus. kurunjiska, to straighten; to justify. Urunji, mau-, righteousness.
kaRUNKURWE, tu-		a smallish mushroom.
	uRURU, mau-	a reedy grass (burnt for salt).
kuRURUKA		to be accustomed to.

117

TUMBUKA	TONGA	ENGLISH
kuRUSKA		to defeat; to overcome; also to excel; to surpass: (better, in comparison of adjectives): as adverb, kwakuruska, especially. Ise tiruskenge vara, we shall defeat them. Ise tiruskenge pa vara, we shall be better off than they.
RUSO, ma-		custom; habit (also karuso tu-). Uruso-uruso, properly.
RUTA-RUTA		often.
kuRUTA		to go; to depart. Kurutirira, to go on, to continue; to advance. Kurutirizga, to cause to go on, or to grow.
	RUTI, ma	the shaft of a spear.
kuRUVYA		to announce (especially a death): nduvyo, (yi-), an offering (e.g. a fowl) sent by the messenger with the announcement.
maRUVUVU (gha-)		fragments; crumbs.
kuRUWA		to forget.
	chiRUWU, vi-	posts for building house: (for the wall).
kuRUWUKA		to eat first-fruits. Mruwuku, mi-, first-fruits.
kuRWA		to struggle; to fight. Kurwana, to do battle; to fight. Murwani, va-, enemy; adversary; foe. Urwani, mau-, danger.
chiRWA, vi-		island.
RWANDE		(with pa or ku) to one side; beside. Rwande...rwande..., On the one hand... on the other hand.
kuRWARA		to be sick, ill, or ailing. caus. kurwazga, to care for the sick; to nurse.
maRWAYO (gha-)		footprints: (sole of the foot).
	RWEGHA	ku rwegha kwa, behind; beyond; on the other side of (e.g. a house which hides the object from view).
uRWIRWI, mau-		pain; anguish. (may be used of e.g. snake venom, which causes the pain).
kuRWITA		to be sorrowful; to be pensive. (of deep grief when one is speechless).

118

TUMBUKA	TONGA	ENGLISH
kuRYA		to eat. As noun, food. Chakurya, vya-, food. Maryero, (gha-), eating: woko la maryero, the right hand. (see kuliska). Uryero (u-), manger.
muRYANGO, mi-		doorway; gate.
	mRYAPASI, mi-	a kind of cassava.
uRYARYA, mau-		guile; cunning.

S

chiSA, vi-		honeycomb. Chisa cha masa (or visa vya masa) honeycomb with larval bees: visa vya wuchi, honeycomb with honey.
viSAUIRO, vi-	kuSAUASAUA	see kusarasata.
	SABWE, zi-	louse (lice).
	chiSACHI, vi-	the lying-in place (and period) of a woman's confinement after child-birth.
kuSACHIZGA		to guess; to suggest; to offer an opinion.
mSAFI, mi-		branch (of a tree).
kuSAGHAMILA		to raise (someone's head) on a pillow.
kuSAKA		(nyama) to hunt (game driven by a company of men). (also of fish—kusaka somba).
SAKARARE		nkuku ya sakarare, a species of fowl with ruffled feathers.
kuSAKATA		to prosper: kusakata vinandi, to gather much property. Usakati, (u-), prosperity.
kuSAKAZA		to squander (money or goods).
SAKAZINJE, va-		a wild creeper used to tie round a finger with a whitlow—as medicine.
mSALALI		a long thin striped snake (harmless).
chiSALI, vi-		rat trap (set with noose on a bent sapling). salu! of the trap being sprung.
kuSAMA	(kwasama)	to open the mouth; to gape.
kuSAMA		to flit village (to new site): wali kusamiranku? where has he flitted to? Sama, (li-), a flitting.

119

TUMBUKA	TONGA	ENGLISH
kuSAMBA		to bathe; to wash. Kusambira to swim. (of woman's monthly period, "Ndawamo mu masambi": kusamba ku rwande, irregular menstruation).
kuSAMBAZGA		to make rich. p.—ika, to be rich (enriched). also kusambazgika, to make rich.
	uSAMBASI, mau-	usambazi, mau-, riches; wealth. —sambazi (adj.) rich: msambazi, ʋa-, a rich person.
SAMBI, ma-		bark cloth.
kuSAMBIRA		to learn; to read; to swim (see kusamba): msambiri, ʋa-, pupil; scholar; disciple: kusambizga, to teach: msambizgi, ʋa-, teacher: chisambizgo, vi-, lesson.
SAMBO, zi-		bracelet (metal).
mSAMILO, mi-		pillow (kusaghamila).
mSAMPA, mi-		trap, of green sapling bent and fixed down by noose.
kuSAMPUKA		to spring up—as the sapling does when the trigger of the trap is touched: mtima wane ukusampukira muchanya, my heart is stirred, or thrilled (leaps up).
	kuSAMUKA	to taste nice.
kaSAMWA, tu-		misfortune (kakawuka pa kaya) —(kusama).
	SANA, zi-	kidney.
	mSANA, mi-	the back: middle of the day; daytime; msana wale, to-day.
kuSANDA		to test; to examine: (also used of making the pattern in beadwork).
kuSANDA-SANDA		to criticise (e.g. a gift).
	SANDU	marundi gha sandu, club feet.
kuSANDUKA		to change; to alter: kusanduska, to cause to change.
kuSANGA		to find; to discover: kusangana, to share in common; to pool together. Masanganaʋana, (gha-) sharing; pooling.
SANGANAVU, ma-		hornet (s).
SANGARAWE, ma-		quartz rock.
SANGU, zi-		The Pleiades (constellation). Sangu zikwera ku mazulo—the rains are near. Vuwa yisuka sangu, the rain washes Pleiades.

120

Tumbuka	Tonga	English
kuSANGURUKA	kuSANGARUKA	to be comforted; comfortable.
kuSANGURUSKA	kuSANGARUSKA	to comfort. Sangaro, (li-), comfort.
kuSANGWA		to be pleased; to be content, happy, or cheerful. Fundo izo mukusangwa nazo, principles well-pleasing to Thee (God).
—SANI		adj. wide; broad; chisani-sani, adv., in general; widespread.
uSANI (u-)		width; breadth.
	kuSANIYA	to find.
kuSANJA		to cut (maize, grass).
SANJI (yi-)		envy; jealousy.
	SANJIKA, zi-	fish—much relished (very bony).
kuSANKA		to choose; to select; to elect: rev. kusankura, to separate (good from bad).
kuSANKARA		to be well aired, or dried (e.g. seasoned timber). Kusankazga, to set out to dry (food or other things which have been dry, have got moist, and need to be aired).
	maSANO (gha-)	graves; graveyard.
kuSANUSKA		to broaden; to enlarge.
	kuSANUWA	to be in heat (bitch).
SANYA, zi-		ray of light (e.g. from sun); also sanyanya, zi-. Sanya zikuchonta maso, the rays hurt the eyes (on looking at the sun).
chiSAPA, vi-		swamp.
maSAPA (gha-)		fringes (on a cloth).
kuSAPALIRA		to overflow (e.g. a river).
kuSAPIKIZGA		to guess.
	kuSARA	(nyuwa) to beat out bark cloth.
maSARA (gha-)		old gardens (overgrown).
mSARA (u-)		kufwa msara, to die of want". To be exhausted on a journey—faint from hunger, thirst and weariness.
kuSARA		(makani or mrandu) to set forth in order.
kuSARARA		(lulimi) to be eloquent.
	kuSARARA	(of a piece of heart wood of mlombwa lighter and softer than the rest).

121

Tumbuka	Tonga	English
	chiSARANDA, vi-	cocoon. (resting stage of insect larva).
kuSARASATA	kuSAUASAUA	to be inconsistent, changeful (as a fretful child, or a patient in delirium).
	viSAUIRO, vi-	poles rejected after trial for roof of a hut: irrelevant arguments in a mrandu.
	chiSARAYI, vi-	tree of which the wood is used for torches.
SARU, zi-		cloth: (dress).
	kuSASA	(manja) to brush dust off hands (by clapping them together): to wash hands of an affair—kusasamo. Sasapo kusi, dust it underneath.
kuSASA		to ferment; to turn sour; to rot; to decay.
mSASA, mi-		booth; temporary hut.
kuSASATURA		to unravel cloth so as to make a fringe.
SASIRA, zi-		rays (e.g. from sun): shooting pains in a limb, or pain and swelling from a wound.
kuSASKA		to offer for sale; to hawk about.
chiSASUNI, vi-		the "ear", or grain-bearing cluster of food plants, e.g. lupoko.
SATO, zi-		python.
kuSAUKA		to need; to want; to be poor, Usauchi, (u-), poverty; need; want.
kuSAURA	kuSAUWA	the return of menstruation after lactation. Ndasauliya mwana uyu le—I have weaned this child now.
kuSAPALIRA		to overflow (e.g. a river).
kuSAVYA		to wash (someone else, e.g. a child).
kuSAYIKA		to insinuate; to hint at something without expressing it clearly; to suggest. (Amenorrhoca—ndasayikanga waka mwezi umoza, I missed one monthly period: i.e. a hint of pregnancy).
kuSAYURA		to depreciate. Kusayuka, to be flavourless (as weak tea); to be washed out (as soil which cannot bear); to lose favour (as cloth in store); to lose interest (as old news).
kuSAZGA		to mix. Kusazgako, to add to.

122

TUMBUKA	TONGA	ENGLISH
ɲiSE, (gha- or yi-)		afternoon or evening. Na mise, in the afternoon. Mise ghano, this evening.
	chiSE, vi-	small basket.
kuSEƲA		to sift (flour when pounding).
kuSEƲERA	kuSEƲE	to play.
	chiSEƲE, vi-	courtyard (also the fence round it),
SEFU, zi-		eland.
kuSEKA		to laugh; to laugh at; to scorn. Kusekerera, to rejoice; to be glad; to be happy.
SEKERA, ma-		a kind of grass with thick strong stems.
kaSEKESERA, tu-		a bushy-tailed rat, nesting in thatch or in holes in trees (not eaten).
SEKETERA, li-		a kind of witchcraft—by medicine the ng'anga makes himself invisible so as to catch the ʋafwiti who come to the grave to take the body for cannibalism.
SEKURU, ʋa-		grandparent; ancestor.
SEMBE, zi-		sacrifice; offering.
SEME, zi-		landslide. Seme yagumuka.
mSEMPA, mi-		tendons; sinews.
kuSENDAMA		to lean over (as in listening to someone).
kuSENDEKA		to tilt, or cause to lean over (e.g. a pot when removing something from it).
kuSENDERERA		to approach, to draw near (e.g. in pupils moving closer together to make room). Kusenderezga, to cause to approach.
SENGA, zi-		harder particles of grain remaining after pounding and sifting, which have to be ground on the stone: (grit). (also lusenga).
kuSENGA		to cut grass, or hair. (Ngoni, to milk cow).
kuSENGULA		to clear grass from among trees &c. (met. of clean speech).
uSENGULI, mau-		a cleared space: safety.
(lu) SENGWE, ma-		horn.
	SENJE, ʋa-	booth (of posts fixed at top and grass thatch).
kuSENTA		to graze (as an arrow or a bullet which just touched).

123

TUMBUKA	TONGA	ENGLISH
kuSENYA		to carry; to bear; to take.
kuSEPA		to pluck; to gather (flowers, mushrooms).
mSEPUKA, ʋa-		boy.
kuSEPETURA		(mlomo) to pout.
SERE		pa sere pa-, behind; beyond; on the other side of (e.g. a house which hides the object from view).
	kuSERE	to enter: caus. kuserezga, to put in.
kuSEREꞄENDA		to be loose (e.g. axe in handle).
chiSERU, vi-		small basket.
luSERU, malu-		large flat basket for winnowing.
kuSERUKA		to be nauseated; to feel sick; caus. kuseruska. Museru, mi-, nausea.
kuSESA		to tell secrets (may be good or bad); to backbite; to slander.
kuSESEMA		to run.
mSESI, mi-		young female goat (without kid).
mSEU, mi-		hoed road.
kuSEWA		to sew by casting (e.g. wurumano).
kuSEWA		v. int. to boil (e.g. water); to float (e.g. a bad egg in water).
kuSEZGA		to push aside; to remove: (to suspend a member from Church fellowship). p. kusezgeka, to be set aside.
—SI		down: pasi, on the ground: musi mu kuni, at the foot of the tree: kusi ku gome, in under the table.
chiSI, (chi-)		darkness.
muSI, mi-		pounding-stick.
	uSI, mau-	smoke.
mSIBWENI, ʋa-		maternal uncles; father-in-law and his brothers; brothers of mother-in-law.
kuSIWA		to be drowsy; to be sleepy.
luSIꞄA, malu-		medicine made by burning roots as charm against lions and leopards.
kuSIDA		to leave; to forsake; to desert. Kusidana, mutual separation (met. to differ in an argument.)
SIGIRO	SIGIRU, zi-	steering oar: rudder: helm.

124

TUMBUKA	TONGA	ENGLISH
	kuSIKA	to descend: caus. kusiska, to lower: adv. kusika, lower down.
	liSIKA, (li-)	siftings of flour; grit.
maSIKA (gha-)		time of reaping: harvest. (met. market, or fair). (cp. vuna).
kuSIKITIKA		to be beaten down. Dongo likusikitika, (newly hoed) earth is beaten down (by rain) also of cutting grass short. caus. kusikitizga.
kuSIKIZGA		to cast a shadow on (when something intercepts the light (or wind) falling on a person); to overshadow.
	chiSIKU, vi-	the lower stick for fire-making— soft, flat on one side, with notch; held by feet.
uSIKU, mau-		night: usiku uno, last night: masiku ghose, always.
kuSIKURA		to cast a spell; to cause ill-luck. Chipiri wandisikura, the adder has warned me—of bad luck (because it was moving instead of lying still).
SIKWA, zi-		small calabash tops—used in game of spinning them through a goal.
SIMA, (yi-)		porridge—the main food dish (the plural, zi-, denotes the separate dishes brought by the women to the mphara).
kuSIMBA		to make marks; to write. Simbo, zi-, tribal tattoo marks.
SIMBI, ma-		the koko plant.
chiSIMI, vi-		spring; fountain; well.
kuSIMIKIZGA		to give evidence; to bear witness; to testify.
chiSIMIKIZGO, vi-	chiSIMISIMI, vi-	token, sign.
kuSIMPA		to wait. Ndasimpa masimpa libwe. I have waited like a stone.
	chiSINA, vi-	trunk (of a tree): stump in path.
kuSINA		to pinch. (also of scratching with claws, as a cat pressing its claws into the skin).
	kaSINAUANA, ka-	a child's portion. (pinched off).
—SINDA		part; (half): ncha sinda, or chiri sinda, it is not full: mwezi uno na sinda, six weeks.
maSINDA		pa masinda, or masinda, behind; after.

125

Tumbuka	Tonga	English
kuSINDA		to smear (a floor) with dung from kraal.
	kuSINDA maso	to close the eyes (of a person dying).
kuSINDAMA		to bow the head; to nod.
SINDI, zi-		grass bangles.
kuSINDIKIZGA		to press: (to print).
kuSINDIRA		to shake together flour or meal in a tin so that it settles down; to press down the earth when filling in a grave.
mSINDO, (u-)		coming out dance of girls (at puberty).
kuSINGA		to wash; to rinse (e.g. dishes): to prohibit. lusingo (lu-), prohibition.
chiSINGA		stump of a tree; stumbling-block.
	liSINGA, ma-	sinew. (used for bow-string; or musical instrument).
kuSINGINIKA		to grumble, to complain.
SINGO, zi-		throat. Kukhara pa singo pera, to be nearly dead.
kuSINIZGA		to beckon—by nod or wink. (kusina).
	mSINJI, mi-	river; stream.
kamSINJI—kamronga		a girls' dance.
kuSINKA muzi		to cleanse (village), ceremonial cleansing referring not only to physical rubbish.
mSINKO, mi-		cleansing: ncha msinko—referring to the heap of rubbish piled outside the village after such a cleansing.
chiSINKO, vi-		the stem, or trunk, of a tree. (the root of a matter.)
mSINKU, mi-		stature.
kuSINTA		to exchange: to change for another of the same kind, e.g. goat for goat; money for money.
maSINYA		(with pa or ku) behind; after. (masinda).
(mu)SINYA, ʋa-		second of twins.
mSIPA, mi-	liSIPA, mali-	blood vessels, sinews (not clearly distinguished): in particular, the temporal artery, which is cut in bleeding with a horn for 'mutu'. (also msipi, mi-).

126

TUMBUKA	TONGA	ENGLISH
uSIPA, (u-)		tiny fish occurring in shoals in lake—caught with small-meshed nets, and dried for dendi.
	SIRA, (yi-)	a disease (?melancholia) supposed to be contracted by drinking water where game has been.
	SIRANGA	nyoli ya siranga, a kind of fowl with ruffled feathers.
	mSIRAWAYINGWE	(u-) fish poison—root (kills the fish).
mSIRIKARI, ʋa-		soldier; policeman.
kuSIRIMULA		to circumcise: p. kusirimuka. Ʋinasilamu. ʋaMohammedans.
chiSIRIRI, vi-		fables; tales (with chorus).
kuSIRISITA		to wipe out. (kusisita).
SIRYA, (li-)		sirya lino, this side: ku sirya, on the other side (e.g. of a river): ku sirya na ku sirya, on both sides.
SISI, ma-		hair (human) of head, face and armpit. (contrast weya).
chiSISI (chi-)		quietness; silence.
mSISI, mi-		root (spreading).
	mSISI, mi-	channel for water; ditch.
	mSISIKO, mi-	medicine to ensure silence of partner in wrong-doing.
SISINYA, zi-		large black ants.
kuSISIPURA		to restore to health; to refresh: kusisipuska to quicken.
kuSISITA		to wipe out; (to blot out).
kuSITA		to buy or sell (barter)—more commonly in reference to slaves —old word.
	kuSITA	to fence. lisito, mali-, a fence.
kuSITA		to iron (clothes).
SITO, zi-		purlins on roof (e.g. for hanging tiles, or binding thatch).
	uSIWA (u-)	lack; want; poverty.
mSIWANE, ʋa-		cousin (children of brothers and sisters: children of brothers are ʋana na ʋana—also children of sisters).
	kuSIWIYA	to dig a trench round (e.g. tent) to carry off water: to break up fallow ground for a garden. (also kusiuwiya).

127

TUMBUKA	TONGA	ENGLISH
	kuSIYA	to leave; to forsake.
	liSIZA (li-)	the butt end of a spear—for sticking in the ground (also called jembe).
kuSIZIBUKA		to dislike; to be disappointed; to be discontented. Kusizibukira, to scowl at.
kuSIZIMIRA		to shut the eyes.
kuSKA		to grind (between stones—e.g. lupoko). Kuska mino, to grind the teeth.
SKAƲA, zi-		ground nut: monkey nut.
	maSKAƲI (gha-)	kuvina maskaʋi to exorcise by dancing (with other accompaniments) the spirits supposed to be causing illness.
mSKAMBO, mi-		herd; flock.
SKAPATO, zi-		sandal; shoe.
uSKARO, mau-		beads.
SKE !		smooth.
kuSKENGEKA		to be worn away by rubbing or grinding.
SKEPA, zi-		husk (of fruits or nuts).
kuSKEPERERA		to cling to (as skin or husk of fruit). Kuskeperera kw'Ayesu, to cling to Jesus. Kuskepererana na Chiuta, to cling to God.
kuSKEREUKA		to be sloping; (to be thin at the buttocks—of cattle).
kuSKESKETESKA		to smoothe.
kuSKIANA		to work in iron. Mskiani, ʋa-, blacksmith.
chiSKO, vi-		face.
kuSKOWA		to take spoils of war; to pillage; to plunder. Mskoli, ʋa-, spoiler. Mskowo, mi-, spoils; plunder. (Also kuskogha).
mSKOMBE, mi-		bamboo.
kuSKUKA		to be lucky.
—SO		suffix meaning again, or also. Chitaso, do it again.
kuSOƲA		to go astray; to be lost; to perish. Chandisoʋa, it has eluded me—i.e. I have lost it. Kusoʋeka, to be lacking.

TUMBUKA	TONGA	ENGLISH
kuSOUERA		to play. rec.—ana, to play together, to get on well together (also, in bad sense, of illicit intercourse). Souero, ma-, games; play. (see kuseuera).
mSOFI, ua-		one who leads worship; priest. (kusopa).
kuSOKA		to warn; to threaten. Soko, (li-), a warning.
SOKA, ma-		misfortune; ill-luck. Masoka ghandiwira, misfortune has befallen me. Soka kwaku iwe, woe to thee!
	chiSOKA (chi-)	compesation paid by husband to wife's relatives for her death.
	kuSOKA	to rise; to stand up.
luSOKO (lu-)		strength; physical, or moral and spiritual power. Kufwa lusoko, or kutika lusoko, to relax effort,; to be indolent; to lose heart.
SOKORA, ma-		large basket.
chiSOKORI, vi-		the chase: (combined hunt of men and dogs).
SOKOROKO !		clear! (of coming out from trees to clear grass land when climbing a hill: of getting out from a crowd).
kuSOKORORA		to gather together.
mSOKOROWE, mi-		a species of tree giving soft timber.
kuSOKWA		to have bad luck; to be desolate, or bereaved (e.g. by death); to be orphaned. usokwano (u-), bereavement. (soka).
chiSOKWE, vi-		the core of a maize cob (without the grains).
	kuSOLONTA	to hop.
	mSOLONTI, mi-	the shin (bone).
	mSOMA, (u-)	the vagina. (msome). (occlusion of vagina we ndi jarawe; or we ndi mwa; or we ndi nguli).
SOMBA, zi-		fish.
kuSOMBA		to try to snare a man in talk (kwavya). Kusomba maso, to dazzle or attract (of worthless things).
kuSOMPA		to dig, or hollow out (e.g. tuli, or chisali).
mSOMPO, mi-		sharp-ended tool for hollowing out tuli &c. (chisel, gouge).

TUMBUKA	TONGA	ENGLISH
kuSOMPORA		to take a wife; to marry without proper ceremony: caus. kusomporeska. p. kusomporwa (of the woman).
kuSONA		to sew (cloth &c.).
kuSONGA		(mino) to sharpen teeth by filing: (nchewe) to treat a dog with medicine to make it sharp on the scent in hunting.
chiSONGA, vi-		a wooden arrow.
mSONGA, mi-		a sharpened stake for digging: the first shoot of a plant.
	SONGA	kuja songa, to sit upright.
SONGAMBWA, zi-		bicuspid teeth.
SONGO, ma-		end (of string, stick &c.).
kuSONGORA		to sharpen to a point (arrow, pencil &c.).
kuSONGEREZGA		to arouse; to stir up; to persuade (to act).
kuSONGONORA		to dissolve: p. kusongonoka: caus. kusongonoska.
	kuSONGONORE	vuwa, to bring forth rain.
SONI, zi-		shame; disgrace. Soni zakora mlomo, dumb with shame. Kukhozga soni, to cause shame. Kulengera soni, to cause disgrace. Kufyura soni, or kutatura soni, to remove the stigma of shame.
muSONJI, mi-		tower (e.g. of church—probably imported word).
SONJO, va-		booth; temporary hut of poles, leaning together at top and thatched.
kuSONKA		to pay tax: kusonka moto, to pile the wood together to make it burn well.
SONKO, zi-		tax. (or musonko, mi-): wamsonko, va-, tax-gatherer; (publican).
SONO		now. Madazi gha sono, the present day.
SONO-SONO	SOSONOKWENI	at once; immediately.
kuSONYEZA		to shew: kusonyezeka, to be shewn; (to be publicly admitted to Catechumens' class).
kuSOPA		to worship; to offer sacrifices chisopo, vi-, sacrifice; offering. Sopero, ma-, act of worship; meeting for worship.

130

TUMBUKA	TONGA	ENGLISH
kuSOPANA		to be reconciled (parties to a quarrel).
kuSOPERA futi		to load a gun.
kuSOPOSKA		to abort, or miscarry: (of cattle).
kuSORA		to pick up; to gather up; to choose; to elect (e.g. by lot).
mSORO, mi-		a species of tree. Kupyora msoro, to break a msoro stick (in token of allegiance to a chief). Kupyorera msoro kwa Yesu, to surrender to Jesus.
	kuSORO	to pull out (a stick from a bundle): to launch (a canoe).
kuSOROTA		to pass right through (e.g. a house, or a district).
kuSOSA		to clean up a garden before the rains—grass, weeds, bush &c. hoed, gathered and burnt.
kuSOSOMORA		to provoke.
kuSOSONTERA		to let fall rubbish (e.g. birds in building nest; or debris of grass during thatching). Tuntu twasosontoka, debris left behind.
chiSOSONYA, vi-		rubbish left lying (sheaths of maize cobs etc.).
chiSOSU, vi-		a garden for lupoko.
mSOTI, mi-		pullet (hen).
chiSOTI, vi-		hat.
	kuSOTO	(nthumbo) to procure abortion, p. kusotwa.
	mSOTORA, mi-	drug for causing abortion.
	kuSOTOPO	to extract (e.g. tooth): kusotopoka, to come out, or burst forth, suddenly.
kuSOWOYEKA		see kusoya.
kuSOVYA		to err; to do wrong; to sin. (kusova).
kuSOYA		to be worn away; to deteriorate. (e.g. a hoe handle in which the hoe is loose): (met. maungano ghakusoya-soya, attendance at the meetings is falling off). Kusowoyeka, to be worn away (as a nut with worn threads; or a person who is thin after an illness).
	liSOYO, mali-	one piece of a nyuwa (in which several pieces are sewn together).

Tumbuka	Tonga	English
kuSOZA		to eat sima without dendi.
(li)SOZI, ma-	SOZO, ma-	tear: kulira masozi, to shed tears.
kaSU, (ka-)		stinginess; selfishness.
	muSU, mi-	sharp stick for digging: the bow (of a boat).
kuSUƲA		to strip, or peel, off (e.g. banana peel, or bark of tree): p. —ika.
kuSUƲIRIRA		to be pre-occupied; to dally with trifles. Kusuʋizga to engage the attention or interest (e.g. of a child to keep it from crying).
kuSUKA		to wash (utensils, not cloth): kusukiska, to scrub.
kuSUKA		to reach to (meaning until)—used as an auxiliary verb—tenses agreeing. Tasuka tavuka, or tikasuka tikavuka, until we were tired. Wasuke wize, till he comes. Wakasuka wiza, till he had come.
	kuSUKA	to be selfish (e.g. to refuse food to someone): ususi, (u-), selfishness.
	mSUKA, mi-	the hind end of an axe or a hoe: the part of a knife within the handle.
	chiSUKA, vi-	the stump of a worn-out hoe.
maSUKU (gha-)		a wild fruit tree common on the hills.
mSUKU, mi-		earthenware pot with wide neck.
kuSUKUMURA		to rinse out the mouth.
	kuSUKUNIKA	to be shaken; caus. kusukuniska.
chiSUKUPIKO, vi-		tail feathers of a fowl.
kuSUKURUKA		to be washed out; to be savourless (e.g. salt ashes, soil, &c.): kusukuruzga, to dissolve the flavour (e.g. of tea by adding water): to wear out old clothes.
kuSUKUTURA		to wash thoroughly—as in rubbing soiled clothes in the tub to wash out the dirt.
	kuSUKUSA	to shake (as the hen does the eggs she is sitting on). Mazira ghakusukusa, addled eggs.
kaSUKU-SUKU, tu-		elbow; funny-bone.
luSUKUTI (lu-)		close forest with thick under, growth: thicket.

Tumbuka	Tonga	English
kaSULI, tuka-		whitlow (of finger).
mSULI, va-		blacksmith.
mSULI, mi-		root: sucker (e.g. from banana root).
	kuSULIKA	to be turned upside down (of a felled tree).
chiSULO, vi-		iron (kusura). (Chisulo is Saturday —the day of the iron (bell)).
kuSUMBA		to chew: kusumbira, to ruminate; to chew the cud.
mSUMBA, mi-		large village; town; city.
SUMBI, ma-		egg. Masumbi mavivya, bad eggs.
	kuSUMBUWA	to knock (e.g. with fist).
	chiSUMBWIYA, vi-	a clod (e.g. of earth and grass).
(lu)SUMU, malu-		song; hymn. (also sumu, zi-).
kuSUMULA	kuSUMUWA	to denounce; to accuse.
kuSUNAMA		to shut the mouth.
kuSUNDA		to put out buds or leaves.
chiSUNDA, vi-		bits of old rotten bark-cloth—used as wick for lamp, &c. (tow in making fire with sticks).
mSUNDO, mi-		the anus.
miSUNDU, (yi-)		worms.
kuSUNGA		to keep; to preserve; to protect; to bury.
kuSUNGIRIZGA		to protect with special care.
SUNGU, zi-		smell; odour. (also plur. ma-).
chiSUNGU (chi-)		sympathy; (also chisungu-sungu).
luSUNGU, malu-		pity; mercy; compassion.
SUNGUMBUWA, va-		a weed with a yellow flower.
	SUNGUNUNGU, zi-	small, black, biting, ants.
kaSUNGUPOTI, tu-		stye on eyelid.
mSUNGWANA, va-		girl; maiden.
SUNGWE, zi-		bamboo.
mSUNI, (u-)		gravy. (sauce).
kuSUNJIZGA		to slight; to insult; to be impudent or rude. Msunjiro, mi-, impudence; disrespect; rudeness. (opposite of kutumbika).
kuSUNKA		to smoke (of fire).
kuSUNKUNYA		to shake. p.—ika.
kaSUNKUNUNU, tu-		ankled (bone or joint).

TUMBUKA	TONGA	ENGLISH
kuSUNTA		to test (e.g. strength).
SUPA, zi-		vessel (calabash) for holding oil; (cruse): good fortune.
kuSURA		to prophesy.
	kuSURA	to work in iron. Msuzi, va-, blacksmith.
SURU (li-)		milk.
kuSURURA		to leak; to ooze (from a vessel).
uSUSI, mau-		selfishness.
kuSUSKA		to accuse; to give judgement against: kususkana, to discuss; to argue; to dispute. Suskano, ma-, disputes; quarrels.
kuSUSUTIZGA		(mwana) to rock (a child)—to quieten it.
SUSUWA, zi-		wart.
kuSUSUWUKA		to cast skin (as snake); to peel off (as superficial skin from dry blister, leaving whole skin below).
kuSUTULA		to loosen; to slacken: p. kusutulika.
SUTURA, ma-		hairy green caterpillar with red head—found on trees and used as dendi.
	luSUWA, ma-	thick forest with strong undergrowth: a thicket.
kuSUZA		to slander; to mock any peculiarity; to tell secrets. (Ngoni, to make a smell).
kuSUZGA		to trouble; to bother; to vex; to harass; to oppress. Suzgo, zi-, trouble; adversity. p. kusuzgika, to be troubled: suzgiko, ma-, trouble. (also visuzgo, vi-, troubles).
	mSUZI, va-	blacksmith. (kusura).
kuSUZURA		to sever connections; to release; to divorce. p. kusuzulika.
kuSWA		to break (pot, plate). p. kusweka.
	muSWA (u-)	white ants.
mSWAJU, mi-		twig for cleaning teeth. (toothbrush).
kuSWANURA		to splinter (e.g. a piece of wood). p. kuswanyuka, or kuswanuka— of the wood being splintered, or a person being pierced by a splinter: kaswanyu, tu- splinter: also swano-swano, zi-.

134

TUMBUKA	TONGA	ENGLISH
viSWA-SWA, (vi-)		refuse; rubbish. (kuswa).
kuSWASWATA		to knock leaves off dry twigs: viswatu, vi-, and swatu, zi-, dry twigs collected for kindling fire.
viSWAULIRA (vi-)		broken stalks of maize—cattle food.
luSWAZU, malu-		birch whip. (a light branch).
kuSWAZURA		to tease out (cotton).
chiSWE, vi-		white ants.
mSWENI, ʋa-		husband.
kuSWERA		to delay.
—SWESI		red. (also yellow or brown).
SWI !		conveys the idea of great distance or time. (also swi-ri-ri-ri-ri!).
maSWIRI (gha-)		clots of blood.

T

TUMBUKA	TONGA	ENGLISH
	kuTA	to go: muta pani? where are you going? wata kuti waza, when he had come.
chiTA, vi-		an impi; an army: (chiefly in, plural).
maTA (gha-)		saliva; spittle. Kufunyira mata to spit at. Mata pa jani! quickly! (before the spit dries on the leaf).
uTA, mau-		bow (for shooting arrows). Kupinda mauta, to stretch the strings on the bows (really to bend the bows).
	chiUTA	Orion (constellation). chaja pa uta, an inadvertence.
TAʋALI, ma-		pond; pool; lagoon.
kuTAʋA-TAʋA		to look, or gaze, about (e.g. in church).
TABWA, ma-		plank; board: mlimo wa matabwa, carpentry.
kuTAFULA		to disobey: mtafu, mi-, disobedience.
kuTAGHARARA		to be parted, or separated (as in straddling the legs, or when something prevents—e.g. a lid—coming down into place). caus. kutaghariska.
	kuTAGHARIKA	to make the meshes wide in net-making: to space wide apart the poles for a hut.

TUMBUKA	TONGA	ENGLISH
maTAKALIMBWE (gha-)		mud. (also matakalambwe).
kuTAKAMIRA		to be very ill.
	kuTAKA-TAKA	to work hard, or diligently.
TAKO, ma-		the buttock.
maTALALA, (gha)		hailstones.
TALI, ma-		iron ore (dug from deposits in the hills).
	kuTAMA	to be ill.
	kuTAMANDA	to praise.
	kuTAMANTA	to moan: (to groan).
TAMBALA, va-		cock.
chiTAMBARA, vi-		head cloth.
kuTAMBARARA		to stretch out (e.g. the legs): to lie flat (of land).
kuTAMBAZURA	kuTAMBAZUWA	to unfold (e.g. cloth; or arms).
chiTAMBARIRO, vi-		footstool.
maTAMBI, (gha-)		the stern (of a boat).
mTAMBI, mi-		a vipya plant, used for dendi.
mTAMBIKO, mi-		beam (e.g. the main beam in a house roof).
mTAMBO, mi-		the sky; the heavens: (the clouds). Mtambo uli birivirviri, the sky is blue.
kuTAMBURA		to stroll about.
kuTAMBWA		to view; or gloat over (possessions).
	kuTAMIKA	to praise: chitamiko, vi, praise; (also tamu, ma-).
kuTAMIRA		to rely on (someone who will help): kujitamira, to be conceited (to praise one's own powers).
kuTAMPA		to groan. Mitampo yikuru, deep groans.
kuTANA		to call (Nyanja kuitana).
kuTANA		to excel; to be superior.
kuTANDA		to spread out; to stretch out (e.g. both hands in politely receiving something): to mend (nets)—i.e. to spread them out for this purpose. Pa mtandasanya, in broad daylight; openly. Kutandika, to spread; to lay down (a mat). Kutandura, (kutandaura) to lift and roll up (mat).
	kuTANDAULIYA	mlomo, to open the mouth (for food).
mTANDA, mi-		portion of sima (in basket).

TUMBUKA	TONGA	ENGLISH
chiTANDA, vi-		corpse.
kuTANDARA		to wait; to linger; to delay: to spend a day or two at a place. Kutandazga, to spread out (e.g. flour on mat to dry).
maTANDAKUCHA (gha-)		the first rays of approaching dawn.
mTANDATO, mi-		bridge.
	TANDAUDI, ʋa-	spider.
chiTANDO, vi-		booth; open rest-house for shade.
TANGA, ma-		sail.
mTANGA, mi-		basket.
	maTANGA (gha-)	the hips.
kuTANGARARA		to straddle (legs). see kutagharara).
TANGI		ku tangi, day before yesterday.
kuTANGWANIKA		to be occupied; to be busy; to be hindered. Ndatangwanika, I am busy: ntangwanika, zi-, hindrance.
TANJE, ʋa-		pumpkin.
kuTANTA		to cross (stream) on stepping stones.
chiTANTALI, vi-		a platform set up on forked posts, for drying flour &c. (compare ntanta).
kuTANTANYA		to pass over (e.g. to omit a point in a speech).
mTANTO, mi-		bridge.
kuTAPA		to take out (some) from a store, or supply. Skulu zikutapuka pano, schools are supplied from here. Pano mpa mtapu, this is the source of supply. Kutapapo, to dock pay.
kuTAPATA		to be watery (of puddled clay too moist for moulding bricks, or porridge made with too much water): to be thin, or fluid. Makani ghanditapatira, the matter has been too elusive for me.
chiTARA, vi-		bedstead.
miTARA (yi-)		polygamy: first wife, mutara (u-); others, mitara (yi-). Reka kukhara mitara, don't flit from place to place.
kuTARAMIRA		to choke; sima yamtaramira, the sima has stuck in his throat. p. kutaramirwa—of a woman unable to bring forth the child in labour.

137

TUMBUKA	TONGA	ENGLISH
—TARI		long; high; tall; deep; distant.
uTARI, mau-		length; height.
uTARI, mau-		a species of mushroom.
kuTARULIRA	kuTARULIYA	to go to excess; to exaggerate, kutarulira pa kurya, to eat excessively.
kuTASKA		to save; to deliver: mtaski, va-saviour: utaski (u-), deliverance.
TATA, va-		(my, our) father: tatavyara, va-father-in-law.
	kuTATA NCHITO	to work; to labour.
luTATA (li-)		bond.
TATAFURU, ma-		bubbles; foam; froth.
mTATAKUYA, va-		the everlasting one. (to one persistently blocking a matter —mukukhumba ghave gha mta-takuya? i.e. never-ending).
chiTATANGA, vi-		crate for carrying fowls.
chiTATATA, vi-		diligence; perseverance.
kuTATAURA		to unravel; to disentangle.
luTATAVI, ma-	luTATAVU, ma-	spider's web.
—TATU		three: chachitatu, third.
kuTATURA		to remove (wipe, or scrape, away) e.g. dust, thorn, shame. Kundi-tatura soni ku vantu, to take away my shame before men.
	kuTAULA	to tell; to declare; to preach.
kuTAUZGA		to greet; to salute.
kuTAWA		to weave (e.g. making a net for carrying things, or as a spider weaves its web); to tie up a parcel; to spread (as a creeper).
	mTAWO, mi-	the rope of a fishing net.
kuTAYA		to throw away; to lose: kutaya pasi, to drop: p. —ika, to be lost. Kutayira (of hen—to lay). Ku-tayirizga, to cast away.
	mTAZI, mi-	trigger, or noose, for trap..
TE-TE-TE!		completely; altogether. (e.g. finish-ed).
	TEVERA, ma-	man's loin cloth (hanging down in front and behind).
kuTEVETA		to serve; to labour: mteveti, va-servant. Kutevetera.
—TECHI		soft; delicate; weak. Utechi, mau-softness.
kuTEFYA		see kutepa.
TEGHA, ma-		grave.

TUMBUKA	TONGA	ENGLISH
kuTEGHERERA		to draw near: kutegherezga makutu, to lend the ears; to listen attentively.
kuTEKA		(maji) to draw water.
	kuTEKA	(pasi) to sit down.
uTEKA, mau-		grass: (thatch).
kuTEKENYURA		to break into small pieces; to smash; to crush (with hammer): p. kutekenyeka.
	viTEKETI (vi-)	fragments (e.g. of a worn-out mphasa).
—TEMA		delicate: mwana mutema, an infant.
liTEMA, mali-		a tender infant.
kuTEMA		to cut.
kuTEMBA		to curse: ntembo, zi-, a curse; also matembo, (gha-).
kuTEMBA		to carry (on a pole between two, as a machila, or a corpse): also kutembeza.
mTEMBO, mi-		a corpse prepared for burial—wrapped in a mat: (bier).
kuTEMBEYA		to take a stroll.
mTEMBWERE, (u-)		peace and contentment: mbwe! many things scattered about—baskets, pots, &c.
kuTEMERERA		to go and meet on the way.
kuTEMPENTA		to be weak: matempentero, (gha-), weaknesses.
kuTEMUKA		to be peeled off (as skin off a blister): met. to clear up (as after rain); to dawn (the darkness rolled away)
kuTEMWA		to love.
mTEMWENDE, mi-		man's loin cloth (hanging down in front and behind).
kuTENA		to castrate (an animal).
muTENDE (u-)		peace.
chiTENDE, vi-		heel (of foot or hand).
kuTENDEKA		to come first; to precede; to be prompt. Tendeka pa mtendeko begin at the beginning. Kutendeka mbembe, to start a quarrel.
kuTENDERA		to prepare (dendi—with nuts, leaves, usipa, &c.).
TENGA, ma-		messenger. utenga, mau-, message.

139

TUMBUKA	TONGA	ENGLISH
	kuTENGA	to take; to bring.
kuTENGA		to take a wife; to marry (of the man). kutengwa, to be married (of the woman). caus. kutezga, or kutengiska, to betroth; to arrange a marriage. Nthengwa, zi-, a marriage, a wedding.
	kuTENGENDUKA	to spread (as an ulcer; or as water in a pond during rain).
kuTENGERA		to mourn; to lament: chitengero, vi-, a mourning (loud wailing of a company of mourners).
TENGERE, ma-		the bush; the woods.
mTENGO, mi-		price; value: mtengo uli? what price? mtengo wa patali, a high price: mtengo wa pafupi, a low price.
chiTENGO, vi-		seat; chair; throne.
mTENJE, mi-		roof.
	TENTE, (li-)	report; rumour.
kuTENTEMA		to tremble; to shiver (with fear or cold); to be afraid: chitente, vi-, fear; fright; terror.
kuTENYA		to cut and bring (firewood).
kuTENYURA		to cast down (as one flings down a load of firewood).
kuTEPA		to be pliable (lacking firmness)—when carried bamboos bend up and down—tepa-tepa-tepa! Zuva likutepa, it is getting cool: caus. kutefya; p. kutefyeka.
kuTEPETA		to be thin (fluid—as thin gruel).
kuTERA		to surrender; to submit (e.g. to a chief): caus. kutereska, to subdue. Zitero, zi- tribute.
kuTEREMUKA		to slip. Uterezi, mau-, slipperiness.
—TESI		false; untrue: utesi, mau-, lie; falsehood. (kuteta).
	kuTESKA	to test; to judge (e.g. character); to make sure (e.g. of the exact time; or the meaning of something said).
—TETA		adj. tender; soft.
kuTETA		to lie; to speak falsely (even by mistake). utesi, mau-, falsehood.
chiTETE, vi-		basket made of reeds.
	mTETE, mi-	pipe (for smoking).
kuTETERA		to cackle (hen wishing to lay).

TUMBUKA	TONGA	ENGLISH
kuTETESKA		to lead by the hand (e.g. child learning to walk).
kuTETEZGA		to tell fibs (lies) (e.g. idle threats or promises).
mTETEZGA, (u-)		fish poison (Tephrosia vogelii).
kuTEURA		to borrow (to owe; to be in debt). Wateura uli? How much have you borrowed, or how much do you owe? Kuteuliska, to lend. Teu, ma-, debt. Ua mateu, debtors.
kuTEZGA		to pretend.
uTEZI, mau-		marriage; wedding: wa utezi, bridegroom.
kuTEZUKA		to decline (sun in afternoon).
kuTHALIKA		to look at; to aim at: thalika kwa ine, look at me.
THAMA, matama		the cheek (face).
	THANULA (li-)	a kind of cassava.
	kuTHAUA	to flee, to run: kuthavya, to put to flight.
	THAYU (li-)	revenge. (A. wrongs B.—B. wrongs C., a friend of A. : B. watayapo thayu pa ku A.). Kuwezgerapo thayu.
kuTHAZA		to spread—of a plant (e.g. a creeper sending out branches or roots).
THE !		snatch! Ncheue the waruta nayo, snatched a dog and went off with it.
THEMBA, ma-		great chief; king.
kuTHENGA		to be flat on top (of hill or table).
muTHENO, mi-		a castrated animal (ox, goat, sheep).
THETE, matete		reed.
kuTHIKA		to respond (to a call): kuura kuthika pa kuchemeka—no response to a call.
	THIPURA (li-)	a kind of cassava.
	kuTHOUA	to notice; to mark; to pay attention to: kuthoua mtima, to observe the heart.
THOKAZI, ma-		heifer (Ngoni).
kuTHOKOZA		to sound the praises (of a chief); to do honour, or pay homage. (Mudange chathokoza, said to a child reading in school, means—first give the title of the book, the chapter, page, &c.).

141

TUMBUKA	TONGA	ENGLISH
	THONDO, (li-)	the Morning Star. (also thondwe, li-).
THONDO (li-)		bush (thick undergrowth).
THONDO matondo		large, spiky, caterpillars (green on foliage, brown on tree trunks: contents are expressed and bodies eaten as dendi).
mTHUUI, mi-		colostrum (the secretion from the breasts during the first week of lactation): bere ndi mthuui.
mTHULO, mi-		tribute; (tax).
THUMBA matumba		bag: met. fine; ransom; marriage payment. Also the mounds into which the weeds are gathered in second hoeing of plantations.
kuTHUMBWA		to be swollen, or puffed up; to abound: kujithumbwira, to boast (of possessions).
THUPI matupi		the body (of man or animal).
kuTHURA		to put down a load (to unload): also to be in spate (of streams in the rains): kuthurwa, to be freed of a load—hence to arrive; to reach (the place of putting down the load).
kuTHUWUSKA		to publish abroad: kuthuwukwa, to be widely known.
—TI—		medial in verb, 1st. pers. pron. plur. accus. us.
kuTI		to say; to speak: the infinitive often has the sense of the conjunction—that. Ndati ndingachita, I said I could do it (i.e. I thought I could). Nyifwa iyo tati tifwenge ise, the death we ought to have died. Mute na kuchita, get on and do it. Wati wachita, and wakati wachita, when he had done it, having done it.
	muTI, mi-	tree.
mTIBI, mi-		fresh beer (unfermented).
kuTIBULA		to wear a path smooth: ntowa tibu tibu!
kuTIFUKA		to be broken (as a green stick or reed—not broken off).
kuTIFYA		to cause to be thin, to weaken.
mTIKA (u-)		moisture; dampness (e.g. in soil): pali mtika pano, there is moisture here.
mTIKAZANA, mi-		small, brown, translucent beads.

142

TUMBUKA	TONGA	ENGLISH
maTIKENYA (gha-)		chigger (pulex penetrans).
kuTIKITA		to flourish; to thrive (of plant): watikita makora—of fresh green grass after the rains have begun.
mTIKO, mi-		porridge spirtle.
kuTIMA		to grow cool.
mTIMA, mi-		heart: kamtima, the germ (e.g. of a bean): chitima, vi-, sorrow; sadness; grief: pa mtima, diarrhoea. Kutore pa mtima, to be impatient.
kuTIMBA		to strike; to beat: ntimbo, zi-, stripes, blows. Kutimba maruzu, to shoot in flight.
kuTIMBANYA		or kutimbanizga, to mix; to confuse.
chiTIMBAHETE, vi-		confusion.
kuTIMBULA		to stir: ntimbu, zi-, sediment stirred up.
kuTINA		to be small—as a child which hasn't grown well: caus. kutiniska.
kuTINDIKA		to pass comprehension; to be too difficult. chikunditindika, it beats me.
kuTINDIUIZGA		to press down (as a heavy load): said of a younger brother outgrowing the elder.
kuTINKA		to hate: utinko, mau-, hatred.
	kuTINTIMIKA	to hurry.
kuTIPA		to weed with a hoe (as in hoeing a maize garden).
maTIPA (gha-)		mud; dirt: matipa gha ng'ombe, dung from the cattle kraal.
	kuTIPITIYA	to thrive (as plant when fresh leaves appear).
	kuTIPUWA	to convey gruel with the fingers from the bowl to the mouth.
kuTIRA		to pour: tira maji agha, pour out this water (cp. kwita): kutirira, to pour into (basin &c.) for use: kutika, to be poured away—kutika lusoko, strength poured away, i.e. to lose hope, to despair: chatiska lusoko, it has caused my strength to be poured out: zitiro, zi-, collection.
kuTIRIMURA		to stir or rouse up to action successfully—(of a leader who carries the crowd along with him).

143

TUMBUKA	TONGA	ENGLISH
kuTIRIMUKA		to throng, to flock together: Ʋantu ʋakutirimuka ʋakwiza ku ng'oma, the people are thronging to the sound of the drum.
chiTIVIRI (chi-)		a boys' dance.
kuTIWA		to be carried away (by a flooded stream); to be destroyed.
kuTOƲA		to cut branches of a felled tree and make a fence with them.
TOƲEROƲE, ʋa		larvae of mosquitoes.
TODWE, ʋa-		large rat (edible).
TOCHI, ma-		banana.
TOFU, ʋa-		pelican.
kuTOFYA		to press; to squeeze (as in feeling if fruit is ripe). kutoska, to feel (as in palpating the body on medical examination).
kuTOKATOKA		to work diligently.
kuTOKOTA		to speak maliciously against a person.
	kuTOKOSKA utokosi,	to speak vile, impure, things.
kuTOKOTOSKA	kuTOKOTEZGA	to whisper (probably accusations against someone).
TOLI, ma-		calf.
kuTOMA		to be greedy; to be in a hurry to eat (e.g. before others; or cutting off a piece of meat and going off to roast it before all is distributed).
	mTOMBO, mi-	first shoot from a growing bean &c.
kuTOMBOROKA		to be weak (in body): untomboro, mau-, weakness.
kuTOMBOZGA		to taunt; to sneer at; to reproach; to upbraid (as a man reminding his wife of the chuma paid for her): to torture or torment (as children may do to an animal before killing it). Ntombozgo, zi-, reproach.
	kuTOMPO ndi janja,	to weigh in the hand.
kuTONDA		to defeat; to overcome: kutondeka, to fail (used also of plants or seeds not growing). Kutondana, to be equally matched in a contest; to draw.
TONDO, ʋa-		small bush rat (edible).
muTONDO, mi-		a species of tree—wood used for axe handles.

TUMBUKA	TONGA	ENGLISH
kuTONDORA	kuTONDO	to pick; to select (e.g. fruit—either fallen, or from the tree).
mTONDORI, mi-	mTONDONI, mi-	small lizard (Mabuya striata).
kuTONDWA		to be astonished; to see an omen.
	kuTONGA-TONGA	to be restless; to move about.
TONGO, ma-		testicle; scrotum.
kuTONGOMARA	kuTONGOMA	to sit on haunches; to squat.
maTONGORORO, (gha-)		excreta of fowls, pigeons &c.
TONJE, ma-		cotton.
	TONTERA, ma-	drops (kuntona).
kuTONTORA		kutondora.
kuTONYA		to drop, or drip (as water): to walk or stroll in a slow and dignified manner (as chiefs do).
kuTONYEZGA		to sprinkle (water); to drop (e.g. drops into the eye).
kuTONYORA		to dally or trifle (e.g. a child not hungry playing with its food); Mtonyoro (u-), wilfulness; impudence.
	TORONG'ONDO, ma-,	lumps in sima.
kuTOPORA		to pluck out (as in taking seedlings from a seed-bed for transplanting): p. kutopoka. Kutopora moyo, to provoke: kutopoka moyo (or mtima), to be provoked.
chiTOPOKO, vi-		the root; the origin; the essence. of a thing.
kuTORA		to pick up; to take; to bring. To marry—mwanarumi wakutora mwanakazi: mwanakazi wakutoreka. Kutoreskana, to wed publicly. (kutorana may refer to coition apart from marriage).
TORI, ma-		boundary mark (claim-peg; cut in tree; knot in grass &c.).
	kuTORA	to be in spate—of streams in flood rains.
	kuTORO	to bore a hole; to perforate; to pierce: p. kutoroka—may be used of a leaky tin.
mTORO, mi-		a bundle (of grass, sticks, reeds &c.); a burden.
kuTOSKA		see kutofya.
	mTOTO, mi-	a kind of tree.
uTOTO, mau-		a white clay used for whitewashing (paint).

145

K

TUMBUKA	TONGA	ENGLISH
	TOTOCHI	kulereska totochi, to gaze fixedly.
chiTOTOKA, vi-		cockerel.
kuTOTORA	kuTOTO	to pluck off one by one (as kabata from cloth). p. kutotoka, to moult (as fowl; to fall off (as wings from flying ants).
	chiTOTOSA, vi-	callosity (e.g. on sole of foot).
mTOVU, mi-		lead (Nyanja).
kuTOWA		to be beautiful (also of inward beauty and holiness): caus. kutoweska, to beautify; to ornament; (to sanctify): kutozga, to cleanse; to make tidy; to adorn: kutowerezga, to seek outward adornment: katowero, ka-, adornment; cleansing; sanctifying.
	kuTOZA	to asperse: tozu, li-, aspersion, reproach. (also chitozero, chi-).
uTOZI (u-)		beauty; cleanliness; goodness; holiness.
TOZI, ma-		bolus of sima (portion taken in the hand and dipped in the dendi).
TRIGU, va-		wheat.
—TU		suffix to verbs, meaning completion —altogether.
	chiTU, vi-	small bundle (e.g. of salt).
muTU, mi-		the head: fever (pain in the head).
—TUVA		adj. white; clean; holy: utuva, (u-), whiteness; holiness.
TUVI, va-		toad.
	uTUCHI, (u-)	sawdust.
chiTUFYA, vi-		a swelling; an abscess (kutupa).
kuTUKA		to rail; to curse; to blaspheme.
chiTUKU, vi-		recrimination (e.g. husband and wife in the house): blame.
TUKU, va-		bin for storing beans or nuts (kutukumuka).
kuTUKIRA		to be hot (e.g. of water in a kettle): caus. kutukizga, to heat: chitukivu, (chi-), heat; warmth. (e.g. of atmosphere).
kuTUKUMULA		to blow up (bag); to shake up (cushion): p. kutukumuka, to be puffed up (e.g. bread dough which has 'risen').
kuTUKURA		to heave about under a covering (e.g. a rat or a snake under covering of earth; or an infant in the womb; or the penis in erection under cloth).

146

TUMBUKA	TONGA	ENGLISH
kuTUKURUKA		to move about (as a restless child).
TUKUTIRA, ma-		sweat; perspiration: samba tukuta, bathe in sweat.
TULI, ma-		mortar (for pounding grain).
TULO, (tu-)		sleep.
mTULO, (mu-)		the great heat just before the rains break.
kuTUMA		to send: also kutumizga: ntumi, zi-, a messenger.
	mTUMBA, mi-	a truss (of calico).
kuTUMBARA		to be pregnant (of animal bearing a litter, as dog, cat).
kuTUMBIKA		to esteem; to respect; to honour (as when a father accepts a son as come to man's estate, or devolves authority on him): adopted to mean to‧ bless. p. kutumbikika. Tumbiko (li-), honour; blessing.
	kuTUMBIRIYA	ndopa zitumbiriya mukati—the swelling of a bruise.
kuTUMBIRIZGA		to wean a suckling child (because pregnancy has occurred): p. kutumbirizgika, to be weaned: ntumbirwa, zi-, the child weaned.
TUMBO, ma-		bowel. Tumbo likucheka— sympathy.
mTUMBUKO (u-)		the breaking of the rains.
kuTUMBURA		to cut open; to disembowel: p. kutumbuka. vula yatumbuka, the rains have broken.
	kuTUMBUZUWA	mujitumbuzuwa waka, you are cutting yourself in vain (in the effort to extract a chigger).
tumiTUMBWE-TUMBWE (tus)		small red and black beads.
kuTUMPA		to exert oneself in something difficult such as lifting a load. (when the husk has come off in the tuli and the maize is ready for sifting—vyatumpa).
kuTUMPURA		to lift up; to raise; to hoist (flag). p. kutumpuka, to be puffed up (as cushion). kutumpura rundi, to hurry.
kuTUMPUSKA		to raise up; to lift. Kutumpuskira maghanoghano na mtima kwa Chiuta, to lift thoughts to God.

TUMBUKA	TONGA	ENGLISH
kuTUNA		to cool down (anger, or inflammation in a wound); to be at peace; to be calm; (to relent). Kutuniska, to pacify, to appease (e.g. a quarrel, or a child crying); to ease pain. Mpinjika yikutuniska zawe, the Cross settles quarrels.
kuTUNUKA		to bend down (with buttocks prominent): kuwera waka chitunu-tunu, to move backwards in a crouching position (i.e. to make a gesture of apology).
kuTUNA-TUNA waka		to twist about restlessly in one's seat.
kuTUNDA		to pass urine; to micturate.
mTUNDA, mi-		land (as opposed to water); the shore; the bank of a stream; rising ground.
chiTUNDU, vi-		large basket.
TUNDU, ma-		thicket.
mTUNDU, mi-		kind; species: (tribe, nation, people): vamitundu, Gentiles.
kuTUNDULA		to heap up accusations (e.g. of witchcraft).
kuTUNDUMARA		to be heaped up; to be higher (of rising ground).
kuTUNDUMULA		to blow up; to fill out; to distend: p. kutundumuka, to be puffed up; to be raised up: caus. kutundumuska, to distend (met. to exalt; to magnify).
	kuTUNDUMUWA	nthengo, to fix hoops in a creel (to distend it).
	chiTUNDWE, vi-	medicinal root for treating haematuria.
	kuTUNGA maji	to draw water.
kuTUNGA		to pierce and sew (as a saddler does); to string beads: mutunge chivindi, pluck up courage.
	kaTUNGA, (ka-)	a wild fibre used for stringing beads.
chiTUNGU, vi-		long needle for sewing reed mats.
mTUNGA, mi-		nyama zikutya mtunga, game faces the wind (scent).
	chiTUNGU (chi-)	perspiration due to a heated atmosphere—(ndavira).
kuTUNGURA		to castrate (an animal).
	maTUNTA (gha-)	bold purposes or designs.

148

kuTUNTIRA		to press on (e.g. on a journey to go further than the intended stop): kutuntika, to be persistent; to get on with the work in hand. (Tonga, vuwa yituntika viʋi, the rain is very persistent). kujituntira, to take pride in something done for one.
chiTUNTULU, vi-		a female slave: (female slaves killed for burial with a chief; or paid as ransom for compensation for manslaughter).
kuTUNTUMULA		kutundumula.
kuTUNYA		to spit out: kutunya mata, to spit.
TUPA, ma-		a file.
mTUPA, mi-		compensation (e.g. for manslaughter).
chiTUPA, vi-		goat pen (also for sheep, fowls, pigeons—roofed and with floor raised off ground).
kuTUPA		to swell (of parts of the body): caus. kutufya: chitufya, vi-, swelling, abscess.
miTUPI, (yi-)		wheals (of a beating).
kuTUPIKA		to steep (e.g. in water). (? kutupa).
	TUSI, ma-	mounds for planting (food crops).
maTUSI (gha-)		slanders.
kuTUTA		to flit (village) to a new site.
	kuTUTUWA	to shift things (pots &c.) out of house.
kuTUTA		to breathe to pulsate: tuti-tuti, sighing respiration: p. kututika, to be invigorated: nkondo yatutika, the army has been reinforced (in numbers and morale).
	kuTUTUKA	to be full to overflowing (of trees bursting into leaf; of lake or river full of water; of the rising of water in a pot when boiling over; of swelling of doors &c. in wet weather; &c.).
mTUTU, mi-		heavy black clouds (piling up): kwachita mtutu lero, or mtutu ulipo lero, clouds are banking up. Ʋantu ʋakwiza kafuru-mtutu, the people are flocking in (to Church); kafuru-mtutu also of sheep flocking into the chitupa—pressing on one another.
chiTUTU		kugona chitutu, to sleep without fire in the hut.

149

kuTUTUƱA		to be fat.
kuTUTUZGA		to push.
TUTWE (li-)		mist: personalised as Nyatutwe, ƲA-.
	kuTUWA	to come out; to go out: kutuzga, to put out; to bring out.
kuTUWURUKA		to fade with the sun (to be brown or pink); caus. kutuwuruska: adj; tuwurufu, faded; (brown, or pink).
kuTUZGA		to make cool (e.g. water that is too hot, by adding cold).
TUZI, ma-		urine. (kutunda).
TUZGA		blister.
chiTUZITUZI, vi-		shadow; picture.
kuTWA		to be sharp; njakutwa, it (the knife) is sharp. Also met. of people, or a person.
	kuTWAMUWA	to snap (e.g. a cord).
	kuTWANGA	to rebel.
kuTWAZURA		to tear (flesh—as a wild beast does).
kuTWEƱA		to stretch (as bow-string in shooting).
TWI !		intensive particle used e.g. of a sting.
kuTWIKA		to help a carrier to lift a load on to his shoulder or head. Ta-mtwikani mtoro, we have laid a burden on you.
kuTWINYUKA		to be ashamed: twinyu-twinyu, 'with his tail between his legs'!
kuTYA		to name; to call (in sense of naming): p. kutyika, to be called (name).
kuTYANA na		to be level with; to be opposite.
kuTYA		chiƲana, to set a trap, or snare.
	kuTYAPA	to thrash (with a switch).
kuTYAPULA		to whip (with whip, or switch).
uTYATYA (u-)		guile.
kaTYETYE, (tuka-)		wagtail.

U

UKO		there; yonder.
	UKONGWA	very; much; greatly.
chUKU, vy-		mould (fungus).

TUMBUKA	TONGA	ENGLISH
maULA (gha-)		bones, sticks, shells, &c. used in kuwukwa maula, to practice divination or witchcraft.
ULI ?		how? what? Pa uli? when? Ndipo uli, never-the-less. Ŭa uli-uli, poor, worthless, people.
chUMA, vy-		iron; property; wealth. (the marriage payment).
chUMBA, vy-		barren (woman or animal).
chUMBI, vy-		hump (or hunch-back).
UMO		in there; in where: how (followed by directive form of verb).
kuURA		to be without; to lack (cp. kwa, mbura). Often used as a negative with noun or verb— kuura urunji, unrighteousness.
chiURAVI, vi-		tender mercy; compassion.
chURU, vy-		anthill.
USANGE		if.
ŭaUSO, ŭa-		(thy-) father.
UVWE		if.
UŬIMBI, mau-		small pumpkin, or marrow.
UWU, UWO		demonst. pron. this, that.
UYU, UYO		demonst. pron. this, that.
chUWU, vy-		heap of derision (stones or branches thrown on a heap at the approach to a village—e.g. of an impotent man).

V

—VE,—vye		suffix to verb denoting negative— palive, mulive.
	mVEKA (u-)	eaves (of hut). Uteka wa mveka, the first row of thatch.
	kuVERUKA	to be thin or translucent (of cloth)
—VI		intensive suffix: kachokovi, very small.
maVI (gha-)		faeces.
VIŬI		much; very; especially.
kuVIKA		njakuvika—of a cow which may be milked without tying its legs.
kuVIKIRIRA		to protect.
kuVIKITA		to break up into small pieces (e.g. a stick, or a reed).

151

TUMBUKA	TONGA	ENGLISH
kuVIMBA		to cover up; to shut from sight: kuvimba makani, to suppress or conceal the evidence in a case. Vya mvimba, things seen; material things (as opposed to spiritual).
mVIMBI, mi-		wheals on skin: clouds overcasting the sky.
chiVIMBO, vi-		birds' nest: cork for a bottle (kuvimba).
kuVINA		to dance; to spin (of a top).
kuVINDA		to conceal; to cover up; to falsify; (e.g. murderer concealing body, or mutilating it to suggest work of wild beasts; or witness falsifying evidence; or chief judging wrongly because of influence or bribe).
	VINDA (vi-)	bribe.
VINYO (li-)		wine. (imported word).
kuVIRINGARA		mavi ghaviringara, faeces are dry and hard; constipation. (man or animal).
kuVIVIRA		to toss and kick arms and legs (as a baby does); kuvivira pasi, to writhe on the ground. Kuvivika, to wallow; to knock about on the ground as a dog worrying another, or lions killing and eating a beast.
chiVIVIRI (chi-)		kuwuka na chiviviri, to start very early.
kuVIVYA		to overcome; to triumph over: ndavivya charu, I have overcome the world. p. kuvivyika—ndavivyika, that beats me! (of something astonishing). If a hen leaves its eggs, yavivya; and the eggs are mavivya.
	VIYO	thus.
	mVIZI (u-)	a furrow hoed; a row; a course.
	VU (li-)	shallow beach for landing a net.
VU		tamkuʋasanga pa moto vu nteura, we shall find them sitting at a fire.
muVUCHI (u-)		breath.
chiVUCHI (chi-)		sweat; heat: kuli chivuchi, it is hot.
maVUCHI (gha-)		sweat.
kuVUKA		to be tired; to be weary (may be of argument): caus. kuvuska, to tire: kuvukuka, to be rested.

152

Tumbuka	Tonga	English
kuVUKUPARA		to grow old and worn (cloth &c.).
VULA, zi-		rain.
	VULI	with pa, ku, or mu, behind.
chiVULUPI, vi-		disturbance, riot.
VUMA (yi-)		east; north-east wind.
kuVUMBA		to cover over: particular use in mourning (chivumbi) when people go to stay at the house (cp. 'prostrate with grief'). p. kuvumbika, to turn over, or cover over. (contr. kuvumbula).
kuVUMBATA		to fold the arms: kuvumbatira, to. clasp in hands or arms: kuvumbatizga, to make one shut the hands.
VUMBA, (li-)		smell: iyi yi na vumba—of nyama or somba which cause hands to smell after eating.
luVUMBU, malu-		blacksmith's forge; smithy.
kuVUMBULA		to uncover, to reveal: p. kuvumbulika or kuvumbukwa.
uVUMBUZI (u-)		revelation.
kuVUNA		to reap (crops): vuna, zi-, harvest.
kuVUNAMA		to lie prone: caus.—iska, to turn over (something or someone face down).
	kuVUNIKA	to turn on face—upside down, e.g. a pot or a basket (khomo le pasi): kuvunikiriya, to cover, i.e. to turn something over on top of it: chivunikiri, a cover.
kuVUNDA		to rot: caus. kuvundiska, or kuvuzga. kuvundika, to hang or store for maturing, e.g. bananas, tobacco. Vundira, ma-, manure.
kuVUNDURA		to stir up, e.g. mud in water.
kuVUNGA		to wrap (rice, salt, &c.) in a bundle of one's cloth at the belt: kuvungira, to hide in the cloth (met. to hide in the heart). kuvungirizga, to wrap securely.
kuVUNGUMARA		to be hollow: kuvungumariska, to cup the hands for receiving something. (salt &c.).
	mVUNGUTI, mi-	a tree with large sausage-shaped fruit.
maVUNGWA (gha-)		feathers. (hungwa).
kuVUNJA		to spoil (e.g. a knife—bent, or loosened in handle); also kuvunjika.

153

TUMBUKA	TONGA	ENGLISH
kuVURA		to undress (take off one's clothes): caus. kuvuriska, to undress (someone else).
kuVURUMUKA		to fade.
kuVURURA		to glean (after reaping of crop).
kuVURUVUNDUKA		to go off in a huff because angered by something said.
	muVURWA, ʋa-	young man: younger brother, or sister (of same sex).
muVUSERERA, ʋa-		maize boiled and stored for future use.
VUVI, ʋa-		a dangerous snake (Naia nigricollis).
kuVUVUTURA		to wash out the colour of cloth.
	VUWA, zi-	rain.
kuVUWA		to paddle (canoe): to stir (sima in a pot).
mVUWA, mi-		mixture of flour and water in preparation for making bara or sima.
kuVUWATA		to hold water in the mouth (also of holding a thermometer in the mouth; or a dog taking fingers into its mouth without biting).
chiVUWO, vi-		large wide-mouthed pot with neck.
	chiVUZI (chi-)	rotten-ness. (kuvunda).
maVUZI (gha-)		hair on genitals (human).
maVWA (gha-)		grain of wood: mavwa gha tabwa ghakurata nteura, the grain of the plank runs thus.
	kuVWA	to perceive; to hear; to feel. p. kuvwika.
	kuVWANA	to believe: chivwano, (chi-), faith.
chiVWAMBA, vi-		a trap.
	chiVWANDA, vi-	a bundle (e.g. of salt).
kuVWANDAMIRA		to seize; to grab; to swoop down on and catch (e.g. rabbit, or bird in trap).
kuVWARA		to clothe oneself; to dress; to put on (cloth or clothes): kuvwarika, to clothe (another). Mavwaro, (gha-), the private parts. (reverse—kuvura).
kuVWASKA		to knock down (fruit—with a stick).
chiVWATI, vi-		a bush; shrub.

TUMBUKA	TONGA	ENGLISH
VWA-VWA !		swampy! (sound of feet squelching in mud).
	kuVWEMA	to be satisfied. (paid in full).
kuVWETEPURA		to snatch (e.g. in a quarrel over nyama one snatches it): p. kuvwetepuka, as when an animal starts suddenly out from bushes.
muVWI, mi-		arrow.
	kuVWIKA	to cover (with a cloth).
	kuVWINKA	to cover (as with a blanket): rev. -ula, to uncover.
kuVWIRA		to help. (same as kovwira).
	VYA	kuti vya ku singu—pyrosis.
kuVYANTA		to skid (slip).
—VYARA		in-law (relation): tata-vyara; mama-vyara; mvyara wane, &c. Pa uvyara pali nthengwa.
—VYE		see —ve above.
	kuVYONTO	ndivyontore ku urongo dodomoke —I press toward the mark (Paul).

W

WA		vocative of address: wa mwana iwe: wa mpusikizgi, you deceiver.
kuWA		to fall: (to be born).
	kuWAMO	to understand. ('to tumble to it').
kuWIRA		to fall into (trap): to happen ('it fell out'): kawiro, (ka-) birth: muwiro, mi-, generation
	kuWIRWA	to be married (of woman).
WAKA		a general negative—nothing, no change, ukuchitachi? waka, what are you doing? nothing. Wachali waka, he is still alive; (i.e. there is no change). Dazi lichali waka, it is still light (sun hasn't set).
zoWALA, zi-		wedding-feast. (Nyanja zobvala).
WANDULO		ku wandulo, on the verandah behind the house.
chiWANGWA, vi-	chiWANGA, vi-	bone.
	chiWANJA, vi-	the raised, beaten, floor of a hut (often persisting after the ruins of the hut have disappeared): (foundation).

TUMBUKA	TONGA	ENGLISH
	kuWARA	to elude; to be lost: chandiwara, it has eluded me (i.e. I have lost it).
luWARA, malu-mawARA (gha-)		the nether grindstone.
mawARA (gha-)		haste; rashness; heedlessness.
—WARO		with pa- or ku-, outside; without.
kuWATALARA		to lie flat: caus. kuwatalariska, to make flat (e.g. to set a roof at too low a pitch).
WATO, ma-		canoe; boat.
kuWAWATA		to talk noisily (of a crowd; also of bees): to make an uproar: chiwawa, vi-, noise; din; uproar; tumult.
	kuWAZGA	to sprinkle: vuwa yiwazga pa charu, a shower of rain passes over the land.
WAZGO, ma-		cross sticks on a bridge (decking).
—WEME		adj. good; beautiful; nice; clean: uweme (u-), goodness; beauty.
WENGU-WENGU		little by little; gently.
kuWERA	kuWE	to return: kuwera ku kaya, to return from the village: kuwerera ku kaya, to return to the village: caus. kuwezga, to cause to return, to restore, to give back: mwere-ranyuma, va-, backslider: kuwe-rezga, to repeat; to revise: kuwerenga, to count: kuweren-khanya, to return (same day) from a visit; or to repeat (work such as drawing water).
	kuWERA	to mock.
	mWERA (wa-)	south-east wind (local geographic reference).
WERE-WERE-WERE		tinkling (e.g. of child's ankle bells).
mWERERO, mi-	mWERE, mi-	chaff (especially that winnowed from millet).
kuWERUKA		chakuweruka, Saturday.
kuWESKA		to stick (something) on the end of a stick (for lifting it up).
WESU		familiar form of address to a friend.
kuWEWETA		to belch out (wind).
WEYA, ma-		hair on body (man); fur or wool (of animal); down and feathers (of fowl). (cp. cheya).
kuWINDA		to miss—in shooting.

TUMBUKA	TONGA	ENGLISH
kuWINYA		to pain; to ache.
WINO-WINO		gently; slowly; properly.
kuWIRA		see kuwa.
kuWISKA		to cause to fall; to cast down. (kuwa).
WISKE, ʋa-		father (3rd. pers. his or her): ʋawiskefwe, our father; ʋawiskemwe, your father; ʋawiskeʋo, their father: ʋawiskekuru, ancestors: wiskevyara, ʋa-, father-in-law.
kaWIZU-WIZU, tuka-		wagtail.
	chiWO, vi-	landing net (for usipa).
	kuWO	to be rotten: chiwoli, (chi-), rottenness.
WOA, ma-		mushroom. (wowa).
kuWOFOKA		to be soft; to be puffy (as over-ripe fruit); to be fluctuant, (as an abscess); (compare the fontanelle of a child's skull—wofu-wofu).
	kuWOJA	to reconcile; muwojo, (u-), reconciliation—the work of a third person between two offended parties—result, kusopana.
	kuWOKA	to transplant (e.g. seedlings).
WOKO, ma-		hand; arm: kuwoko, (kwa-), hand; forearm.
muWOLI, ʋa-		wife: ʋana ʋa muwoli, twins—the first (if male) mwiza, ʋa-; (if female) muwoli, ʋa-: the second is sinya, ʋa- or nyuma, ʋa-.
	kuWOMBA	to be soft.
luWOMBO, (lwa-)	liWOMBO (li-)	the fontanelle (soft hollow on an infant's head).
kuWOMBA		to plait (e.g. the frame of a nkokwe of withes or twigs, which are bent in the process).
kuWOMBA mawoko	kuWOMBA manja	to clap hands: womba bell, strike the bell: (also womba ng'oma; womba futi).
kuWOMBEZA		maula, to divine by striking the bones (&c.).
kuWOMBORA	kuWOMBO	to redeem: p. kuwombokwa: uwombozi, (u-), redemption: chiwomborero, vi-, ransom.

TUMBUKA	TONGA	ENGLISH
kuWONA		to see; to behold: p.—cka, to be seen; to appear: intens.—eska, to see for certain: chiwonesko, vi-, a sign: kujiwonerera, to see for oneself: cha mbonekera, something visible: mboniwoni, zi-, a vision: chiwoniwoni, vi-, mirror.
liWONDWE, mali-		the young shoots and leaves which precede the breaking of the rains (on which caterpillars appear).
kuWONGA		to thank: chiwongo, vi-, surname (the thanking name which it is polite to use); also the return gift accompanying the thanks.
muWONGO, mi-		the back; the spinal column. (see -ongo).
kuWONGONDORA		(mino) to break (teeth) (with a blow).
	kuWONGOZGA	to conciliate.
kuWONJA		to trap (small birds); the trap is a net stretched on a hoop buried in ground; hair nooses attached to this stick above the surface on which gaga is strewn—tuyuni tukuwira: kuwonjora, to take the birds out of the nooses. (konja).
kuWOROFOKA		to be weak with a body that should be strong.
WOWA, ma-		mushroom: wowa ukuvunda mu lukoro—'there's many a slip between the cup and the lip'.
kuWOWOTA		to lay flat (grass or crops): vula yikuwowota uteka mu dambo: chiwowota, vi-, flood (coupled with the rain causing it).
kuWOZGA		to sting: luwozga, malu-, sting (of bee, scorpion &c.).
luWUGHA, malu-		an open swept space (in village or bush): an open enclosure behind hut.
kuWUKA		to rise; to awake; to start off: Chiwuka, (chi-), the Resurrection: kuwukirana, to rise up against one another (in a quarrel): muwukirano, va-, an adolescent (of either sex): caus. kuwuska, to lift; to raise; to rouse: kuwuskapo, to remove; to take away.

TUMBUKA	TONGA	ENGLISH
kuWUKURA		to vomit; to be sick: kuwukuska, to cause to vomit; to shell maize from cob.
	kuWUKUWA	karungunjazi, to vomit red matter like blood.
WUKWA, ma-		envy; jealousy.
kuWUKWA		maula, to divine (by bones &c.): (to cause the bones to reveal): muwukwi, va-, a diviner; a sorcerer.
	chiWULI, vi-	dew (and the cold accompanying).
kuWUMA		to be alive: wumi, (u-), life.
	liWUMA (li-)	perseverance; stubbornness.
WUMBA, ma-		a crowd.
	chiWUMBA, vi-	a great heap.
kuWUMBA		to mould (pots &c. bricks): muwuvi, va-, a potter; a moulder
	muWUMBI, va-	a potter; a moulder.
	muWUMBWI, mi-	galleries in an ant-hill.
kuWUNDA		to heap up (earth &c.); to fill in a grave: rev. kuwundumula, to dig earth away from a heap: p. kuwundumuka, to fall away (earth from a bank, or from roots of a tree).
muWUNDA, mi-		grave. (see above).
chiWUNDA, vi-		young pigeon (young of nkhunda).
luWUNDA, malu-		the loins.
kuWUNGA		to gather: chiwunga, vi-, a heap (e.g. of maize stalks): rec.—ana, to meet together; to assemble: caus. kuwunganya, or kuwunga-niska, to gather together, to call together: (wungano,) ma-, meeting; assembly.
kuWUNGURURA		to skim (as cream off milk).
kuWUNGUZURA		to cut off; to twist off (e.g. fruit); to slice off (ears, or nose—in the old days).
kuWUNJIKA		also kuwunjiska, to gather up; to collect: kuwunjikirana, to assemble—umo tawunjikirana pano: kachiwunji-wunji, all haddle together (people).
	chiWUNU, vi-	loins.
	kuWUNUKIYA	to lust after; to covet: mbunu (yi-), desire.

159

TUMBUKA	TONGA	ENGLISH
WUPU, ma-		council: in a mrandu one party may go aside to take counsel together—tiʋike wupu, or tikhare wupu.
chiWURAVI, (chi-)		tender mercy.
maWURONGOMA (gha-)		clods (lifted by hoe in garden).
chiWURU, vi-		a heap; a crowd; a company (of people or game).
kuWURUKA		to fly; to jump.
kuWURUMA		to growl (lion, cat); to rumble (storm, bowels).
WURUMANO (u-)		small millet.
kuWURUNGA		to form in a lump; to round off. (burunga).
kuWUTURA		to lessen; to decrease (e.g. a debt); p. kuwutuka.
chiWUVI, vi-		dew (with accompanying cold).
WUWO		also; too (much): ʋose vaʋiri wuwo, both.
	kuWUZIRIYA	to blow upon (e.g. a whistle): kawuzi, ka-, a whistle (also kayuzi).
kuWUZGA		to tell; to relate; to preach.

Y

kuYA		to go; to travel: kuyamo, to suit; to 'go with': kuti chikuyamo icho chara, that is not seemly: mayiro, yesterday (occasionally, to-morrow):
	muYAYA	muyirayira, for ever.
kuYAUA		to gather (e.g. mushrooms); kuyaʋa mayani, to pluck young leaves (for dendi).
chiYAUIRO, ʋ-	chiYAUI, ʋi-	vessel (for domestic use).
kuYAGHA-YAGHA		to shake—the wave-like motion of the surface of a bog, or floating grass, when trodden upon.
chiYAMBO, vi-		the beginning. (kwamba).
kuYANA		to be equal to; to be like; kuyana na—, to agree with...; kwaku-yana na, according to...
kuYANGAZUKA		to be perplexed.
maYANI, (gha-)		young leaves (of cassava &c.) for dendi.

160

chiYAO, ʋi-		yam.
kuYARUKIRA		to be incensed against.
YEUO		yes; thank you, polite acknowledgement of a greeting.
	kuYEGEME	to lean (on).
kuYEGHA		to carry.
chiYEKWETI, vi-		a rattle.
muYEMBA, ʋa-		parent-in-law.
YEMBE, zi-		mango.
—YENI		strange; foreign: muyeni, ʋa-, stranger.
kuYENJAMA		to float: caus. kuyenjamiska.
	—YERA	adj. orange (uli ndi zira): red (uli ndi ndopa).
maYERE (gha-)		tricks; conjuring; magic.
kuYEREZGA		to compare: kuyerezgera.
chiYERUZGO, vi-		parable; illustration. (kweruzga).
kuYETCHEMURA		to sneeze. (mwetcha! mwetcha!).
	chiYEU-YEU, vi-	earthquake.
kuYEYA		to despise; to belittle.
kuYEZGA		to try; to taste; to tempt; (viyezgo, vi-, temptations): to copy; to imitate. p.—eka: dir. kuyezgera, to imitate. chiyezgo, vi-, straight-edge, plumb-line &c.
miYI (yi-)		ya nyinda, nits of lice.
	uYI (u-)	sharpness (e.g. of knife).
YIFWA		see nyifwa.
	muYIGHA, mi-	clots (of blood).
YII !		vacancy; calm; quiet: waruta nayo waka yii, he has disappeared with it: ndasanga yii, I found (the village) deserted.
kuYIMA		to stand. (kwima).
kuYINGA-YINGA		to wander about; to travel about.
kuYINGISUKA		to stroll to and fro (e.g. at a market)
kuYINIKA		to please; to honour (e.g. with a good present).
muYIRA-YIRA		everlasting. (kuya).
maYIRO (gha-)		yesterday: mayiro ghanyake, another day; cha mayiro ghene, something recent (not old).
maYIYI, (gha-)		desolate, uninhabited country. (yi-i!).

L

TUMBUKA	TONGA	ENGLISH
	YO	see iyo.
kuYORA		to gather (e.g. fallen fruit).
kuYOWOYA		to speak; to talk: rec. kuyowoye-skana, to converse; to argue; to dispute.
kuYOYOKA		to drop; to fall (leaves, flowers &c.): dongo liyoyoka, the earth is loose (sandy).
	kuYUKA	to rise: kuyuska, to raise; to lift.
kuYUMA		to be dry: dongo liyumo, dry earth: pa yumo, on a dry place.
kuYUNGA		to be slack, to be loose (e.g. a parcel whose wrappings have become slack; or a nkokwe which has got slack and leans over). kuyungwa, to be harassed.
chiYUNI, vi-		bird; kayuni, tu-, little bird.
—YUYU		adj. light; easy.
viYUYU (vi-)		floats (for nets—of wood or cork).
	kuYUYUNDUKA	to be puffed up.
kuYUYURA	kuYUYUWA	to make light of; to scorn; to despise; to debase: kujiyuyura, to be humble.
kuYUZGA		to overwork; to harass; to oppress. (cp. uzga).

Z

	kuZA	to come.
uZAGHALI, mau-		unclean-ness, filth (putting filth in food; cursing; fornication &c.).
chiZAKAZAKA		kuwirirana chizakazaka, to hug one another.
muZAMBA, va-		midwife (an experienced old woman.
kuZAMBIKA		to instruct girls at puberty (by old women); to help in child-birth: uzamba (u-), the coming of age of girls. (see msindo).
ZAMBWE		ku zambwe, to the west.
	ZANA	yesterday.
kuZARA		to be full; to abound; to have plenty.
kuZANTA		to spring; to leap. (of a child in its mother's arms tossing its arms and legs; also of quickening in the womb).

TUMBUKA	TONGA	ENGLISH
chiZARA, vi-	chiZA, vi-	rubbish heap, or pit. (chizara cha vyoto, or chizara cha viswaswa).
ZARO, ma-		junction of rivers; or of stream with lake.
mZATI, mi-		pillar or post in house.
ZAWE, ma-		quarrel; strife; wrath.
kuZAYA		to dance for joy.
ZAYI, ma-		large green fruit (some edible). (Kaffir orange).
	kuZAZA	to fill.
maZAZA (gha-)		authority; power.
ZAZI, (li-)		pins and needles: kufwa zazi, (of hand or foot numbed in a cramped position.)
kuZENGA		to build; (to edify): uzengi (u-), building; edification: mzenge-zgani, va-, neighbour.
ZENGO, ma-		poles for wall of hut.
ZENJE, ma-		pit.
maZERE (gha-)	maZE (gha-)	woko la mazere, the left hand, or arm.
mZERE, mi-		row; line; measure.
kuZEREZEKA		to be silly; to be mentally deficient: mzereza, va-, a fool; a simpleton: uzereza (u-), folly; stupidity.
kuZEREZGA		to ignore, to be inattentive to, or to intentionally falsify a matter; mweruzgi wakuzerezga, a judge who falsifies judgement.
chiZEREZERE		kuyowoya chizerezera, to speak with a hidden meaning.
kuZEREZENDUKA		to become silly, or weak in the mind.
ZERU, zi-		sense; wisdom; cleverness. (vinje-ru).
kuZERUKA		to be devoid of wisdom.
chiZETI, vi-		maggot fly. (maggot gets into the skin).
ZEZE, va-		musical instrument with iron keys on a board, and a calabash below.
kuZEZERUKA		to be startled.
uZGA (u-)		slavery; (kuyuzga): muzga, va-slave.
viZGA-ZGA, (vi)		dawdling.
kuZGEVA		to elude; to be lost: chandizgeva, it has eluded me.—I can't find it: uzgevu, (u-), mu uzgevu, in secret.

kuZGEUEREKERA		to disappear (e.g. a rash from the skin).
kuZGERERA		to cheat: chizgezge, vi- (or muzgezge, mi-), shadow of a person chizgere-zgere, or chizgetu-zgetu shadowy: kuwona chizgetu-zgetu, to see imperfectly.
kuZGOUERA		to be accustomed; to be in the habit of; to be tame: caus. kuzgovezga, to tame.
kuZGORA		to turn; to reply; to alter; to change; to answer; to interpret; to translate: p. kuzgoka, to be turned &c.; to become; to repent; to rebel.
ZGORANYA (li-)		regret.
liZGU, ma-		(liu also heard rarely) word; voice; call (e.g. of fowl calling her chickens): kutaya lizgu, to call loudly: uzgu wa fumu, a decree of the chief.
mZGUKI, va-		ghost. (kuzgura).
chiZGUMBU (chi-)		dizziness; giddiness.
muZGUMBU, mi-		crest of crested crane.
kuZGURA		to pull up by the roots (e.g. cassava, ground nuts): kuzguka, to be rooted up; to rise from the dead.
uZI, mau-		thread; wool.
luZI, malu-		inner bark of tree—used as rope or string.
muZI, mi-		village; town.
chiZIUA, vi-		pool of water (in course of a stream).
	kuZIUA	to know; kuziviska, to understand: mziviro, mi-, knowledge.
kuZIUANIZGA		to ignore; to distract attention.
	kuZIUIRIYA	to be accustomed; to be in the habit of: kuzivirizga, to tame.
kuZIUIZGA		to refrain from; to abstain from; taboo (cp. mziro): kuzivizga kurya, to fast.
	mZICHI, va-	brother to sister; sister to brother.
kuZIGHA		to bring trouble upon: wazigha futi ya fumu, he has caused trouble over the chief's gun.
	chiZIGHIRI, vi-	plug (e.g. to fill up the old hole in an axe handle).

164

TUMBUKA	TONGA	ENGLISH
kuZIKA		to be quiet; to be calm; to be at peace: to be meek; to be patient: mitima zikiti, calm: kuziska, to make quiet or patient: kuzikiska, to quieten; to tame.
kuZIKA		to make firm (e.g. to set poles firmly for a house wall).
kuZIKIZGA		to trouble; to persecute.
ZIKO, ma-		fireplace in hut; hearth.
—ZIMA		adj. living: uzima, mau-, life: ndi mzima, he is alive.
	mZIMBI, mi-	feather.
kuZIMBWA		to be depressed (by trouble or illness).
mZIMU, mi-		spirit.
kuZIMYA		to put out; to extinguish (fire or light): to quench; to cool; chikuzimya marupya— the rains that quench the grass fires.
kuZIMWA		to be extinguished; to be put out: (also used in active sense like kuzimya).
chiZIMI-ZIMI		maso chizimi-zimi, blind (the light of the eyes quenched—see kuzimya).
ZINA, ma-		name.
kuZINA		to have a grievance against: mwatizina tavanyinu, you are annoyed with us.
kuZINA-ZINA		to be heedless or neglectful (e.g. not to answer when called, or spoken to).
kuZINDA		to repair (net or basket &c.).
mZINDA, mi-		crowd; multitude.
kuZINGA		to encircle; to wind: kuzingizga, to roll up; to wind; to wrap: kuzinga makutu, to close the ears (by making a noise): kuzingirira, to surround: kuzingirizga, to encompass; to besiege: p. kuzingirizgika or kuzingwa, to be surrounded: kuzingiziwa, to be harassed: kuzingura, see kuzungura.
	ZINGA, ma-	pot-sherd.
mZINGA, mi-		a section of the bark of a tree—used for bee-hive. (adapted to mean cannon).
ZINGANO, zi-		needle.

TUMBUKA	TONGA	ENGLISH
	muZINGU, mi-	strips of meat cut for drying.
kaZINYANE, tuma-		goat-kid (Ngoni).
	ZIPE !	kukiya limu zipe! gone for good.
kuZIRA		to despise a gift (e.g. refusing to take food because too small a portion given): kuzirira, to reject (e.g. a man dissatisfied with wages throws down the money and leaves it).
	ZIRA, ma-	egg: mazira gha nkhunda, necklace of large white stones (old fashion).
kuZIRA		to abstain from certain things because of mourning (e.g. shaving bathing, dressing hair).
chiZIRA, vi-		floats for net.
muZIRA, mi-		cattle tracks (near village).
kuZIRIKA		to be faint; to be unconscious: kuziririka, to be delirious; to be in a death agony. vizirisi, vi-, convulsions; epilepsy.
—ZIRIMA		adj. whole; entire.
	kuZIRIMITIYA	to rub out (writing, picture): kuzirimitika, to be rubbed off; to be faint; to be indistinct; to disappear (as nkhama from a pot).
mZIRO, mi-		an imprudent or rash act, such as the breaking of a taboo: ndi mziro, it is not done; it is forbidden. (kuzira).
uZIRO, (u-)		blacklead.
maZIRO, (gha-)		comings. (see kwiza).
kuZIRWA		to be valuable; to be precious: kazirwiro, (ka), value; worth: vakuzirwa, people of worth, important people: ivyo vakazirwanga navyo, the things which made them people of substance.
—ZITU		adj. heavy; difficult: something not to be lightly done (e.g. using the name of one's parent, or of God).
maZIU, (gha-)		gum (exuding from trees).
	mZIWO, mi-	bundle (of firewood).
kuZIWUKA		to be chipped (a piece out of a brick, or a knot out of a plank).
	kuZIWULIKA	to delay; to tarry: wa chiziwu, a slacker.
kuZIYA		to be hungry.

166

TUMBUKA	TONGA	ENGLISH
kuZIZA		to be calm; to be firm; to be sober.
chiZIZI, (chi-)		a quiet spot: yikupenja chizizi, of a fowl seeking a place to lay its egss.
mZIZI, (u-)		moisture.
kuZIZIKA		to puzzle; to bewilder: p. kuziziki-ka, to be bewildered.
kuZIZIMA		to be cold; to be wersh, or insipid (dendi without salt).
—ZIZIMU		adj. cold: maji ghazizimu, cold water.
kuZIZIPIZGA		to be long-suffering, patient; to bear; to endure: dir.—ira, to forbear; to endure on behalf of.
kuZIZIRA		to be cold: maji ghakuzizira, cold water: zi-zi-zi-zi ! numb with cold!
kuZIZWA		to be surprised; to be astonished; to wonder: caus.—iska, to astonish.
ZOBARA, zi-		fruit; (esp. lemons). (Nyanja, from kubara).
chiZOKONO, vi-		'cobbler's pegs': (seeds which stick to clothing).
ZOMBE, va-		locusts (eaten).
	chiZOMBO, vi-	a kind of white ant: (hills with a deep hole, very damaging to houses).
ZOMBWE, ma-		stick insect (not eaten).
kuZOMERA		to agree; to accept; to confess; to consent: kuzomerezga, to allow; to permit: chizomerezgo, vi-, acceptance; profession.
kuZONDA		to spy upon.
kuZONGOKA		to be deep (e.g. looking down a well)—also kuzongoza: uzongo-vu (u-), depth.
ZONGWE, ma-		pit (e.g. deep pit in an ant-hill).
	chiZONONO (chi-)	a venereal disease; (gonorrhoea).
kuZONTOKA		to be high: also as noun, height.
	ZORI, va-	an old hole in an axe or hoe handle (a new hole having been made).
	kuZOROKE	to sink in mud (feet).
kuZOTOPA		to be heavy: maso ghakuzotopa, eyes are heavy (with sleep): also kuzitopa— uzitu, (u-), weight: caus. kuzotofya (and kuzotope-ska), to oppress, to trouble: p. kuzotofyeka, to be burdened, weighed down.

TUMBUKA	TONGA	ENGLISH
ZOVU, zi-		elephant; tusks; ivory.
	ZOZGERA, zi-	skin covering handle of spear.
uZU, mau-		thread; wool.
	maZU, (gha-)	words. (sing. liu, lizwe, also heard rarely).
ZUƲA, ma-		sun; day: mazuʋa ghose, day by day; always: zuʋachi? when ?
ZUKA-ZUKA, zi-		wild cat (like a small lepoard).
kuZUKA		to be oppressed (with work or worry): p. kuzukika, to work hard; to try hard.
uZUKUKU, mau-		fowl fleas.
kuZUKUMA		to be amazed; to wonder; to marvel caus. kuzukumiska, to surprise; to astonish.
mZUKURU, ʋa-	mZUKU, ʋa-	grandchild.
— chivu	— chivu	great grandchild.
— nyenye	— nyenye	great, great, grandchild.
— mavi	— sonjeru	great, great, great, grandchild.
	ʋaZUKURU, (ʋa-)	the men of the village whose duty it is to bury the dead.
uZUKUSI. (u-)		selfishness; greed.
	maZULO, (gha-)	afternoon or evening.
	ZUMA, zi-	large flying white ants which appear after the chizizimya rupya rains.
mZUMALI, mi-		nail (joiner's).
chiZUMBE, vi-		a raised part of the floor of a hut; platform: the seat of the chief: (throne).
	chiZUMBI, vi-	small perforated pot (strainer for salt).
kuZUMBWA		to be damp: caus.—iska, to moisten chizumbwa matoli, early rain showers.
ZUMBWE, ʋa-		wild cat.
muZUNGU, ʋa-		European; white man.
kuZUNGURA		to unwind; to disentangle, to undo knots in string. (rev. of kuzinga).
kuZUNGUNYA		to swing on a string.
	kuZUNGURIYA	to surround; to be round about.
	uZUNGURU, mau-	small birds (with white breast) in flocks.
kuZUNULA		to mention; to pronounce.

TUMBUKA	TONGA	ENGLISH
kuZURA		to be full: kuzurafura, to be full to overflowing: caus. kuzuzga, to fill.
	kuZUUWA	to undress.
kuZUWUKA		to come up out of the water (lake or river). (of a woman—to conceive in the womb).
	mZUWURA, (u-)	moss gathered from stones in streams and burned for salt.
kuZUZGA		see kuzura.
uZUZI, (u-)		guile: mzuzi, ʋa-, a guileful person (fwiti is mzuzi).
	uZUZU, mau-	mosquito. (or cloud of buzzing flies).
uZUZUNDI, (u-)		something astonishing; a portent (e.g. an aeroplane—when first seen).
kuZWAZWANDULA		to tear off small pieces (as thorns do from clothing); to catch and tear the skin: p. kuzwazwanduka, met. to be suddenly angry without cause in peaceful talk: wạli na zwazwandu, he is irritable.
kuZWETA		to turn aside; to be tortuous (of a path).

ENGLISH TONGA TUMBUKA DICTIONARY

ENGLISH	TONGA	TUMBUKA
ABBREVIATE, to		kufupiska. (*see* -fupi *and* -finyi).
ABDOMEN		nthumbo, ya za.
ABHOR, to		kunyanyara.
ABLE, to be		kumanya.
ABOMINATION		ukazuzi, wa; vinyara, vya.
ABORT, to		kusoposka.
ABORTION, to cause	kusoto nthumbo.	
ABORTIFACIENT	msotora, wa, ya	
ABOUND, to		kuzara; kuthumbwa.
ABOUT		na.
ABOVE		pachanya; kuchanya.
ABRADE to		kuparapata.
ABSCESS		chitufya, cha, vya.
ABSENT oneself, to		kugwenta.
ABSOLUTELY		nkanira.
ABSORBED in, to be		kudekanya na.
ABSTAIN, to		kuziuizga; kuzira.
ABSTINENCE		dongololo, la, gha.
ABUNDANCE		fumpha, ya; kuzara.
ACCEPT, to		kupokera: kuzomera.
ACCEPTANCE		chizomerezgo, cha, vya.
ACCIDENT		ngozi, ya, za.
ACCOMPANY, to		kurongozgana na; kuperekeza; kulinda.
ACCORDING to		nga; kwakuyana na; kwakulingana na.
ACCUSE, to		kususka; kusumula; kuchombola; kutundula: kugulizgira.
ACCUSTOMED, to be	kuziuiriya.	kuzgovera; kururuka.
ACHE, to		kuwinya; kuuaua.
ACNE		ntenku, ya, za.
ADD, to		kusazga: *see* kurunda *and* kubampikira.

English	Tonga	Tumbuka
ADDER	chipi, wa, ʋa.	chipiri, wa, ʋa.
ADDLED EGGS	mazira ghakusukusa.	
ADEQUATE, to be		kukwana.
ADJOIN, to		kupakana na.
ADMIRE, to		kurumba: kudaʋira.
ADMONISH, to	kuchinyiya.	kuchinyira; kuchinyinta; kuchinyintizga.
ADOLESCENT		muwukirano, wa, ʋa; muhurwa, wa, ʋa.
ADULT		murara, wa, ʋa.
ADULTERY		uleʋe, wa, gha: *to commit adultery* kuleʋa.
ADVANCE, to		kurutirira: (*pay* &c.) kukuzga.
ADVERSITY		suzgo, ya, za; suzgiko, la, gha; unonono, wa gha.
ADVICE		fundo, ya, za.
ADVISE, to		kupereka fundo
ADVOCATE		nkoswe, ya, za.
ADZE		mgomora, wa, ya.
AFFIRM, to		kuneneska.
AFRAID, to be		kopa; kutentema; kunjenjema.
AFRAID, to make		kofya; kutentemeska; &c.
AFTER		*see* -ntazi; -nyuma: *later on,* mwenekale; mwenembere.
AFTER-BIRTH		chibaliro, cha, vya.
AFTERNOON	mazulo, gha.	mise, ya (*or* gha): *see* kupendama.
AFTERWARDS		mwenekale; mwenembere.
AGAIN		-so (*suffix to end of verb*—chitaso)
AGE		uchekuru, wa; *see* msinku.
AGED, to be		kukaramba: *the aged,* —karamba: nkaramba, ya, za. (*see* kukokonyara).
AGREE, to		kuzomera.
AGREE with, to		kuyana na; kulingana na.
AGREEMENT, to make		*see* kupangana.
AID, to		kovvira.
AIL, to		kurwara.
AIM (goal)		marati, gha.
AIM, to	kuʋanga.	kurazga; kuʋerenga; kuthalika: kulinga.
AIR		mpepo, ya: *in the air;* padera, mudera.

172

ENGLISH	TONGA	TUMBUKA
AIR, to (dry)		kusankazga.
ALAS!	mbaya, we! ma-ko-to!	okwe! owe!
ALIKE, to be		kukozgana.
ALIVE, to be		kuʋa moyo; kututa; kwenda: wachali waka, *he is still alive*.
ALL		-ose: ʋantu ʋose, *all men*.
ALLEGIANCE, to offer		kukhoza.
to withdraw		kupunta.
ALLOW, to		kuzomerezga.
ALONE		-eka. (*see* kupera, *and* mpatu).
ALREADY		kale; mbere.
ALSO		-so; wuwo; na kwenenako: *he also*, iye naye.
ALTAR		kavuʋa, wa, ʋa; kazumbi, wa, ʋa; jochero, la, gha.
ALTER, to		kuzgora.
ALTHOUGH	chingana.	nanga: (*see* kupera).
ALTOGETHER	limu.	nkanira: (*see* -tu).
ALWAYS	mazuʋa ghose.	madazi ghose: masiku ghose.
AMAZED, to be		kuzukuma.
AMBIDEXTROUS, to be		kuʋa mphiri-woko.
AMBUSH, to lie in		kukhazga.
AMENORRHOEA		kusayika: (*see also* kusaura).
AMONG		mu; mukati.
AMOUNT		unandi, wa.
AMULET		njirisi, ya, za.
ANCESTOR	wiskekuru, ʋa.	sekuru, wa ʋa: *ancestry, see* kukumba
ANCHOR	ndondowa, ya, za.	nyangulo, ya za.
AND	ndi.	na: ndipo.
ANGER		ukali, wa; mbembe, ya, za: kuʋira m'mtima. *to cease from anger*, kugowoka.
ANGLE		(mu) fyakanya.
ANGRY, to be		kukaripa; kukwiya; kucheruka; kuvuruvunduka: *see* kuzwazwanduka.
ANGUISH		urwirwi, wa.
ANIMATED, to be		kukwezgeka nkumbi.
ANIMOSITY		ndundumbi, ya, za.
ANKLE BELLS		mliwo, wa, ya; njuwuru, ya, za; mangenjeza, gha.
ANKLE BONE		kasunkununu, ka, twa.
ANNOUNCE, to		kuruvya; *see* kuthokoza.
ANNOYED, to be	kung'ondo.	

English	Tonga	Tumbuka
ANSWER, to	kudanika.	kuzgora; kwamuka; kuchemeka.
ANOINT, to		kuphaka; kuphakazga.
ANT—house	nyere, za.	nyerere, za.
white	muswa, wa.	chimehe, cha, vya; chiswe, cha, vya;
	karandi, wa, ʋa.	chikumbi, cha, vya; chimbombombo, cha, vya.
	mapepi, gha.	
	nthende, za.	
	chizombo, cha.	
red, biting		nkurandi, ya, za.
black, biting	sungunungu, za.	
large, black		sisinya, ya, za.
smelling	chibomboni, cha.	pomboni, wa, ʋa.
flying	lupumi, lwa.	mbulika, za; mparata, za; jarama-kutu, la, gha, manyenye, gha.
	zuma, za.	
sugar	vya mnkhwiro.	
nest in tree	nkungumkoma, za.	
	mpampa, za.	
ANTELOPE (roan)		chirembwe, wa, ʋa.
ANTHILL	nkura, ya, za.	churu, cha vya; chikura, cha, vya.
ANTICIPATE, to		kujandizga; kutendekera.
ANUS	pa ng'o (pa).	msundo, wa, ya.
ANXIOUS, to be		kwenjerwa.
ANYONE		see ngana.
ANYTHING		see kantu, ka.
APART, to sit		kujungata.
APATHY		daka, la.
APPEAL (court)	kupazga bwalo.	kupazga mphara.
APOLOGY		see kutuna: chitunutunu.
APPEAR, to		kuwoneka; kubulika: (a small part) kulinga: (unexpectedly) kubuchizga.
APPEASE, to		kupepeska; kutuniska; kuʋeteka: to be appeased, kutuna.
APPLAUD, to		kurumba; kukuʋira; kukuʋa mawoko.
APPROACH, to	kuʋandika.	kusenderera: kuneng'enera; kuparamira.
ARAB		Mrungwana, wa, ʋa.
ARCH		see kupinda.
ARGUE, to		kususkana; kuyowoyeskana; kupindana; kudafyana.
ARISE, to	kuyuka.	kuwuka; kunyakuka.
ARITHMETIC		kupenda.
ARM	janja, manja.	woko, la, gha, kuwoko, kwa.

ENGLISH	TONGA	TUMBUKA
ARMS	vidya, vya.	mahomwa, gha.
ARM-PIT		(mu) nkwapa, ya, za.
ARMY		chita, cha, vya: *chiefly in plur.* vita, vya.
AROUSE, to		kuwuska; kupampuska; kusongere-zga.
ARRANGE, to		kunozga; kundondomeska.
ARRIVE, to		kufika; kwiza; kuturwa; kutiwa; kunenekera; kugota (*of place or conclusion*).
ARROW		(*iron tipped*), muvwi, wa, ya; (*wooden*) chisonga, cha, vya; mpusu, ya, za.
ARROW-POISON		ulembi, wa.
ARTERY	lisipa, la.	(*especially the temporal artery, the site for cupping with a horn*).
AS (conj.).		nga; nga ndi; nga ndi umo (*with dir. form of verb*): mumo; pakuti; mwakuti. As long as he lives, wacha-li na umoyo. *It was as if......* kukaʋa nga ndi para......
ASCEND, to		kukwera.
ASHAMED, to be		kujinyumwa; kutwinyuka (twinyu-twinyu); kulengeskeka.
ASHES		choto, cha, vya: dotarota, la, gha.
ASIDE		pa dera; *see* mbeyeka: *to go aside,* kugweʋera.
ASK, to		(*question*) kufumba: (*ask for*) kuro-mba; kuʋeya: *see* kwavya.
ASLEEP, to be		kugona tulo.
ASPERSE, to	kutoza: *aspersion,* tozu, la.	
ASS		mbunda, ya, za.
ASSAULT, to		kudumira.
ASSEMBLE, to		kuwungana; kuwunjikirana; ku-motoka: *to assemble (e.g. soldiers)* kukumbira.
ASSEMBLY		wungano, wa, gha.
ASSENT, to		kuzomera.
ASSERT, to		kuneneska; *I assert,* nkufiska nkani-ra.
ASTONISHED, to be		kuzizwa; kuzukuma; kutondwa; *see* kuvivya.
ASTONISHMENT, an		uzuzundi, wa.
ASTRAY, to go		kupuruka; kuzgeʋa; kusovya; ku-randa: *to lead astray,* kupuruska.
ASTRINGENCY		nkhanya, ya.

175

English	Tonga	Tumbuka
AT		pa (*place or time*).
ATMOSPHERE		*see* mpepo.
ATROPHY, to		kuphapa.
ATTACH to, to		kubata; kudemerezga.
ATTACK, to		kurotokera.
ATTEMPT, to		kuyezga.
ATTEND, to	kuthova.	kutegherezga; kuvanika; kulola: khutupulika!
ATTRACT, to		kusomba maso.
AUNT (paternal)	ada, va	(*father's side*), nkazi, wa, va.
(maternal)	mama, wa, va.	(*mother's side*), mama, wa, va. mother's family, chikazi, cha.
AUTHORITY		mazaza, gha.
AVOID, to		kulambarara. (*see* kufyura soni).
AWAKE, to		kuwuka; kupampuka; kuva maso. *To remain awake (at night)*, kucherezga.
AXE	see mphompo, za.	mbavi, ya, za; macheza, wa, va; mpompwe, ya, za.

B

BABBLE, to		kuvereveta.
BABE, baby		kana, ka, twa; litema, la, gha; bonda, wa, va.
BABOON		mkweri, wa, va.
BACHELOR		wa mphara, wa, va.
BACK, the	msana, wa, ya.	muwongo, wa, ya.
BACKBITE, to		kusesa.
BACKSLIDER		mwereranyuma, wa, va.
BAD, to be		kuhenipa: bad, -heni: *badness*, uheni, wa.
BAG	khanda, la, gha.	thumba, la, gha.
BAIL (boat) to		kukapa.
BAIT	nyambo, ya, za.	
BALL	*see* mphumpu.	mpira, wa, ya.
BAMBOO		sungwe, ya, za: mskombe, wa, ya.
BANANA	dochi, la, gha. (*see* ndifu)	tochi, la, gha.
BAND		(*of warriors*) livanja, la, gha.
BANDEAU (bead)		chibereveza, cha, vya; kamubambi wa, va.
BAND (S)		(*fetters*) vikondo, vya.
BANG (on door)		kukong'oska.
BANGLE (grass)		chipeka, cha, vya; sindi, ya, za.

English	Tonga	Tumbuka
BANJO		chiding'indi, cha, vya.
BANK (river)		mlima, wa, ya; mtunda, wa ya; mpepete, ya, za. (*also of shore of lake &c.*).
BANKING up		(*of clouds*) kututuka mtutu, wa.
BAPTISE, to		kubapatiza: *baptism*, ubapatizo, wa.
BAR (of door)		(*inside*) mpinjirizgo, ya, za; mgogo, wa, ya: (*outside*) mphinga, wa, ya.
BAR, to		kupiringizga; kujarizga.
BARK (of tree)		kungwa, la, gha; *bark canoe*, chikungwa, cha, vya; chikwa, cha, vya.
BARK (tree), to		kukomora.
BARK, to (dog)		kubwenta.
BARK-CLOTH	nyuwa, ya, za. lisoyo, la, gha.	nyanda, ya, za; sambi, la, gha.
to beat out	kusara nyuwa.	
BARREN		(*woman or cow*) chumba, cha, vya.
—(soil)		kusukuruka.
BASHFUL		kuphotoka.
BASKET	chise, cha, vya. of bark) chikwa, cha, vya.	(*small*) chiseru, cha, vya; koma, wa, ʋa; (*for* sima) chibu, cha, vya; lusero, la, gha; (*for sifting*) luparo, lwa, gha; luhengo, lwa, gha; (*large*) sokora, la, gha; chitundu, cha, vya; chitete, cha, vya; jamanda, la, gha; (mtanga, wa, ya). (*crate for fowls*) lwanga, lwa, gha; chitatanga, cha, vya.
BASTARD	mwana wa mu dondo.	
BAT		kasusa, wa, ʋa; (*large*) mlema, wa, ʋa.
BATHE, to	kowa	kusamba; kubira: (*trans*). kusavya.
BAY		(li) pota, la, gha.
BE, to		kuʋa; kuli. Copula, ndi—*is, it is*.
BEACH	vu, la.	dowoko, la, gha; chirowoko, cha, vya.
BEADS		mkanda, wa, ya; kaʋere, wa, ʋa uskaro, wa, gha; (*large stone*) mazira gha nkhunda; (*small brown*) mtikazana, wa, ya; (*small red and black*) tumitumbwe-tumbwe, twa.
BEAM		(*roof*) mchiko, wa, ya; mtambiko, wa, ya; mgororo, wa, ya; mgorobedi, wa, ya; (*post*) mzati, wa, ya.
BEANS	njuyu, za; nthamba, za; mkarasonga, ya; kobwe, ʋa.	nchunga, ya, za; nthamba, ya za; &c.

BEAR, to

burden	kupinga.	kusenya.
endure		kuzizipizga.
fruit		kupasa, kupambika.
children	kupapa	kubaba: *to be born,* kubabika, *or* kuva. *a matron who has borne children,* nyakatema, wa, va.

BEARD — mwembe, wa.

BEAT, to — kupuma; kukhwema. — kutimba; kukong'onta; kubwanya: *(drum)* kulizga: *(to beat down)* kusikitizga: *(it beats me)* kutindika *(see).*

BEATERS, — nkhwemi, za.

BEAUTIFUL, to be — kutowa; *(see* kukongora).

BEAUTIFY, to — kutozga; kutoweska.

BEAUTY — utozi; wa; uweme, wa.

BECAUSE — chifukwa; pakuti; mwakuti: *(see* kuti).

BECKON, to — kukonozga — kukopezga; kucheura; kukupizga: *see* kusinizga.

BECOME, to — kuva; kuzgoka.

BED — chitara, cha, vya.

   (for plants) — mgando, wa, ya.

BEE — njuchi, ya, za.

BEESWAX — pura, la, gha.

BEER — phere, la; moa, wa; mtibi, wa, ya; *(of third day)* mulamba, wa, ya.

BEFORE — pa (ku) urongo. — pa- *(or* ku-) ntazi; pa mbere: *(of time)* mbere; kale.

BEG, to — kulava. — kuromba.

BEGET, to — kupapa. — kubaba; kubara.

BEGIN, to — kwamba; kwanda; kudanga.

BEGINNING — chiyambo, cha; jando, la; mtendeko, wa.

BEHALF — *(on behalf of)* chifukwa, cha:. *or the directive form of verb may be used.*

BEHAVE, to — kukhara (makora—*or otherwise*). Kwenda.

BEHAVIOUR — kendero, ka; mendero, gha.

BEHIND — pa- (or ku-) vuli. ku rwegha. — (pa- *or* ku-) nyuma; -manyuma; -masinya; -masinda: pa sere pa.

BEHOLD! — ehe! ehena!

BEHOLD, to — kuwona: kutava-tava.

BEING — untu, wa; *a being,* muntu, wa, va.

BELCH, to — kubagha; kuweweta.

BELIEVE, to — kuvwana. — kupulikana; kugomezga.

ENGLISH	TONGA	TUMBUKA
BELITTLE, to		kuparamura; kuyeya.
BELOW		kusi; musi; pasi: *down a slope*, kusika.
BELT	likwamba, la.	lamba, la, gha; lukwamba, lwa, gha; chikowa, cha, vya.
BENCH (seat)		mpando, wa, ya.
BEND, to		kugoυa; kubendera: *to be bent down*, kubwantuka. (*see also* kurandara, kutunuka, kupontoka, kukokonyara, kukokoυara).
BENEFIT		wanduzgo, wa. (mwaυi, wa).
BENEFIT, to		kovwira; kwandula.
BEREAVEMENT		uranda, wa; usokwano, wa; kusokwa.
BESEECH, to		kuυeya; kuninizika.
BESIDE		pamoza na; pa rwande pa; pa chiri pa.
BESIEGE, to		kuzingirizga.
BETRAY, to		kupereka; (*oneself*) kujinyumwa.
BETROTHED		chibwezi, cha, vya.
BETTER, to be		kuruska; kuchirako; mphanyiko!
BEWARE, to	kuchewa	kuchenjera: do!
BEWILDER, to		kuzizika.
BEWITCH, to		kulowa: *to be bewitched*, kutondwa.
BEYOND	pa rwegha.	pa *or* ku sirya; pa *or* ku sere: *see* kutagharara; kutapata.
BHANG		chamba, cha, vya.
BICYCLE		njinga, ya, za: *to ride b.* kuchova njinga.
BIER		mtembo, wa, ya.
BIG		—kuru.
BILE		ndulu, ya za.
BILL (bird's)		mlomo, wa, ya.
BIN (for grain)		tuku, wa, υa.
BIND, to	kumanga.	kukaka; kukurunga.
BIRD		chiyuni, cha, vya; kayuni, ka, twa-
BIRDLIME	ulimbo, wa.	
BIRTH, to give	kupapa.	kubaba: *at his birth*, pa kuwa kwake: *to help at birth*, kuzambika: *birth customs, see* makumbi.
BITE, to		kuruma; kukampa: *see* nkwenyu!
BITTER, to be		kuυaυa: kunchanchamira.
BLACK		—fipa: *to be black*, kufipa; kubinka: bi!
BLACKLEAD		uziro, wa.
BLACKSMITH	msuzi, wa, υa.	mfuzi, wa, υa; mskiani, wa, υa.

179

English	Tonga	Tumbuka
BLAME		dapi, la; chituku, cha, vya.
BLASPHEME, to		kutuka; kwerura.
BLEED, to		(*with cupping horn*) kununa.
BLESS, to		kutumbika; *blessing*, tumbiko, la; vitumbiko, vya: *blessed*, ʋa mwa ʋi.
BLIND, to be		kubulumutira; *to blind*, kubulumutizga; *a blind person*, wa chibulumutira; wa chinturu: maso chizimi-zimi.
BLISTER, to		kuʋamba: *blister*, tuzga, la, gha.
BLOCK		nguli, ya, za. (*e.g. top of centre pillar in hut*).
BLOOD	(ropa, wa)	ndopa, za.
BLOODVESSEL	lisipa, la.	musipa, wa, ya.
BLOT OUT, to		kusisita.
BLOW, to	kuwuziriya.	kuputa; kupuputa; (*of storm*) kuwuruma; *to blow up* (*bag*) kutukumula.
—the nose	kumina mamphina.	kupenka mpuno.
BLOWS		ntimbo, ya, za.
BLUNT		—bumpu: *to be blunt*, kubulumutira; kufunyuka.
BOARD		tabwa, la, gha.
BOAST, to		kujikuzga; kujithumbwira.
BOAT		wato, wa, gha; ngarawa, ya, za; chombo, cha, vya.
BOBBIN	njinga, ya, za.	
BODY	liʋavu, la, gha.	thupi, la, gha.
BOIL	bumba, la, gha.	pumba, la, gha.
BOIL, to		(*intr.*) kuʋira; kusewa; kubwata: (*tr.*) kuphika: *to boil over*, kufuza.
BOLD, to be		kuganga.
BOLDNESS	matunta, gha.	chiganga, cha, vya: chikanga, cha, vya.
BOLUS (of sima)	dozi, la, gha.	tozi, la, gha, mphiri, ya, za.
BONDAGE		ukoli, wa; umikoli, wa; wuzga, wa
BOND (S)		chikondo, cha, vya; lutata, lwa; magwedi, gha.
BONE	chiwanga, cha, vya.	chiwangwa, cha, vya.
BONE MARROW		mongo, wa.
BOOK		buku, la, gha.
BOOTH	senje, wa, ʋa.	msasa, wa, ya; sonjo, wa, ʋa; chitando, cha, vya.

180

English	Tonga	Tumbuka
BORDER on, to		kupakana na: *border*, mpaka, ya, za.
BORE, to	kutoro.	kudorora; *pass.* kudoroka.
BORERS (in wood)		fufuzi, ya, za.
BORROW, to	kulamba.	kubwereka; kuteura; kukongora; kudirira; kopeza.
BOTH		—ose—*viri* wuwo.
BOTHER, to		kusuzga: *unwilling to take trouble*, kudonda.
BOTTOM		*firm, in lake*, mtunda, wa.
BOUGH (of tree)		mnthavi, wa, ya.
BOUND, to be		(*obliged*) kwenera.
BOUNDARY		mpaka, ya, za; chipuli, cha, vya; tori, la, gha.
BOW		uta, wa, gha: *bow-string*, lukuzi, lwa, gha.
BOW (of boat)	musu, wa.	
BOW, to	kuverama.	*to bow the head*, kukovama: *body*, kusindama; kubendama; kubwantuka; kukotama; kujikama; kurandara; kuvenda; kuvezga.
BOWEL		tumbo, la, gha.
BOWL		ngwembe, ya, za: (mbali yakufukulika).
BOY	mhurwa, wa, ya.	msepuka, wa, va.
BRACELET	goza, la, gha.	(*ivory*) koza, la, gha; (*metal*) sambo, ya, za; (*grass*) chipeka, cha, vya; (*brass wire*) mkono, wa, ya.
BRACKEN	barivari, la, gha.	
BRAIN		wongo, wa, ya.
BRANCH	ntambi, ya, za.	mnthavi, wa, ya; msafi, wa, ya; mpanda, ya, za. (*see* ntevere).
BRASS		mkuva, wa, ya.
BRAVE, to be		kukhoma mtima; kukhwima mtima; kuva chivindi.
BRAVERY		chikanga, cha, vya; chivindi, cha.
BREAD		chingwa, cha, vya; chibama, cha, vya.
BREADTH		usani, wa, gha.
BREAK, to	kufyo.	(*stick*) kupyora; *pass.* kupyoka.
		(*dish*) kuswa; (*bread*) kumenya.
—maize	kuchoko.	kuchokora.
(*see also*)	kupwituka, kupwanyuwa.	kubantula; kubaula; kubowora; kubwangandula; kutekenyura; kuvikita; kutifuka; kuwongondora.

181

English	Tonga	Tumbuka
BREAKING of rains		kurowoka, kwa, mtumbuko, wa.
BREAK—dry spell in rain	barawara.	ng'amba, ya, za; mlanga, wa, ya.
BREAST	be, la, gha.	bere, la, gha; (*bosom*) chipakato, cha, vya; (*chest*) chifuwa, cha, vya.
BREATH		mvuchi, wa, ya.
BREATHE, to		kututa.
BREATHLESS, to be		kuchita befu.
BREEZES	machiwa, gha.	
BRIBE (S)	vinda, vya.	chimbundi, cha, vya.
BRICK		njerwa, ya, za.
BRIDE		*see* mwali.
BRIDEGROOM		wa utezi, wa, υa.
BRIDGE		uraro, wa, gha; mtanto, wa, ya; mtandato, wa, ya: *cross decking of bridge,* wazgo, la, gha.
BRIGHTNESS		*of metal object,* kugadima.
BRIM		*see* kaυende.
BRINDLED		—bidi.
BRING, to	kutenga.	kutora; kwiza na; *to bring in,* kunjizga.
BROAD		—sani: *to broaden,* kusanuska.
BROOM		cheyu, cha, vya; chipyerero, cha, vya.
BROTHER		mwana munyake; mbali, wa, υa.
to sister	mzichi, wa, υa.	mdumbu, wa, υa. (*and vice versa*).
elder	mku, wa, υa.	mukuru, wa, υa.
younger	mvurwa, wa, υa.	munung'una, wa, υa.
kin		mbumba, wa, υa.
-in-law		mlamu, wa, υa.
BROTHERHOOD		ubali, wa.
BROWN		—swesi; *see* kutuwuruka, *and* bi!
BRUSH, to	kusesa.	kupuputa; kuparasura. (*noun see broom*).
BUBBLE		tatafuru, la, gha; mpovu, ya, za.
BUBBLE, to		kuυira; kubwata.
BUCK		(*bush-*) mpatu, ya, za; (*reed-*) mpoyo, ya, za; (*water-*) chuzu, wa, υa.
BUD, to		kusunda.
BUFFALO		njati, ya, za.
BUG		nkunguni, ya, za; nkufu, ya, za.
BUGLE		lipenga, la, gha; mbata, ya, za.

English	Tonga	Tumbuka
BUILD, to		kuzenga.
BULL		nkuzi, ya, za; nkambako, ya, za: *young bull*, bongwani, la, gha.
BULLOCK		nkhaʋi, ya, za.
BULRUSH GRAIN	ucheʋere, wa.	
BUNDLE, grass	nchinda, ya, za.	mpundwe, ya, za; mtoro, wa, ya.
—salt	chitu, cha, vya. mphinda, ya, za. chivwanda, cha.	chikwati, cha, vya.
—wood	mziwo, wa, ya.	chifinga, cha, vya. *see also* chipupu *and* mpiminta.
BURDEN	mphingu, ya, za.	katundu, wa, ʋa; nthundu, ya, za; mphingu, ya, za.
BURDENED, to be		kulemerwa.
BURIAL		kuʋika: *to prepare body for*, kufungira.
BURN, to	kufya.	(*tr.*) kocha; (*intr.*) kupya: kunyeka: *to be scorched (food)* kudokotera.
—intertrigo	kufya fyuku.	
—grass		(*round village, for protection*), kuʋawulira.
BURST, to	kuphumuka.	(*tr.*) kupwatura; kubaula: (*intr.*) kupwamuka: (*seed pod*) kupanta.
—cord	kudomo.	
BURY, to		kuʋika; kusunga: *men responsible for burial of the dead*, ʋazukuru, ʋa.
BUSH	dondo, la, gha.	thondo, la, gha; tengere, la, gha: *a bush*, chivwati, cha, vya: *to go to the bush (for excretion)* kupatuka; *or* kuruta ku tengere, *or* thondo. *Bushes cut and laid for burning in garden*, nteʋere, za.
BUSY, to be	kucheka-cheka.	kutangwanika: *see* kukwata-kwata.
BUT		kweni: *but because*, nchankuru.
BUTTER		mafuta, gha.
BUTTOCK		tako, la, gha.
BUY		kugula; kuguliska; kusita.
BY		na. *By themselves*, pa -eka; pa lwaʋo.
BY-AND-BY		mwenekale; pa dazi linyake.

C

English	Tonga	Tumbuka
CACKLE to (hen)		kutetera.
CAJOLE, to		kuʋeteka.
CALABASH		(*small*) chandi, cha, vya; nkombo: ya, za: (*large*) chipindi, cha, vya, (*for oil*) mfuma, wa, ya; supa, ya, za.
—plant	nyungu, ya, za.	

183

English	Tonga	Tumbuka
CALAMITY		chipakarara, cha, vya.
CALF		toli, la, gha; ngwata, ya, za.
CALL, to	kudana.	kuchema; kutana: *to call out*, kukuta; kugazamuka; kutaya lizgu: *to name*, kutya: *see* kusinizga. n. nchemo, ya, za.
CALLOSITY on hand or foot	chitotosa, cha, vya.	chimbata, cha, vya.
CALM		bata, la. *to be calm*, kubata; kuzika- (*calm spirit*, mtima zikiti); yii! *to calm anger*, kutuna.
CAN (be able)	kuziva.	kumanya: -nga- *before verb stem*— ndingachita, *I can do*.
CANNIBALISM		*see* ufwiti *and* uhavi.
CANOE		wato, wa, gha; (*bark*) chikwa, cha, vya; chikungwa, cha, vya.
CAP (for gun)	ching'anda, cha, vya.	
CAPTIVATED, to be		kudovera.
CAPTIVE		mufu, wa, va; mkoli, wa, va.
CAR (bush)		gareta, la, gha.
—motor		garimoto, la, gha.
CARDS, playing		juga, za.
CARE ABOUT, to		kulola; kupwerera.
CARE, to take		kuchenjera; kupwerera na; *you don't care*, muli kufwa daka.
CARELESSLY		bweka; dara.
CARPENTER		mbazi, wa, va. (kuvaja).
CARRY, to	kupinga.	kuyegha; kusenya; kutemba: (*child on back*) kubaba: *to carry away* (*as stream*) kukukura; kutiwa.
CART		gareta, la, gha.
CARTILAGE		mpuputura, ya, za.
CARVE, to		kuvaja (*e.g. hoe handle*).
CASE at law		mrandu, wa, ya: *to bring an action against someone*, kuronga mrandu na ngana.
CASSAVA	chigawo, cha, vya.	chigawo, cha, vya; (jiyawo; chinangwa).
—kinds	kabinyo, thanula. kapanti, thipura. mryapasi, &c.	mpando, mpozwa, nkowa. &c.
—steeped	phumu, la, gha.	
CAST, to		kuponya.
—away	kujowo.	kutaya; kujowora.
—down		kuwiska; kutenyura.
—lots		kudula makungwa.
—skin (snake)	kufundurwa.	kufundumuka; kususuwuka.

184

ENGLISH	TONGA	TUMBUKA
CAST, n.	chifundurwiya, cha, vya.	chikwakururu, cha, vya; chipapururu, cha, vya.
CASTOR OIL		mafuta gha mono, gha; (plant) mono, ya, za.
CASTRATE, to		kutungura; an eunuch, nthunguli, ya, za. (animals) kutena: mutheno, wa, ʋa a castrated animal.
CAT	mbuyau, wa, ʋa.	chona, wa, ʋa: wild cat, zumbwe, wa, ʋa; chiʋaraʋara, cha, vya; kacheʋere, wa, ʋa.
CAT'S CRADLE	mwadi, wa.	madgha, gha.
CATCH, to		kukora; (ball) kwanka; (fly) kubaka: to be caught (trap) kuwira; (in tree) kuparamira.
—fire	moto wawa, (see kupuka).	
CATERPILLAR		kapali, wa, ʋa; thondo, la, gha; doʋerampuno, wa, ʋa; sutura, la gha; mpherebungu, ya, za; nyirenda, ya, za.
CATTLE		ng'ombe, ya, za.
CAUSE		chifukwa, cha, vya.
CAVE		mpanji, ya, za.
CEASE, to		kureka: (rain) kukata.
CENTIPEDE	jereka, wa, ʋa.	bongororo, wa, ʋa.
CERTAIN, to be	see kuteska.	kumanyiska; kufikapo.
CERTAIN person	muntu wa mwenga.	ngana; muntu yunji.
CHAFF		mwerero, wa, ya; gaga, la.
CHAIN		unyoro, wa, gha.
CHAIR		chitengo, cha, vya; mpando, wa, ya.
CHAMELEON	lwenda, wa, ʋa.	lwivi, lwa, gha.
CHAMPION		nkanku, ya, za.
CHANCE		mwaʋi wa, ya; by chance, nga ndi mwaʋi.
CHANGE, to		kuzgora; kung'anamula; kusinta: (intr.) kuzgoka.
CHANGEABLE, to be	kusaʋasaʋa.	kusarasata.
CHANNEL		mugoronga, wa, ya.
CHARACTER	kendedu, ka; kararidu, ka.	nkharo, ya, za; kendero, ka; kakhariro, ka.
CHARCOAL	maka, gha.	makara, gha, (made from mukarakati; musokorowe; muʋanga).
CHARGE at law		mrandu, wa, ya; chifukwa, cha, vya.

185

ENGLISH	TONGA	TUMBUKA
CHARGE, to		(*enjoin*) kulayizga: (*war*) kurotokera.
CHARM		njirisi, ya, za; mphiyi, ya, za; munkwara, wa, ya.
CHASE away, to		kuʋinga; kuʋinka; kudikiska.
CHASE, the (hunt)		chisokori, cha, vya.
CHATTELS		mpango, ya, za.
CHEAT, to		kuzgerera.
CHEEK, the	dakama, matama, la, la, gha.	thama, matama, la, gha.
CHEERFULNESS		kusangwa.
CHEST, the		chifuwa, cha, vya.
CHEW, to		kusumba: *to chew the cud*, kusumbira,
CHICKEN		kapiyu-piyu, ka, twa; kachipyoropyoro, ka, twa.
CHICKEN-POX		kalira, wa.
CHIEF		fumu, mafumu, ya, gha. mwenecho, wa, ʋa.
CHIGGER		tikenya, la, gha.
CHILD		mwana, wa, ʋa; (*little child*) kana, ka, twa; kanichi, ka, twa; mwanichi, wa, ʋa; bonda, wa, ʋa: (*only child*) kananda, wa, ʋa. (*see also* -pyu). (*to be with child*): kuʋa pachanya.
CHILDBIRTH		kubaba: (*to be unable to bring forth*) kutaramirwa.
CHILDHOOD		wana, wa; wanichi, wa. (*see* -jedu).
CHIN		kalezu, ka.
CHIP (of wood)	chipadwa, cha, vya.	(*to be chipped*) kuziwuka.
CHIRP, to		kuchweta.
CHISEL		*see* msompo, wa, ya.
CHOKE, to	kukwiya	kukwira; kutaramira: kufyorongara, (*to be choked with weeds*).
CHOOSE, to		kusora; kusanka.
CHUCKIES (game)		kwanka ntura; kwanka mbaba.
CHURCH, the		ekleziya, la, gha. (*not building*).
CINDER		kara, la, gha.
CIRCUMCISE, to		kuchinja; kukotora; kusirimula.
CITY		msumba, wa, ya.
CLAIM, to		*see* kukontora.
CLAIM-PEG		chipuli, cha, vya; tori, la, gha; *see* chikochi-kochi.

English	Tonga	Tumbuka
CLAMBER, to	kubaramatiya.	
CLAP hands, to	kuwomba manja.	kukuʋa mawoko (or nkufi, or mafi).
CLAW		njoʋe, ya, za.
CLAY		dongo, la, gha; (white) utoto, wa.
CLEAN		—weme: (heart) mtima mpye-mpyemu. To clean a garden, kusosa.
CLEANLINESS		ukhovu, wa.
CLEANSE, to		kutozga; kuphotora; kusinka (mu-zi).
CLEAR		mbi! see sokoroko and kulengama.
CLEAR, to		(grass from path) kusengula: (to clear up after rain) kutemuka, kungweruka.
CLEARLY		fwantu!
CLEFT		mwanya, wa, ya: (of hoof) gawu, la, gha.
CLENCH teeth, to		kuruma sayati.
CLEVER		—chenjezi: (in mirandu) nkocho, ya, za; kusalala lulimi.
CLEVERNESS		zeru, za; mahara, gha; mano, gha; vinjeru, vya.
CLIMB, to		kukwera: to climb over, kuʋenuka: see nda!
CLING, to		kubatika; kudemerera; kuskepere-ra.
CLITORIS, the		kongo, la.
CLOD (of earth)	buma, la. gha; chipu-tu, cha, vya; chisu-mbwiya, cha, vya.	marongo, gha; magadi, gha; ma-wurongoma, gha.
CLOSE (shut) to		kujara: to close eyes of the dying, kusinda maso.
CLOSE (near)		pafupi pa (or na); kufupi ku: to stick close together, kumatikana; kubatikana.
CLOTS (blood)	muyigha, wa, ya; vi-nthuli, vya; mafigha, gha.	mayigha gha ndopa; maswiri, gha.
CLOTH		saru, ya, za; hiya, la, gha; buka la, gha; cloth with fringes, chigwe cha, vya; cloth for carrying child nguwo, ya, za.
CLOTHE, to		(self) kuvwara; (another) kuvwarika
CLOUD		bingu, la, gha; mtambo, wa, ya.
CLOUDY, to be		kufumpira; kufurukira.
CLUB		ntonga, ya, za.

187

English	Tonga	Tumbuka
CLUSTER		chisasuni, cha, vya: *to cluster* (*as maize on cob*) kupamba.
COAX, to		kukopa-kopa.
COBBLER'S PEGS	kabata, ka.	
COCK		tambala, wa, ʋa: *cockerel*, chitoto-ka, cha, vya.
COCOON	chisaranda, cha, vya.	
COCKROACH		chembere, wa, ʋa.
COITUS		kutorana; kuleʋana.
COLD		mpepo, ya, za: (*adj.*)—zizimu.
COLD, to be		kuzizira; kuzizima.
COLD (a cough)		chifuwa, cha, vya.
COLD SEASON		chifuku, cha, vya; chipwepwe, cha, vya.
COLLECT, to		kuwunjiska.
COLLECTION		zitiro, za: *see* kutira.
COLOSTRUM		mthuʋi, wa, ya.
COLOURED cloth		saru ya madyeka.
COMB, to	kupesa.	
COMB	chipeso, cha, vya.	
COME	kuza.	kwiza.
COME back, to		kuwera.
COME down, to	kusika.	kwikha.
COME first, to	kudanjiya.	kudangira; kutendekera.
COME in, to	kusere.	kunjira.
COME near, to	kuʋandika.	kusenderera ku.
COME out, to	kutuwa.	kufuma; (*from water*) kuzuwuka.
COMINGS		maziro, gha.
COMFORT, to	kusangaruska.	kupembuzga; kusanguruska.
COMFORTABLE, to be	kusangaruka.	kusanguruka.
COMMAND, to		kulangula; kulayizga; kurapizga.
COMMANDMENT		dango, la, gha; chilayizgo, cha, vya
COMMENCE, to		kwamba; *commencement*, jando, la, gha.
COMMUNION		(*service*) monesko, wa, ya.
COMPANION		mwanase, wa, ʋa.
COMPANY	guru, la, gha.	mpingo, wa, ya; chiwuru, cha, vya; bumbwe, la, gha.
COMPARE, to		kuyerezgera.
COMPASSION	lisungu, la, gha.	lusungu, lwa, gha; chiuravi, cha, vya.

ENGLISH	TONGA	TUMBUKA
COMPEL, to		kuchichizga; kukanchizga; kupemberezga; kukoserezga.
COMPENSATION	chisoka, cha, vya.	chitunturu, cha, vya; mtupa, wa, ya; ngozi, ya, za.
COMPETITION		kupharazgana.
COMPLAIN, to		kunyunyuta; kudinginyika; kudagha; kukwininika; kusinginika; kudandaula.
COMPLETE, to		kufiska.
COMPLETELY	limu.	nkanira; te-te-te! mya! pwa! zi-zi-zi!
COMPREHENSION		(to pass) kutindika.
COMPRESS, to	kundekuwa.	
CONCAVE, to be		kubabafuka.
CONCEITED, to be		kujitamira; kujivikamo; a conceited person, kajirumbi, wa, va.
CONCEIVE, to		kuzuwuka; kuva pachanya: to be treated with 'medicine' to ensure conception, kwimikika.
contraceptive	munkwara wa mapinga.	
CONCERNED, to be		kwenjerwa.
CONCERNING		na; nga ghave makani agha; &c.
CONCILIATE, to	kuwongozga.	
CONCLUSION		fundo, ya, za.
CONDUCT		see kukhara.
CONDUCT, to		kurongozga; kuperekeza.
CONFERENCE		chidumbirano, cha, vya.
CONFESS, to		kuzomera.
CONFUSE, to		kutimbanizga.
CONFUSION		chitimbahete, cha, vya; ntimbanya, ya, za.
CONGREGATE, to		kukochera.
CONGREGATION		mpingo, wa, ya.
CONJURING		mayere, gha.
CONSCIENCE		mavyevye, gha; njuvi, ya, za: to be conscience-stricken, kujinyumwa.
CONSIDER, to		kufumbana; kupima.
CONSIDERATION		kupwerera.
CONSTIPATION		kuviringara.
CONTEMN, to		kuyuyura.
CONTEND, to	kulimbana.	see contest.
CONTENT	mlere, wa.	kukhorwa (to be content).

189

English	Tonga	Tumbuka
CONTEST, to		kulimbana; kupharana; kupharazgana.
CONTINUE, to	kukiyakiya.	kurutirira: *see* chitatata.
CONTRACT, to		kufinyiska; kujipapatizga.
CONTRITE, to be		kupera.
CONVALESCENT, to be		*see* kubanta.
CONVERSE, to	kukamba.	kudumba; kuyowoyeskana.
CONVULSIONS		njiri, za; kuziririka.
COOK, to	kubika; kukoziya ba.	(*boil*) kuphika; (*gruel*) kuchirigha; (*roast*) kocha; kuvumbika: *to be cooked*, kupya.
COOL, to	kupozga.	(*water*) kutuzga.
COOL, to be		*see* cold.
COOL, to grow	kupo.	kupora; (*weather*) kutepa; kutima; (*anger*) kutuna.
COPY, to		kuyezga.
CORD		mkusa, wa, ya; chingwe, cha, vya.
CORK		chivimbo, cha, vya; *cork tree*, muvali, wa, ya.
CORN		(*maize*) vingoma, vya; (*millet*) mapira, gha.
CORN (on foot)		kafurukutu, ka, twa.
CORNER		chingodya, cha, vya.
CORPSE		chitanda, cha, vya; (*wrapped in mat*) mtembo, wa, ya.
CORRECT, to		kuchonga.
CORRUGATED IRON		rata, la, gha.
COTTON		tonje, la, gha.
COUGH		chikoso, cha, vya; chikosokoso, cha, vya; chifuwa, cha, vya.
COUGH, to		kukosomora.
COUNCIL		wupu, wa, gha.
COUNSEL		fundo, ya, za: *to counsel*, kupereka fundo.
COUNT, to		kupenda; kuwerenga.
COUNTERACT, to		*see* kuropora.
COUNTRY		charu, cha, vya.
COURAGE	unturumi, wa.	chiganga, cha; chikangalizga, cha: kutunga chivindi.
COURSE	mvizi, wa.	
COURT	chiseve, cha,	mphara, ya, za: luwugha, lwa gha.
COUSIN		msiwane, wa, pa.
COVENANT		chipangano, cha, vya. (kupangana).

ENGLISH	TONGA	TUMBUKA
COVER, to	kuvunikiriya; kuvwika; kuvwinka.	kubenekera; kuvimba; *to cover with a cloth*—(*self*) kudika; kujibundirizga; (*another*) kudikiska: *see* kukupika *and* kumbonya.
COVER	chivunikiri, cha.	chibenekerero, cha, vya.
COW		ng'ombe, ya za: nkomokazi, ya, za.
COWARD		mofi, wa, va.
COWARDICE	ugwara, wa.	wofi, wa.
COWHAGE		ukasi, wa, gha.
COVET, to	kuwunukiya.	kudoka; kudokera.
COVETOUSNESS	mbunu, ya.	udokezi, wa.
COY, to be		kupotoka.
CRAB	nkha, ya, za. nkano, ya, za.	nkhara, ya, za.
CRACK		rumwa, lwa, gha; (*in feet*) chenya, la, gha; (*mouth*—mlomo ukuchenyuka).
CRAFTY		—chenjezi: *to be crafty*, kufyafyara.
CRAMP		kufwa zazi.
CRANE (blue)		ngaro, ya, za.
CRANE-FLY		kamuchenjezi, twa-.
CRATE		lwanga, lwa, gha: chitatanga, cha, vya.
CRAVE, to		kuphukwa; kunweka; kukhumbiska.
CREATE, to		kwata; kulenga : *created things*, vilengiwa, vya.
CREATOR		chata, wa, va; mlengi, wa, va; mwati, wa, va.
CREEL (fish)		mono, wa, ya.
CREEP, to		(*child*) kukwava: (*plant*) kutawa; kuthaza.
CREST (of crane)		muzgumbu, wa, ya.
CRICKET (s)		chenje, wa, va.
CRINKLED, to be		kukwinyirira.
CRIPPLE, a		chiti, .cha vya; mkwakwa, wa, ya; chibotela, cha, vya; chilima, cha, vya.
CRIPPLED, to be		kukhara chiti; kulemara.
CRITICISE, to		kusandasanda.
CROCODILE	mng'ona, ya, za.	ng'wina, ya, za.
CROOKED, to be		kubendera.
CROSS, to		(*e.g. river*) kwambuka; kurowoka; kugomera: (*on stepping stones*) kutanta: *to lie cross-wise*, kupingama; *to lay cross-wise*, kupinjika: *to tie criss-cross* (*e.g. a bundle*) kupiska.
CROSS, a		mpinjika, ya, za; champinjika, cha, vya.
CROSS-EXAMINE, to		kukochora.

ENGLISH	TONGA	TUMBUKA
CROUCH, to		kubwantuka.
CROW	chahore, cha.	chihove, cha, vya.
CROW, to		kulira; kuvilikira; kukokovalika.
CROWD		mzinda, wa, ya; chiwuru, cha, vya, mgwirivindi, wa, ya; vantu vali nde-nde-nde, see kufumpira, kufurukira.
CROWD, to		kufinyirizgana.
CROWN		mphumpu, ya, za; chilemba, cha, vya; to crown, kubofya.
CRUELTY	phuzo, la.	nkaza, ya, za.
CRUMBS	makuntwa, gha.	maruvuvu, gha.
CRUSE (oil)		supa. ya, za; muleu, wa, ya; mfuma, wa, ya.
CRUSH, to		kung'anya; kubwanya; kudinya; kutekenyura; kunyakata; kukonya; kunyukuta: (of a crowd) kung'anulirana.
CRY, to		(weep) kulira: to cry out, kukuta; kuchemerezga; kubangura; kukoromoka.
CRY, a		nkuto, ya, za.
CRY-BABY		kaliriliri, wa, va; mwana wa nkuto.
CUD, to chew		kusumbira.
CUNNING		uchenjezi, wa; uryarya, wa.
CUNNING, to be		kuchenjera.
CUP, to (bleed)		kununa.
CUP, a		chandi, cha, vya; nkombo, ya, za; jomera, la, gha.
CURE, to		kuchizga: to be cured, kuchira; kupora.
CURRENT		mweza, wa, ya.
CURSE, to		kutuka; kutemba: a curse, ntembo, ya, za.
CURTAIN		chihiya, cha, vya.
CURVED, to be		kubendera; kugombetara.
CUSHION		chikunku, cha vya.
CUSTOM		ruso, la, gha; karuso, ka,. twa; nkharo, ya, za; kendero, ka, gha: customs, midauko, ya.
CUT, to		kutema; kucheka; kuhemba.
—across	kudumuwa	kudumula; kupikita.
—off		kucheka; kucheketa; kukotora; kuwunguzura.
—hair &c.		kusenga; (grass) kwipa; kupupa.
—maize		kukhata; kusanja.
—open		kutumbura.
CUTLASS	chipura, cha.	mgwandara, wa, ya.

D

ENGLISH	TONGA	TUMBUKA
"DADDY-LONG-LEGS"		kamuchenjezi, ka, twa.
DALLY, to		kutonyora; kusuʋirira.
DAMAGE, to		kunanga.
DAMP, to be		kuzumbwa; kunyewa: *to moisten,* kuzumbwiska.
DAMPNESS		mtika, wa.
DAMSON (wild)	fungu, ya, za.	
DANCE	gurutu, la.	guli, wa, ʋa; ngoma, ya, za; virere, vya; chitiviri, cha; kamsinji-kamronga, ka.
DANCE, to		kuvina.
—(for joy)	kwangara.	kugiya; kupinga: kuzaya: (*flames or fire-flies,* kung'anima).
DANGER		urwani, wa, gha; chido, cha, vya.
DANGLE, to		kuning'ina.
DARE, to		kujikangalizga.
DARK		—fipa: *it is dark,* kwafipa.
DARK, to be		kukoromera: *to make dark,* kufipiska.
DARKNESS		chisi, cha; mdima (bi!), wa, ya; munkhorwe, wa, ya.
DAWDLE, to		kudonda; kudalika; (viderezi; vi-zgazga).
DAUGHTER		mwana-msungwana, wa, ʋa.
—in-law	mkumwana, wa.	mkamwana, wa, ʋa.
DAWN		kwacha, kwa; kudamuka, kwa; chimphara, cha, vya; *before dawn,* pa matandakucha.
DAWN, to		kucha: *to start with the dawn,* kucherera.
DAY		dazi, la, gha; zuʋa, la, gha;
by day	ndi msana.	na muhanya.
to-day	msana wa le.	muhanya wa lero; *daylight,* muhanya, wa: *another day,* mayiro ghanyake.
DAY by DAY		madazi (*or* mazuʋa) ghose.
DAZZLE, to		kusomba maso.
DEAF, to be		kwambura makutu.
DEAL cards, to	kuchova juga.	
DEAR, to be	kwanjiwa.	kutemweka.
DEAR (price)		*it is dear,* ncha mtengo wa patari.
DEATH		nyifwa, ya, za.

193

English	Tonga	Tumbuka
DEATH-AGONY		kuzirika, kwa; kukhara pa singo pera.
DEBASE, to		kuyuyura.
DEBRIS		chisosonyo, cha, vya.
DEBT	ngongori, ya, za.	teu, la, gha; ngawa, la, gha: *to be in debt*, kuteura; kudirira.
DEBTOR		wamateu, wa, va.
DECAY, to		kuvunda; kusasa; kufota.
DECEIVE, to	kupenevya.	kupusika; kupuvya; kunyenga.
DECIDE, to		kudumula (*e.g. a* mrandu).
DECLARE, to	kutaula.	kuphara; kupharazga; kukonkhoma.
DECLINE, to		kukana.
DECLINE, to (sun)		kutezuka; kupendama.
DECREASE, to		kuwutura.
DECREE		langulo, la, gha; uzgu, wa.
DEEP, to be		kuzongoza; kuzongozoka; kunyang'amira.
DEFAECATE, to		kunya; (*see* kupatuka).
DEFAME, to		kupikiska.
DEFEAT, to		kutonda; kugoda; kuruska.
DEFEND, to		kuvikirira; (*in court*, kudapira).
DEFICIENT, to be		kuchepa; kuperewera; kugwitika. (*mentally*) kuzerezeka.
DEFILE, to		kukazuzga; *defilement*, ukazuzi, wa.
DEFORMED, to be		kupendera; kulemara; kuva chiti.
DEJECTED, to be		kugongowa.
DELAY, to	kuziwulika.	kuchedwa; kuswera; kutandara; kudeka; kukava: *to cause delay*, kuchedweska; kusuvizga.
DELICATE,		—tema; —techi.
DELICIOUS, to be		kunowa. (*see* dendi).
DELIGHT in, to	kukankhaviya.	kudemwera.
DELIRIOUS, to be		kuziririka: (mwanjira viverevesi).
DELIVER, to		kutaska; (*give up*) kupereka; kukombora.
DEN		mpanji, ya, za.
DENOUNCE, to		kuchombola.
DENY, to		kukana; kupandira; kudapira: (*withhold*) kwima; kunora.
DEPART, to	kutuwapo.	kuwuka; kuruta.
DEPRECIATE, to		(*tr*,) kuchonjora; kuparamura: (*intr*.) kusayura.

ENGLISH	TONGA	TUMBUKA
DEPRESSED, to be		kuzimbwa.
DEPTH		ndimba, ya; uzongovu, wa; luji, lwa; kwika, kwa.
DERIDE, to		kwerura; kunyoza; (*heap of derision*) chuwu, cha, vya.
DESCEND, to	kusika.	kwikha; kwikira; kukira; kujitika.
DESCRIBE, to		kupokotora.
DESERT		(malo gha) mapopa, gha; chiparamba, cha, vya; (*bare soil*) charu cha lunkamwa.
DESERT, to	kusiya.	kusida.
DESERVE, to		*see* kwenerera.
DESIRE, to	kuwunukiya.	kukhumba; kunweka; kuphukwa; kulakalaka.
DESIRE	mbunu, ya.	khumbo, la, gha; khumbiro, la gha.
DESOLATE, to be		kusokwa; (*see* mphururungwa).
DESPAIR, to		kutika lusoko.
DESPISE, to		(*person*) kuyuyura; kuyeya: (*thing*) kuzira.
DESPOND, to		kufipa mtima; kugongowa; kutika lusoko.
DESTITUTE, to be		kukhara mphururungwa; *destitution*, uranda, wa; ukavu, wa.
DESTROY, to		kwananga (kunanga); kuparanya; kupankura; kupasula: *to be destroyed*, kuparanika; kutiwa.
DESTRUCTION		paraniko, la, gha. (pwanku!).
DETAIL		lukonko, lwa: *to set forth a matter in detail*, kupataula; kukonkoska.
DETERIORATE, to		kusoya.
DETERMINED, to be		Kungangamika.
DETOUR, to make	kuvambara	kulambarara.
DEVOUR to		kumyangura.
DEW	chiwuli, cha.	jumi, la, gha; chiwuvi, cha, vya; (*see* dyonko!).
DHOW		chombo, cha, vya.
DIARRHOEA	chigwewu, cha.	pa moyo; pa mtima: (*see* kucheka).
DIE, to	kumwarika.	kufwa: (*leaves*)—kufota: (*fire*) kupwalalikira; kuzimwa.
DIFFER, to		kusidana.
DIFFERENT, to be		kupambana.
DIFFERENTIATE, to		kupatula.
DIFFICULT		—nonono;—zitu: *it is difficult*, nkunonono: *to make difficult*. kupindirizga. (*see* kutindika).

195

ENGLISH	TONGA	TUMBUKA
DIFFICULTY		unonono, wa, gha.
DIG, to		kujima; kukumba; (*ditch*) kuka-wura: (*as in hollowing out a* tuli) kusompa.
DIGIT		munwe, wa, ya.
DILIGENCE		pampu, la, gha; chitatata, cha, vya kutokatoka.
DILIGENT, to be		kupwerera; kupa kuchita.
DIM, to be		kuzgeʋa.
DIN		chiwawa, cha, vya.
DIP, to	kutipuwa.	kukovya; kubwenga.
DIRT		liko, la, gha: *dirty,*—fipa.
DIRTY, to be		kufipa; kufipirwa; kubinka; kuga-ndirwa: *to make dirty, to soil,* kufipiska.
DISAGREE, to		mtima ukukwinyata chomene: ku-pambana.
DISAPPEAR, to	kuzirimitika.	kuzgeʋa; kuzgeʋerekera.
DISAPPOINTED, to be	kumpweneneka.	kukwiya; kukwinyimbuka; kusizi-buka; kufyota: *to disappoint,* kuronkora.
DISCHARGE	see luji and ntete.	ufira, wa, gha: *to discharge,* kupo-mpa; kusurura.
DISCIPLINE		*see* kulanga.
DISCOURAGE, to		kurombotora; (*pass.* kurombotoka).
DISCONTENTED, to be		kusizibuka.
DISCOVER, to		kusanga.
DISCUSS, to		kufumbana; kudumbirana; kusu-skana; kuyowoyeskana.
DISEASE		ntenda, ya, za.
—(of cattle)	chigodoro, cha.	
DISEMBOWEL, to		kutumbura.
DISENTANGLE, to	kudadauwa.	kuzungura; kutataura.
DISGRACE		soni, ya, za: *to disgrace,* kulengera soni.
DISH		mbali, ya, za; ngwembe, ya, za.
DISLIKE, to		kupata; kusizibuka.
DISLOCATE, to	kugwererura.	kugwedura: (*pass.* kugweduka).
DISMISS, to		(*e.g. a meeting*) kuchutuska.
DISOBEDIENCE		mtafu, wa, ya: *to disobey,* kutafula.
DISPARAGE, to		kuparamura.
DISPERSE, to		kuchunka; (*see dismiss*).
DISPLACE, to		kugwedura.

ENGLISH	TONGA	TUMBUKA
DISPLEASED, to be		kubidwa.
DISPOSED, to be		mtima uli muchanya kale ku......
DISPUTE, to		kususka; kususkana; kupindikana.
DISPUTE (noun)		suskano, la, gha.
DISQUIETED, to be		kukweveka; kutampa.
DISRESPECT, to		kusunjizga.
DISSATISFIED, to be		mtima ukukwinyata chomene.
DISSOLVE, to		kusongonora; (*pass.* kusongonoka; *caus.* kusongonoska).
DISTANT		—tari.
DISTEND, to	kutundumuwa.	kutundumula.
DISTRACT, to		kuzivanizga.
DISTRIBUTE, to		kugava; kufukunyura.
DISTURBANCE		chivulupi, cha, vya.
DITCH	ntembwe, ya, za.	mpaka, ya, za; ngarandi ya za.
—round tent	kusiwiya msisi.	
DIVIDE, to		kugava; kugavira; kupatula.
DIVISION (part)		chigava, cha, vya; chivaro, cha, vya; pandi, la, gha.
DIVINE, to		kuwukwa; kuwombeza maula.
DIVORCE, to		kupata; kusuzura.
DIZZINESS		chizgumbu, cha.
DO, to		kuchita: *to do for* (*serve*) kuchitira.
DOCK, to (wages)		kutapa.
DOCTOR		ng'anga, ya, za.
DOCTRINE		chisambizgo, cha, vya.
DODGE, to	kuverama.	
DOG	garu, wa, va.	ncheve, ya, za; (*wild*) mpumpi, ya, za.
DOLL		mwanchi, wa, va; ngoza, wa, va.
DONKEY		mbunda, ya, za.
DOOR	khomo, la, gha.	chijaro, cha, vya; lwiji, lwa, gha; phondo, la, gha.
DOOR-POSTS		mpanjizgo, ya, za.
DOORWAY		muryango, wa, ya.
DOUBT, to		kukayika; kukanganya; kudodoma.
DOVE		njiva, ya, za.
DOWN (feathers)		weya, la, gha.
DOWN (below)		pasi, musi, kusi.
DOWNCAST, to be	chisko chabwantuka.	kufipa mtima; chisko chakwinyata: kugururuka.

197

English	Tonga	Tumbuka
DOWRY (bride-price)		chuma, cha, vya; chimaro, cha, vya; thumba, la, gha; chikoro, cha, vya.
DRAG, a (e.g. for a lost net)	nkokoto, ya, za.	
DRAG, to		kuguza; kukoka.
DRAW, to		kuguza; kukoka: (a bow) kukweva.
—(water)	kutunga maji.	kuteka maji; (from a vessel) kunegha:
—near	kuvandika.	kuneng'enera; kuparamira; kusenderera: to draw up in line, kundanda: to draw up taut, kukwinja: to draw out (sword) kukwetura: to draw tooth, kukhura: to draw (supplies from store) kutapa.
DRAW, to (game)		kutondana.
DRAW out, to		(in sticky strings like glue, mucus &c.) kunanampuka.
DREAD, to		kopa.
DREAM		loto, la, gha: to dream, kulota.
DRESS		saru, ya, za; (li)raya, la, gha.
DRESS, to		(self) kuvwara; (another) kuvwarika.
DRIBBLES		(from an infant's mouth) dozo, la.
DRIFTWOOD		makochezi, gha.
DRINK, to		kumwa.
DRIP, to	kuntona.	kutonya; kuntonya.
DRIVE, to		(cattle) kukhwema: to drive away, kuchimbizga: to drive out, kufumya.
DRIZZLE, to	kumeme; kupemere.	kumera-mera; kumeka-meka; kupema: vula ya mteki-teki. (see jumi).
DROP, to	kuntona.	kutonya; kuntonya: to drop drops in eye, kutonyezga: (leaves &c. falling) kupururuka; kuyoyoka: to let fall, kutaya pasi. (see kulendemuka; kudyampuka).
DROP, a		kadonto ka, twa; katonye, ka, twa.
DROPSY		mburu, ya.
DROUGHT	lilanga, la,	chilanga-langa, cha. (see chiparanta).
DROWNED, to be		kubira.
DROWSY, to be	kugompo.	kusiva; kugompora.
DRUM		ng'oma, ya, za: (large) mbiriviri, ya, za.
DRUNK, to be		kulovera: drunkenness, ulovevu, wa.

198

ENGLISH	TONGA	TUMBUKA
DRY	—yumo	—yumo;—mizo (dongo ndomizo).
DRY, to		kunyaska; komizga; komiriska.
DRY, to be		komira: *to dry up* (*stream*) kupwa; kukamuka; kuyuma.
DRYNESS		(*soil*) lunkamwa, lwa, gha: (*mouth-in fever*) ndota, ya; chikwanga, cha, vya.
DUCK		(li)υata, la, gha.
DUIKER	puru, wa, υa.	nyiska, ya, za;
DUMB person		wa mbuwu, wa, υa.
DUNG		mavi, gha; bibi, la, gha; urongwe, wa, gha; tipa, la, gha.
DUST		fuvu, la, gha: (*see* mafukuzi).
DUST, to	kusasa.	kupuputa; kuphata.
DWARFED, to be		kutina.
DWELLING-place		chikhazi, cha.
DYSENTERY	chigwewu, cha.	pa mtima; pa moyo.
DYSMENORRHOEA		cheka, la.

E

EACH		uyu...uyu; munyake...munyake.
EAGERNESS	kufwiririya.	pampu, la.
EAGLE		nombo, ya, za; chipungu, cha, vya; *fish eagle*, nkwazi, ya, za.
EAR	gutu, la, makutu, gha.	khutu, la; makutu, gha: kuzinga makutu, *to deafen with noise:* (*ear of corn*) mponje, ya, za.
EARLY		na mlenje; namacherochero; na chiviviri: *to get up early*, kucherera.
EARNEST, to be	kufwiririya.	kupwerera; kuυikapo mtima.
EARTH		dongo, la, gha.
EARTHQUAKE	chiyeuyeu, cha; chididirizi, cha.	chindindindi, cha, vya.
EASE, to be at		kufwasa.
EAST		ku mafumiro gha dazi; vuma, ya; mwela, wa.
EASY		—pusu: *it is easy*, nkupusu.
EAT, to	kurgha.	kurya: (*together*) kusangana: (*early*) kurauka: (sima *without* dendi) kuchemula; kusoza: (*greedily*) kutoma.
—raw cassava	kukwayuwa.	
EAVES of hut	mu mveka.	

English	Tonga	Tumbuka
EBONY TREE		kasarasara, wa, ʋa.
ECONOMY		lwizga, lwa.
ECZEMA		chimasa, cha, vya: muna, wa.
EDGE		mpepete, ya za.
EDIFY, to		kuzenga: *edification*. uzengi, wa
EEL	mnaka, wa, ʋa; mnjorwa, wa, ʋa.	
EFFERVESCE, to		kufuza.
EGG	zira, la, gha.	sumbi, la gha; (*white of egg*) utuʋa wa sumbi; (*yolk*) sumbi liswesi la mkati; (*white lining*) nembanemba, ya, za.
EGGS (bad)	mazira ghakusukusa.	masumbi mavivya.
EGG-SHELL		chikonkonimbwa, cha, vya.
EIGHT		nkonde na vitatu.
EITHER-OR		panji......panji.
EJECT, to		kufumya.
ELAND		sefu, ya, za.
ELAPSE, to		kujumpa.
ELASTIC, to be	kudoromoka.	
ELBOW		kasuku-suku, ka, twa.
ELDER		murara, wa, ʋa; *the* (*honoured*) *elders*, nkaramba, za.
ELECT, to		kusora; kusanka.
ELEPHANT		zovu, ya, za.
ELOQUENT, to be		kusarara lulimi.
ELSEWHERE		kunyake; panyake.
ELUDE, to	kuwara.	kuzgeʋa.
EMBER	ka la moto.	kara la moto.
EMBOLDEN oneself, to		kujikangalizga.
EMBRACE, to	kuvumbatiya.	kupakata.
EMERGE, to	kutuwa.	kufuma; kubulika; kufunka; kurokoka.
EMPHASIZE, to		kukokomezga.
EMPTY		mwazi; *to be empty*, kuʋa mwazi: kwambura kantu: chitete chiri mwazi—*of a basket with very little in it.*
EMPTY out, to	kukhutuwa; kukapa.	kukhutula; kufumiska.
ENCLOSE, to		kuʋigha; kubundira; kuvumbika.

200

ENGLISH	TONGA	TUMBUKA
ENCOURAGE, to		kuwuska mtima; kukhwimiska; kukhomeska; kukuʋirizga.
END		songo, la, gha: (*ends of earth*) mpererekezgo, ya, za.
ENDEAVOUR	kwesa.	kuyezga.
ENDLESS	muyaya.	muyirayira; swi: see mtatakuya.
ENDURE, to		kukuntirapo; kuzizipizga: (*continue*) kurutirira.
ENEMY	wa maʋongo.	murwani, wa, ʋa; wakupindikana, wa ʋa; chimpindikwa, cha, vya; nyarurya, wa, ʋa.
ENERGETIC		an *energetic person*, chikurupati, cha, vya.
ENFOLD, to		(*e.g. child in arms*) kupakata; kukumbatira; kufukatira.
ENGAGE, to		(*workers*) kulembera.
ENJOIN, to		kulangula.
ENLARGE, to		kukuzga; kusanuska.
ENOUGH	mbweno !	ndipera ! *to be enough*, kukwana.
ENQUIRE, to		kufumba.
ENRAGE, to		kukaripiska; kuʋembuka.
ENRICH, to		kusambazga; kusambasiska.
ENSNARE, to		(*in talk*) kusomba; kwavya.
ENTER, to	kusere.	kunjira.
ENTIRE		—zirima.
ENTIRELY		nkanira; fyopo ! -tu (*suffix to verb*).
ENTREAT, to	kuʋeyere.	kuʋeya.
ENVY	mbunu, ya, za.	chiʋinu, cha, vya; sanji, ya, za; wukwa, wa, gha; ʋina, la.
ENVY, to		kuʋiniwa.
EPILEPSY		viziririsi, vya.
EQUAL, to be		kuyana; kulingana; kufwana.
ERECTION		kuzenga: (*sexual*, kupikuka; kutukura).
ERR, to	kulakwa.	kubuda; kusovya; kujuvya.
ERUCTATE, to		kubagha.
ERUPTION		viʋawo, vya: *to cause an eruption*, kuʋawura.
ESCAPE, to	kulimbuka.	kupokwa; kupona; kupaza; kufyorowoka; kufwantamuka.
ESPECIALLY	viʋi.	nkanira; *see* kuruska.
ESSENCE (of a matter)		chitopoko, cha, vya.
ESTABLISH, to		kukhozga.

ENGLISH	TONGA	TUMBUKA
ESTEEM, to		kutumbika.
ETERNITY		muyira-yira; ndanda; *Eternal God*, Mtatakuya.
EUNUCH	mutheno, wa, ya.	nthunguli, ya, za.
EUPHORBIA		(*round stockades, graves, &c.*) nkhazi, ya.
EUROPEAN		mzungu, wa, ʋa.
EVENING	mazulo, gha.	mise. ya, (*also* mise ghano).
EVER, for	muyaya.	muyira-yira; kwa ndanda.
EVERLASTING		*see* mtatakuya.
EVERY		—ose: *everyone*, yumo na yumo.
EVERYBODY	muntu we yose.	muntu wali yose.
EVIDENCE	chisimisimi, cha, vya.	ukaboni, wa; chipanikizgo, cha, vya; chirozgo, cha, vya.
—to give	kusimikizga.	kupanikizga.
EVIL		—heni : (*noun*) uheni, wa ma: (*see sin*).
EVIL-SPEAKING	kutokoska utokosi.	
EXAGGERATE, to		kufuchizga; kupurungizga; kutarulira; (*noun*) njerulira, ya, za.
EXALT, to		kukwezga; (*self*) kujikuzga: (*see* kutundumula).
EXAMINE, to		kusanda: (*in* mrandu) kukochora.
EXAMPLE		bambiro, la; chirongolero, cha, vya.
EXCEL, to	kuperemera.	kuruska; kutana: (*see* chiʋinda).
EXCESS, to go to		kutarulira.
EXCEPT		kwambura kuti.
EXCHANGE, to		kugula; kugulana; kusita; kusinta.
EXCORIATION		(*in fork of legs*) kupya mpyuku.
EXCRETA		mavi, gha: (*of fowls, pigeons, &c.*) matongororo, gha.
EXCUSE	mpandira, ya, za.	mpandira, wa, ya: chigulizgo, cha, vya.
—to make		kupandira; kudapira.
EXERT oneself, to		kutumpa.
EXHAUSTED, to be		*see* kuraghara.
EXHORT, to		kuchichizga.
EXORCISE spirits, to	kuvina maskaʋi.	kuvina virombo, or vimbuza.
EXPECT, to		kulindirira; kulaʋirira.
EXPECTORATION	mankoro, gha.	mankororo, gha.
EXPERIENCE, to learn by		kumamuka

ENGLISH	TONGA	TUMBUKA
EXPERT, an		fundi, wa, ʋa; nkwanti, ya, za: *see* chilimbi *and* chiʋinda.
EXPLAIN, to	kukonkomo.	kwandulira; kubaulizga; kukonkoska; kupataula; kudandaula.
EXPRESS, to		kurokora (*to squeeze*).
EXTINGUISH, to		kuzimya; kuzimwa.
EXTORTION	chipanira, cha.	
EXTRACT, to	kutuzga.	kufumya; kufumiska; (*tooth*) kukhura.
EXUDE, to		kumwerera; kurokoka.
EYE		jiso, la, gha.
EYE-LIDS		nkopi, ya, za.
EYE-WASH		munkwara wa gurumuro.

F

FABLE		ntano, ya, za; ntanti, ya, za; chintanguni, cha, vya; chisiriri, cha, vya; chidokonyo, cha, vya.
FACE		chisko, cha, vya: (*also* maso).
FACE, to		*see* kulingizga *and* kuchirikizga.
FACT		nenesko, la, gha.
FADE, to	kuchujuka.	(*with the sun*) kutuwuruka; (*with washing*) kuvuvutuka, kuvurumuka; (*flowers*) kufota.
FAECES		mavi, gha: *see* matongororo, gha.
FAIL, to		kutondeka: (*run short*) kuchepa; kuperewera.
FAINT, to		kuzirika: *to be faint*, kudengenduka: kufwa msara.
FAINT		(*not clearly marked*) kuzirimitika.
FAITH	chivwano, cha.	chipulikano, cha, vya: chigomezgo, cha, vya; chigomekezgo, cha, vya.
FALL, to		kuwa: (*leaves*) kurakata: (*rain*) kunya; (*fall on and crush*) kudinya (*trap*) kudyampuka.
FALL off, to	kupozomoka.	kupajuka.
FALSE		—tesi; *falsehood*, utesi, wa, gha.
FALSIFY, to	kuvinda makani.	kugulizga; kugulizgira; kutetezga.
FAME		lumbiri, lwa, gha.
FAMILY		mbumba, ya, za; (pa lwaʋo); (fuko, la, gha).
FAMINE		njara, ya, za; chideru, cha; lunkhuwa, lwa.

203

ENGLISH	TONGA	TUMBUKA
FAR		—tari.
FAREWELL	marayi, gha.	kulayira; kulaliska.
FAST		luviro.
FAST, to	kufunga.	kureka kurya; kuzivizga kurya.
FAT		mafuta, gha: (*marrow*) mongo, wa, ya.
FAT, to be		kututuva; (*of meat*) kununa.
FATE		*see* leza.
ˑ FATHER (my)	ada, va.	dada, wa, va.
— (our)	auskefwe, va.	vawiskefwe, va.
— (thy)	auso, va.	vauso, va.
— (your)	auskemwe, va.	vawiskemwe, va.
— (his)	wiske, wa, va.	wiske, wa, va.
— (their)	wiskevo, wa, va.	wiskevo wa, va.
— (in-law)	msibweni, wa, va.	wiskevyara, wa, va: tatavyara, wa, va.
FAULT		ubudi, wa, gha.
FAVOUR, to		kucha na.
FAVOUR		ulemu, wa: *to lose favour*, kusayuka.
FAWN		nyiska, ya, za.
FAWN on, to		*see* kuveta.
FEAR		wofi, wa, gha ; chitente, cha, vya; manta, gha.
FEAR, to		kopa; kutentema; kunjenjema; kufipa mtima.
FEARSOME		*a fearsome thing*, chofyo, cha, vya.
FEAST		chiphikiro, cha, vya; monesko, wa, gha, (*see* koneska): *wedding feast*, zowala, (Nyanja).
FEATHER	mzimbi, wa, ya.	luhungwa, lwa, gha; weya, la, gha.
FEED, to		kulera; *to feed child by hand*, kuchinga: (*flocks*) kuliska. (*see* kukorokota).
FEEL, to	kuvwa; kupuzga.	kupulika.
—(palpate)	kuparapaska.	kupapaska; kutofya; kutoska.
FELLOWSHIP		wenenewene, wa; wendezgani, wa; kupokerana.
FEMALE		—kazi; (mwanakazi &c.).
FENCE	lisito, la, gha. lichinga, la. mpanda, wa, ya. chiseve, cha.	lusito, lwa, gha; linga, la, gha; mchinga, wa, ya; luvigho, lwa, gha.
FENCE, to	kusita.	kusita; kuvigha; kutova.
FERMENT		chirungo, cha, vya; ndungu, ya, za.

204

ENGLISH	TONGA	TUMBUKA
FERRY across, to		kurowoska.
FETCH, to	kuto; (firewood) kudeva.	kutora; (*water*) kunegha; (*firewood*) kutenya.
FETTERS		magwedi, gha; unyoro, wa, gha: goriwori, la, gha.
FEW	—mana.	—choko; —doko; —ntini; —dono.
FIBRE	katunga, ka.	(*hemp*) vikorokoto, vya; lumburwe, lwa; murara, wa.
FIBS		myati, ya; vidokonyo, vya.
FIERCE		—kali: *fierceness*, ukali, wa, gha.
FIG		nkuyu, ya, za; *fig-tree*, mkuyu, wa, ya; chikuyu, cha, vya.
FIGHT, to	kubayana; kuvambiska homwa.	kukomana: kulimbana: kupindikana.
FILCH, to		kukwakwarizga.
FILE		tupa, la, gha: to *file*, kukwenta; kukunta.
FILL, to	kuzaza.	kuzuzga; kutundumula: (*bottle with powder*) kurongezga; (*pit with earth*) kuwunda. (*see also full*).
FILTH	wiyu, wa.	(vya) nthonto, ya, za; vinyara, vya; ukazuzi, wa; uzaghali, wa, gha.
FIND, to	kusaniya.	kusanga; kusora; kubowozga.
FINE		thumba, la, gha.
FINGER		munwe, wa, ya.
FINISH, to		kumarizga; kufiska: to *be finished*, kumara.
FIRE		moto, wa, ya; *to build up a fire*, kusonka; *to warm oneself at a fire*, kota moto; *to sleep without fire*, kugona chitutu.
—to make		(*with sticks*) kupuka moto.
—sticks	*upper*, mpheka; *lower*, chisiku.	
FIREFLY		mpando-mpando, ya, za.
FIREPLACE	chipara, cha.	chipembo, cha, vya: ziko, la, gha.
FIREWOOD		nkhuni, ya, za.
—to bring	kudeva.	kutenya.
FIRM, to be	kulimba.	kukhora; kukhoma; kuzika: *to set firmly*, kukhazika.
FIRST		(wa) chimoza: *to be first*, kudanga: *to go first*, kudangira.
FIRST-BORN		mwana wa uvere.
FIRST-FRUITS		mruwuku, wa, ya.

205

English	Tonga	Tumbuka
FISH		somba, ya, za.
—(kinds of)	usipa; vyambo; mlamba; mbuvu; nkhomo; dokotu; sanjika; vigumbuli; vigong'o; kampanga; katunguru; chidindiri; bongowongo.	(*fabulous big fish*) ntanda, ya, za.
FISH, to (net)	konja.	kurova.
— (hook)		kuveja.
FISHERMAN		mrovi, wa, va.
FISH-POISON	msirawayingwe.	mtetezga, wa.
FIT (epileptic)		viziririsi, vya: (*infantile convulsions*) njire. ya, za.
FIT, to		kuyana: to *fit* (*axe to handle*) kupanjira: *to fit in,* kupanjwa: *see* kudompeka: *to fit an arrow to a bow,* kukoroveka.
FITTING, to be		kwenera.
FIVE		—nkonde.
FLABBY, to be		kukovama; kulipwitika.
FLACCID, to be	—	— —
FLAG		ndembera, ya, za.
FLAME		dimi, la, gha: *to flame,* kulilima.
FLASH, to		kumwetuka.
FLAT, to be		kupavama: *a flat place,* chidika, cha, vya; *a flat plain,* charu chiri kutambarara; charu chiri waka nyete! kuthenga.
FLATTENED, to be		(*as a cushion*) kupapatara (*adj.* papati): (*as a punctured tyre*) kupwafuka (pwafu); kubwatalara.
FLATTER, to	*see* lilimi.	kupepeka.
FLAVOUR		dendi la, gha, munonkoro, wa, ya.
FLAVOUR, to		kunoweska; *to be flavourless,* kusayuka.
FLAY, to		kufuwa.
FLEA		mpanti, ya, za; *fowl-fleas,* uzukuku, wa, gha.
FLEE, to	kuthava.	kuchimbira.
FLESH		nyama, ya, za; mnofu, wa.
FLICK, to		*see* kukwapa.
FLICKER, to		kumwetuka.
FLIT, to		kuduka: (*village*) kusama; kututa. (*see* mitara).

ENGLISH	TONGA	TUMBUKA
FLOAT, to		kusewa; kuyenjama:
—(for net)	chizira, cha, vya.	
FLOCK		mskambo, wa, ya; mpingo, wa, ya.
FLOCK into, to		kututuka; kulipitika.
FLOOD		bumba, la, gha; chigumura, cha, vya; chiwowota, cha, vya; bumbwe, la, gha.
FLOOD, to be in	kutora.	kutura; kuleta.
FLOUR	ufwa, wa, gha.	ufu, wa, gha.
—(cassava)	kondowoli.	
FLOURISH, to	kupakasa.	(of a plant) kutikita.
FLOW, to		(water) kwenda; kupompa; kugurumuka: (oil) kulipitika: current, mweza, wa.
FLOWER		luva, lwa, gha.
FLUCTUATE, to	kukhabwiya.	
FLUID, to be		kuchumburuka.
FLUTE		foliro, wa, va.
FLUTTER, to	kukhabwiya.	
FLY		membe, ya, za; nyezi, ya, za:
—(on lake)	nkhungu, za.	
—(biting)		kamdoni, ka, twa; kaskembe, wa, va;
—(maggot)		chizeti, cha, vya;
—(honey)		munye, wa.
FLY, to		kuduka; kuwuruka.
FLYPE, to	kufundumuwa.	kufundumura.
FOAM		mpovu, ya, za; tatafuru, la, gha.
FOLD		lukutu, lwa, gha; chitupa, cha, vya.
FOLD, to		kupeteka; kufuka.
—(arms)		(across chest) kupinda mawoko; kukumbata.
—(in arms)	kuvumbatiya.	kupakata; kufukatira; kukumbatira.
FOLK SONG		chidokonyo, cha, vya.
FOLLOW, to		kurondora; kurondezga; kukonka; kundondoroska.
FOLLY	phuzo, la.	ubereweza, wa, gha.
FOOD		kurya, kwa; chakurya, cha, vya; (for workers) poso, la; (provision for a journey) mpako, wa, ya.
FOOL		chindere, cha, vya; mzereza, wa va.
FOOLISH, to be		kupusa; kuva chindere; kuzerezeka.

ENGLISH	TONGA	TUMBUKA
FOOT		rundi, la, gha; (*foot-print, or sole*), rwayo, la, gha; (*foot-step*), bundi, la, gha; (*game*) bondo, la, gha.
—(club feet)	marundi gha sandu.	
FOOTSTOOL		chitambariro, cha, vya.
FOR		(*conj.*) pakuti; chifukwa: (*prep.*) *use appropriate form of verb, or connecting particle.*
FORBEAR, to		kukuntirapo; kuzizipizga.
FORBID, to		kukana; kukanizga; kulanga; kurapa; kuchenjezga.
FORCE, to		kukanchizga; kukoserezga; ku pemberezga.
FORD (river)		jambuko, la, gha; *to ford*, kwambuka.
FOREARM		mkono, wa, ya.
FOREHEAD		chene, cha, vya.
FOREIGN		—-yeni: *foreigner*, mufu, wa, va
FORELEG		mkono, wa, ya.
FOREMAN		kapitao, wa, va.
FOREST	lusuwa, la.	nkorongo, ya, za; nguyi, ya za; lusukuti, lwa, gha.
FORETELL, to		kuloska.
FORGE		luvumbu, la, gha.
FORGET, to		kuruwa.
FORGIVE, to	kureke; kukhururukiya.	kugowokera; kurekerera: *forgiveness*, chigowokero, cha.
FORK		(*between legs*) ntangararo, ya, za.
FORKED stick		mpanda, va za.
FORM, to		kuwumba; kuwurunga.
FORNICATION		uzaghali, wa, gha.
FORSAKE, to	kusiya; kujowo.	kusida: kujowora
FORTUNE (good)		mwavi, wa, ya; supa, ya, za.
FORTUNATE		wa mwavi; wa supa.
FORWARDNESS		pampu, la.
FOUNDATION	chivanja, cha.	lufura, lwa, gha: *see* figha, la, gha.
FOUNTAIN		chisimi, cha, vya.
FOUR		—nayi; —nai: *fourth*, cha chinai, &c.
FOWL	nyoli, ya, za.	nkuku, ya, za; nyakutu, wa, va; nyatazi, wa, va: *fowl-disease*, chideru, cha.
—(guinea)		nkanga, ya, za.

English	Tonga	Tumbuka
FOX		kambwe, wa, va.
FRAGMENTS	makuntwa, gha.	maruvuvu, gha.
FRAY, to		kupomborora; kupombonyezga.
FRAYED, to be	kupombonyuka.	kukuntika.
FRECKLES		madova, gha.
FREE		—anangwa: *freedom*, wanangwa, wa.
FRIEND		mbali, wa, va; bwezi, la, gha.
—(familiar address)	nganya!	wesu! mwesu!
FRIENDSHIP		ubali, wa; ubwezi, wa: *to from friendship*, kukorana ubwezi; kuparana ubwezi; kwenderana na.
FRIGHT		manta, gha; chitente, cha, vya. (kopa).
FRIGHTEN, to		kofya; kofyiska: *a frightful thing*, chofyo, cha, vya.
FRINGE		sapa, la, gha.
FROG	chuwa, wa, va.	chuli, wa, va.
FRONT, in	ku urongo.	pa (*or* ku) ntazi; pa mbere pa; pa maso gha.
FRONT, the		(*of an animal's skull*) chikakayo, cha.
FRONT, to go in		kudangira.
FROTH		mpovu, ya, za; tatafuru, la, gha.
FROWN, to	mankwinya ghaza.	kukwinyirira.
FRUIT		chipasi, cha, vya; chipambi, cha, vya.
FULL, to be	kuzaza.	kuzura (fwa!); (*after eating*); kukhuta: *to be full to overflowing*, kuzurafuru; kufuruka; kutumpuka; kutukumuka: *it is not full*, chiri sinda.
FUNNY-BONE		(*elbow*) kasuku-suku, ka, twa.
FURNACE		(*smelting*) ng'anjo, ya, za, chiramba, cha, vya.
FURROW	mvizi, wa, ya.	mgando, wa, ya, mufwerenje, wa, ya.

G

English	Tonga	Tumbuka
GABBLE, to	kubwetuwa.	kubwetura.
GAG		bano, la gha.
GAIN, to	kwanduwa	kwandula: *gain*, chandulo, cha, vya.

ENGLISH	TONGA	TUMBUKA
GALL		ndulu ya, za, ...
GALLERIES in anti-hill	muwumbwi, wa, ya.	
GAME (flesh)		nyama, ya, za.
GAME (play)		sovero, la, gha.
GAME-PIT		mbuna, ya, za.
GANGLION		ntundung'oma, ya, za.
GAP		mwanya, wa, ya.
GAPE	kwasama.	kusama.
GARDEN		munda, wa, ya; dimba, la, gha; nyata, ya, za; (for lupoko) chisosu, cha, vya: (old gardens), masara, gha.
—(cassava)	chivera, cha, chikweta, cha.	
GARLAND		mpambo, wa, ya; kambambi, wa, va.
GARMENT		raya, la, gha; munjirira, wa, ya.
GATE		(of stockade) phondo, la, gha.
GATEWAY		muryango, wa, ya; chipata, cha, vya.
GATHER, to (intr.)		kuwungana; kuwunjikana; kumotoka; kukochera.
—(tr.)		kuwunjika; kuwunjiska; kusepa; kukusa.
—(maize)		kukhata; kukorora; kukoka.
—(grass)		kwipa; kuviva.
—(leaves)	kuyava mayani.	kuyava.
—(firewood)	kudeva.	kutenya.
—(fruit)	kutondo.	kuyora.
—(flour)		(after spreading out to dry) kwanula.
GAZE, to		kulaviska dodoli; kudavira.
GENEALOGY		see kukumba.
GENERAL		chisani-sani.
GENERATION		ntanga, ya, za; mpapu, ya, za; muwiro, wa, ya: (fuko, la, gha.).
GENTILES		vamitundu, va.
GENTLE, to be	korowa.	
GENTLY	kamana-kamana.	makora; wino-wino.
GERM		(e.g. of bean) kamtima, ka.
GET, to	kuronde.	kupokera.
GET UP, to	kuyuka.	kupampuka.
GHOST		mzguki, wa, va; chivanda, cha, vya.

210

ENGLISH	TONGA	TUMBUKA
GIANT		*see* chinkhara, cha, vya.
GIDDINESS		chizgumbu, cha.
GIFT		chawanangwa, cha, vya: (*to look a gift horse in the mouth*) kusandasanda.
GINGER	chikasu, cha.	
GIRD LOINS, to		kuphinya.
GIRL		msungwana, wa, ʋa; mwali, wa, ʋa; buto, la, gha. (*see* uzamba).
GIVE, to	kupaska.	kupa; kupereka; kuninka.
GLAD, to be		kukondwa; kusekerera; kucha; kusangwa.
GLANCE, to		kuchereʋara : (*to glance aside, as a spear*) kugunya; kuteremuka.
GLARE	chilanga-langa, cha; ching'arang'ara, cha.	
GLEAN, to		kuvurura.
GLEN		chipata, cha, vya; mwanya, wa, ya.
GLITTER, to		kugadima; kung'anima; kunyetuka.
GLOAT over, to		kutambwa.
GLORIFY, to		kuchindika: *to be glorious*, kuchindama.
GLORY	unkanku, wa.	nchindi, ya, za; uchindami, wa, gha.
GLOW (of fire)		dangalira, la: *to glow*, kunyeka.
GLUTINOUS, to be		kulenda; kunanampuka.
GNASH teeth, to	kukukuta minyo.	kumemena mino.
GNAW, to		kusumba.
GO, to	kuta.	kuya; kuruta; kurata.
GO back, to	kuwe	kuwera.
GO down, to	kusika.	kwikha.
GO in, to	kusere.	kunjira.
GO off, to		(*in a huff*) kuvuruvunduka.
GO often, to		(*in vain*) kumbwata.
GO on, to		kurutirira: (*see* ntoko).
GO out, to	kutuwa.	kufuma.
GO round, to	kuʋambara.	kulambarara.
GO through, to		kusorota.
GOAL		marati, gha.
GOAT		mbuzi, ya, za; (*he -goat*) chipongo, cha, vya; (*castrated*) nthondoro, ya, za; (*young female*) msesi, wa, ya; (*kid*) kazinyane, ka, twa.

ENGLISH	TONGA	TUMBUKA
GOD		Chiuta, wa, va; Mlungu, wa, va.
GOITRE	chidukuruku, cha.	
GONORRHEA	chizonono, cha.	
GOOD	—mampha; (noun) umampha.	—weme; (noun) uweme, wa, gha.
GOOD-BYE	ruta umampha.	paweme; ruta paweme; khara paweme.
GOODS		(chattels) mpango, ya, za; (barter) maronda, gha.
GOOSE-SKIN		wundi, wa.
GORGE		mpata, wa, ya; chinkwawo, cha, vya.
GOSSIP		lwere, lwa, gha.
GOUGE		see msompo, wa, ya.
GOURD	mungu, wa, ya.	chandi, cha, vya; chipindi, cha, vya.
GOVERNMENT		(and/or its station) boma, li, gha.
GRAB, to		kuvwandamira.
GRACE		wanangwa, wa; wezi, wa; uchizi, wa; ulemu, wa; upeti, wa.
GRAIN		mbeu, ya, za; mbuto, ya, za; njere, ya, za; (maize) mpuzi, ya, za.
GRAIN (of wood)		mavwa, gha.
GRANDCHILD		muzukuru, wa, va: (which see for great-grandchildren &c.).
GRANDPARENT	mbuya, wa, va.	gogo, wa, va; sekuru, wa, va.
GRAPE		(vine and fruit) mpeska, ya, za.
GRASS		uteka, wa, gha: (green, in dambo) luhari, lwa, gha:
—(kinds of)	kanyumbo, mrunguzi.	sekera; lumamba, duru, kaza.
GRASSHOPPER	mphazi, ya, za.	mpazi, ya, za.
GRASS LANDS	vifya, vya.	(on mountains) vipya, vya.
GRAVE	muwunda, wa, ya.	dindi, la, gha; tegha, la, gha; (see mpungo).
GRAVEYARD	masano, gha.	mararo, gha.
GRAVY		msuni, wa, ya.
GRAZE, to		(as an arrow just touching) kusenta.
GREAT		—kuru; greatness, or size, ukuru, wa.
GREATLY	ukongwa.	chomene.
GREED		chilyoko, cha.
GREEDY, to be		kwima; kutoma: (see kukampa &. kunora).

English	Tonga	Tumbuka
GREEDINESS		uzukusi, wa; udokezi, wa.
GREEN		—visi. (viri-viri-viri !)
GREET, to		kutauzga; kuronjerana: *greetings*, maronje, gha.
GRIEF		chitima, cha.
GRIEVANCE		(*to have a grievance*) kuzina; kudunda.
GRIND, to	kupera.	kung'anya; kuska: (*grist*, senga, ya, za, *is ground and becomes* ufu): kugaya, *to grind whole meal in a mill.*
—teeth		kumemena mino; kuska mino.
GRINDSTONE	mphe, ya, za.	(*nether*) mpero, ya, za; luwara, lwa, gha: (*upper*) mwanasko, wa, ya.
GRIT (of grain)	lisika, la.	senga, ya, za.
GROAN, to	kutamanta.	kutampa: *groaning*, mtampo, wa, ya.
GROIN		ntangararo, ya, za.
GROPE, to	kuparapaska.	kupapaskira.
GROUND		mtunda, wa, ya.
GROW, to		kumera; kukura; kudimba; (lupoko) kubanta.
GROWL, to		kuwuruma.
GRUB	chibungu, cha.	fufuzi, ya, za; kapuchi, wa, va; mkunka, wa, ya.
GRUEL	ba, la.	bara, la, gha: (*see* ntimpwa).
GRUMBLE, to		kunyunyuta; kudinginyika; kukwininika; kuninizika; kusinginika.
GUARD to		kuvikirira. (*see protect*).
GUESS, to	kusachizga.	kusapikizga.
GUIDE, to		kurongozga: *a guide*, chirongozi, wa, va.
GUILE		uryarya, wa; uchenjezi, wa; uzuzi, wa; utyatya, wa.
GUILT		*see* dapi, *and* kususka.
GUINEA-FOWL		nkanga, ya, za.
GUITAR	pangwe, la, gha.	chiding'indi, cha, vya; bango, la, gha.
GULF		pota, la, gha.
GULLET		mumizo, wa, ya; chigoromiro, cha, vya.
GULLY		buwu, la, gha; chinkwawo, cha, vya.
GUM (of trees)		maziu, gha.
GUM (in mouth)		chavu, cha, vya.
GUN		futi, ya, za; *cap gun*, futi ya fataki.

H

ENGLISH	TONGA	TUMBUKA
HABIT	kendedu, ka; kajaridu, ka;	ruso, la gha; karuso, ka; kendero, ka; nkharo, ya; makhaliro, gha; kaviro, ka.
—to be in habit of,	kararidu, ka. kuziviriya.	kuzgovera.
HACK in pieces, to		kupikita.
HAEMATURIA	likojo, la.	lukojo, lwa.
—medicine	chitundwe, cha.	
HAILSTONES		matalala, gha.
HAIR		human—(*head*) sisi, la, gha; (*body*) cheya, cha, vya.
—grey	nyivu, ya, za.	mbuha, ya, za; nyivwi, ya, za.
—soft and lank		(*as in illness*) sisi lakuti nyankarara.
—genital		mavuzi, gha.
—animal		weya, la, gha.
HALF		nusu : *half-again*, na pachanya vighavigha:—sinda (mwezi uno na wasinda).
HAMMER		nyondo, ya, za.
—sledge	nkama, ya, za.	
HAMMOCK		machila, gha; kasara-sara, wa, va.
HAND	janja, manja.	woko, la, gha; kuwoko, kwa.
HAND OVER, to		kukombora : *see* kupazga.
HANDLE		chakukorera, cha, vya; (*hoe*) chaka, cha, vya.
—of spear	ruti, la, gha.	
HANDMAID		chidandani, cha, vya. (Ngoni).
HANDSHAKE		chasa, cha, vya.
HANG, to		(*intr.*) kulendera; kuning'ina: (*tr.*) kupayika; *see* kunenekezga: *to hang oneself*, kujigwinjirira.
HAPPEN		kuwira. (*see* mwavi).
HAPPY, to be		kukondwa; kusangwa; kusekerera; kucha.
HAPPY		wa mwavi; wa supa.
HAPPINESS	manyanda, gha.	
HARASS, to		kuyuzga; kusuzga : *to be harassed*, kuzingiziwa; kuyungwa.
HARD		—nonono : gwa ! *it is hard*, nkunonono.
—to be		kunonopa; kukurungara : (*see* kufuwa).

214

English	Tonga	Tumbuka
HARDNESS		unonono, wa, gha; nkaza, ya, za.
HARDEN, to		kunonofya; kunonopeska; kukurungazga.
HARM		urwani, wa. (*see* mapinga).
HARP		chiding'indi, cha, vya.
HARSHNESS		nkaza, ya, za.
HARVEST		vuna, la, gha; masika, gha.
HASTEN, to	kutintimika.	(*intr.*) kungofira; kuphinda; kukankamika; (*tr.*) kukuvirizga.
HASTY	kutore ρa befu.	wa chivefu; wa mawara.
HAT	chipewa, cha.	chisoti, cha, vya.
HATCH, to		(*out of shell*) kukonkomora.
HATE, to		kupata; kutinka; kuvemba.
HATRED		utinko, wa, gha.
HAVE, to		kuva na.
HAWK		kavandwe, wa, va; chimphanga, cha, vya.
HAWK, to		(*for sale*) kusaska.
HAZE	lifuvi, la.	
HE, HIM		iye, iyo.
HEAD		mutu, wa, ya.
—(back of)	gonto, la.	nkonto, ya, za.
HEAD-CLOTH		chitambara, cha, vya.
HEADMAN		(*of village*) mwenecho, wa, va; chiroro, wa, va.
HEADLONG		kapindizgori.
HEAL, to (intr.)	kupo.	kupora; kuchira.
—(tr.)	kupozga.	kupozga; kuchizga.
HEALTH		umsuma, wa: (kuva msuma).
—to restore	kusisipuwa.	kusisipura.
HEAP	chiwumba, cha.	chiwuru, cha, vya; chirundu, cha, vya; chiwunga, cha, vya: (*rubbish*) chizara, cha, vya.
—together, to		kurunda.
HEAR, to	kuvvwa.	kupulika. (makutu ngachoko, *I don't hear*).
HEART		mtima, wa, ya;
—to set h. on	kufwiririya.	kuvika mtima pa......
—to lose		kuwa nkumbi.
HEARTBROKEN	*see* kukhabwiya.	
HEARTH		ziko, la, gha.

ENGLISH	TONGA	TUMBUKA
HEAT	chifundizi, cha.	chitukivu, cha. vya:
—of sun	dungurungu, la.	muhanya, wa, ya:
—of fire	fukunyira, ya.	
—sweat	chitungu, cha.	chivuchi, cha: *before rains*, mtulo, wa.
HEAT, to be in (of bitch)	kusanuwa.	
HEAT, to	kurunguzga. kufundiska.	kutukizga; kunyaska.
HEAVE, to		*see* kutukura.
HEAVEN		kuchanya; machanya, gha: *the heavens*, mtambo, wa, ya; kudera; mlengalenga, wa, ya.
HEAVY		—zitu : *heaviness*, uzitu, wa; kulema.
HEEDLESS, to be		kuzina : *heedlessness*, mawara, gha.
HEEL over, to		kurandara; kugodoboka.
HEEL		(*of hand or foot*) chitende, cha, vya.
HEIFER		thokazi, la, gha. (Ngoni).
HEIGHT		(*of person*) msinku, wa, ya : *a great height*, kuzontoka.
HEIR		*see* kuhara.
HELM	sigiru, ya, za.	sigilo, ya, za.
HELMET		chikupiko, cha, vya.
HELP, to		kovya, kovwira : *to help to shoulder a a load*, kutwika; *to help to put down a load*, kuthurwa. (*see* kugoska).
HELPER		movwiri, wa, ʋa.
HEM, to		kubinyira.
HEMP (sisal)		vikorokoto, vya.
HEN		nyakutu, wa, ʋa; nyatazi, wa, ʋa.
HER		iye, iyo: (*possessive*) -ke.
HERD		mskambo, wa, ya; mpingo, wa, ya.
HERD, to		kukhwema; kuliska.
HERE		apa; pano; penepano—*also* muno, kuno, &c.
HEREDITARY		(*of family likeness &c.*) nchikozgo.
HERO		ngwazi, ya, za.
HESITATE, to		kukayika.
HICCUP		mkuʋi, wa, ya.
HIDE, to		(*tr.*) kubisa; kujowa; kunyevya : *to hide in the heart*, kuvungira mu mtima; kumbonya (*intr.*) kubisama; *to hide behind*, kudinganya ; kunyenkama.

ENGLISH	TONGA	TUMBUKA
HIGH		—tari : *to be high*, kuzontoka. *The most high God*, Chiuta wa mdengwende.
HIGHER, to be		(*ground*) kutundumara.
HILL		phiri, la, gha; lupiri, lwa, gha: *hilldwellers*, ʋa matanje.
HILLOCKS		tuntundumwe, twa.
HIM		iye ; iyo.
HINDER, to		kukanizga; kujandizga: *to be hindered*, kutangwanika.
HINDRANCE	mpindamsoro, ya.	chipakarara, cha, vya.
HIND LEG		mulezi, wa, ya; chigha, cha, vya.
HINT, to		kusayika.
HIPS	matanga, gha.	(*hip-bone*) nyonga, ya, za.
HIPPOPOTAMUS		chigwere, wa, ʋa.
HIS		—ke.
HITHER		kuno.
HIVE		mzinga, wa, ya.
HOARSE, to be		kukaramura; mazgu ghadodwa ku singo.
HOE		jembe, la, gha.
—(hind end)	msuka, wa, ya.	
HOE, to		kulima: *see* kugampa, *and* kutipa.
HOG (wart—)		munjiri, wa, ʋa.
HOIST, to		(*e.g. flag*) kutumpura.
HOLD, to		kukora : *to hold in the hand*, kufumbata : *to hold in the arms*, kupakata : *to hold fast*, kulimbikira.
HOLE	ntha, ya, za; dangazi, la; mphekezi, ya, za: *see* zori.	mpuwu, ya, za ; kululu, la gha; mpako, ya, za; mchembo, wa, ya; (*hole in upper lip*) nthona, ya, za: (*hole in hoe or axe*) handle) jiso, la, gha : *to make holes*, kudorora.
HOLLOW		(*in bamboo or bone &c.*) mpuwu, ya, za ; chibokororo, cha, vya ; *see* chigoroʋezi, cha, vya.
HOLLOW, to		kufuka; kusompa: kuvungumariska.
—to be	mwankhu !	kubabafuka; kufukulika; kuvungumara.
HOLY		—tuʋa : *holiness*, utozi, wa; katowero, ka; *see also* mziro, wa, ya.
HOLY, to be		kutowa; kupatulika.
HOME		kwitu, kwinu, *&c.* mafita, gha : *at home*, ku kaya : *to go home*, kuwera.

217

ENGLISH	TONGA	TUMBUKA
HONEY		uchi, wa, gha.
HONEY-COMB		chisa. cha, vya; *wax*, pura, la, gha.
HONOUR		tumbiko, la; nchindi, ya, za; ulemu, wa; uchindami, wa.
HOOF		bondo, la, gha.
HOOK		mbeja, ya, za.
HOOPOE (?)	kampupupu, wa.	
—(crested (?)		nkumbaruru, ya, za.
HOOP (in creel)	nthengo, ya, za.	
HOP, to	kusolonta.	kugolontika; kujwantira.
HOPE, to		kugomezga; kulindirira; kulindizga.
HORN		sengwe, la, gha ; *to sound the horn*, kulizga mbata ; *for cupping*, chinunu, cha.
HORNET		sanganavu, la, gha; bumbuzi, ya, za.
HORSE		kavalo, wa, va.
HOSTAGE		mkoli, wa, va.
HOT, to be		kufunda ; kutukira; kurungura; *see* kukonda: *it is hot now*, kuli chivuchi sono.
HOUND, to		kucherukira.
HOUSE		nyumba, ya, za; (*boys'*) mphara, ya, za ; (*girls'*) ntanganene, ya, za.
HOW ?		uli ? mbu ? (*relative*) umo—*with dir. form of verb.*
HUDDLE together, to		kuwunjikana.
HUG, to		kufukatira ; kupakata : *see* chizakazaka.
HUM, to	kuhihita.	
HUMBLE, to be	kujorovya.	kujiyuyura : *to humble*, kuchefya.
HUMP		(*of ox*) honyo, la, gha ; lirunda, la, gha : (*of man*) chumbi, cha, vya.
HUMP-BACK		chifumbu, cha, vya.
HUNGER	nja, ya, za.	njara, za, ya.
HUNGRY, to be		kuziya.
HUNT		(*a combined hunt*) chisokori, cha, vya.
—to	kusaka.	kuvinga; kuvamba : kupenja nyama.
HUNTER		chivinda, wa, va.
HURRY, to	kutintimika ; kwenda mkwaramkwara.	kwendeska ; kungofira ; kupusumpa; kuphinda; kukankamika; kuva pa luviro; kwenda ndavara.

English	Tonga	Tumbuka
HURT		kupweteka.
HUSBAND		mfumu, wa, ʋa; msweni, wa, ʋa.
HUSK		kanta, la, gha.
—to	kukonora.	kuchokora: see kutumpa.
HUSTLE, to		kung'anuzga.
HUT		nyumba, ya, za:
—(booth)	senje, wa, ʋa.	msasa, wa, ya; sonjo, wa, ʋa; ndinda, ya, za.
HYENA		chimbwe, cha, vya.
HYMN		sumu, ya, za; lusumu, lwa, gha.
HYPOGASTRIUM		chinena, cha, vya.

I

English	Tonga	Tumbuka
I		ine; (with verb) ndi-, ni-, n-: I, a sinner, ine nda wakwananga.
IDEA		fundo, ya, za.
IDIOT, to be an	kuherewuka.	kuzerezeka.
IDLE, to be		kukhara waka: to make idle threats, kutetezga.
IDOL		ngoza, wa, ʋa.
IF	asani.	usange; uvwe.
IGNORANCE		ujira, wa, gha; ulemwa, wa, gha.
IGNORE, to		kuziʋanizga.
IGUANA		kaʋaʋa, wa, ʋa.
ILL, to be	kutama.	kurwara; kutakamira.
ILLNESS		urwari, wa, gha; ntenda, ya, za.
ILLUSTRATION		chiyeruzgo, cha, vya.
ILL-WILL		see kupindika.
IMAGE		chikozgo, cha, vya; chiyeruzgo, cha, vya; cheruzgiro, cha, vya; mwanchi, wa, ʋa; ngoza, wa, ʋa.
IMAGINE, to		kurokota.
IMBECILE, to be	kuherewuka.	kuzerezeka. an imbecile, bephe wa, ʋa.
IMITATE, to		kuyezga.
IMMEDIATELY	sosonokweni.	sono-sono.
IMPALA		mpala, ya, za.
IMPATIENT, to be	kutore pa befu; kutore pa mtima.	
IMPERFECTLY		mpuvya.
IMPOTENT (male)		mbomi, wa; (or ya).
IMPOVERISH, to		kumazga.

219

ENGLISH	TONGA	TUMBUKA
IMPUDENCE	phuzo, la.	msinjiro, wa, ya; mtonyoro, wa, ya.
IN		mu; mukati mu.
INADVERTENCE	chaja pa uta.	
INASMUCH AS		pakuti; mwakuti.
INCENSED AGAINST, to be		kuyarukira.
INCONSISTENT, to be		kusarasata.
INCREASE, to		kwandana.
INDEED		nadi; nkanira: (surprise) kware!
INDIAN		Mwenyi, wa, ʋa.
INDIGNANT, to be		kubidwa.
INDISTINCT, to be	kuzirimitika.	
INDOLENCE		see kufwa lusoko; mphwayi, ya, za.
INFANT		kana, ka, twa; mwanichi, wa, ʋa; bonda, wa, ʋa; mujedu, wa, ʋa; litema, la, gha.
INFECTION		ntenda yakwambuka.
INFINITE		(distance or time) swi......!
INFLUENCE (bad)		fuzi, ya.
INFORM		kuruvya.
INHERIT, to		kuhara.
INIQUITY		ubendezi, wa, gha.
INITIATION		see kulanga.
INJURE, to		kunanga.
INSERT, to	kuserezga.	kunjizga.
INSIDE		mukati: to turn inside out, kufundumura.
INSINUATE, to		kusayika.
INSIPID, to be		kuzizima.
INSIST, to		kungangamika; kukokomezga; kumiririra; kukanchizga.
INSPECT, to		kusanda: see kupempura.
INSTEAD of		pa malo gha.
INSTINCT		see kupangwa.
INSTRUCT, to		kulanga; kunjirikizga.
INSTRUCTIONS		vipango, vya.
INSULT, to	kufyonya fyonyo.	kusunjizga.
INTEND, to		kuʋa muchanya: mtima wawukira muchanya kuchita.
INTERCEDE, to		kuʋeyerera: (kutaska).
INTERCESSOR		nkoswe, ya, za: (mtaski, wa, ʋa).

220

ENGLISH	TONGA	TUMBUKA
INTERCOURSE		(*sexual*) kuchinda; kusoverana.
INTEREST, to		kusuvizga.
INTEREST (gain)		chandulo, cha, vya.
INTERPRET, to		(*meaning*) kwandulira; (*language*) kuzgora; kung'anamula.
INTERROGATE, to		kukororoska.
INTERRUPT, to		kugwaza lulimi: *see* pampu.
INTERSTICES		mu fyakanya.
INVITE, to	kudana.	kuchema.
IRASCIBLE, to be		kuzwazwanduka.
IRON		chuma, cha, vya; chisulo, cha, vva:
—ore		tali, la, gha: *a mass of iron after smelting*, chipurumba, cha, vya.
—corrugated		rata, marata, la, gha.
—to work in	kusura.	kuskana; kufura.
IRON clothes, to		kusita.
IRRELEVANCE	chisaviro, cha.	
IRRITATING plant (cowhage)	ukasi, wa.	
ISLAND		chirwa, cha, vya.
IT		iyo, ilo, &c. (*as concord*); *its*, -ke.
ITCH (disease)		mphere, ya, za.
ITCH, to		kunyenyera
IVORY		zovu, za.

J

JAW (lower)		mhlati, wa, ya.
— (upper)	njegheyu, ya, za.	
JEALOUSY		sanji, ya, za; wukwa, wa, gha.
JERKS		(*going down hill*) jiti! jiti! jiti!
JEST		mwati, myati, wa, ya.
JOIN, to		kurunga; kubampikanya.
JOINT		fundo, la, gha; marunga, gha.
JOKE, to		kupekula; kuyowova myati.
JOSTLE, to	kugunyuwa.	kukanchizga; kugunda.
JOURNEY		ulendo, wa, gha.
JOY	likondwa, la.	chimwemwe, cha, vya; kukondwa; kusekerera.
—(dancing)	kwangara.	kugiya.
JUDGE		mweruzgi, wa, va.
—to	kuteska.	kupima; kweruzga: (*to condemn*) kususka.

221

ENGLISH	TONGA	TUMBUKA
JUMP, to		kuduka; kuwuruka; kuchirifuka; ngwi! (*flea or spark from fire*) kubanta.
JUNCTION (of streams)		zaro, la, gha.
JUSTIFY, to		kurunjiska; kunyoroska; *see* kudapira.

K

ENGLISH	TONGA	TUMBUKA
KEEP, to		kusunga.
KELOID		duna, la, gha.
KICK, to		kupafula.
KID		kazinyane, ka, twa. (Ngoni).
KIDNEY	sana, ya, za.	ziso, za. (Ngoni).
KILL, to	kubaya; kukoso.	kukoma; kupuzura.
KIND		mtundu, wa, ya.
KINDLE, to		(*fire*) kupemba; kupuka: *the fire kindles*, moto ukugolera: *kindlings*, viswatu, vya.
KINDNESS		wezi, wa; ulemu, wa.
KING		karonga, wa, va; themba, la, gha.
KINGDOM		ufumu, wa, gha.
KISS, to		kufyofyonta.
KNEAD, to		kukonya.
KNEE		khongono, la, gha.
KNEEL, to	kugwada.	kujikama.
KNIFE		mpeni, wa, ya; chimayi, cha, vya.
KNOCK, to	kugunyuwa; kubwefuwa;	kugunda; kukuva. kugong'oska; kukong'oska:
—(on door)		kugong'onta; kujurizga.
—(down)	kung'anuwa;	
—(down fruit)	kupauwa; kuponto.	kupaura; kuvwaska.
—(dust off hands)		kukuvura mawoko. *see* kubumura; kuvivika; kudirimura.
KNOT		fundo, la, gha: *slip-knot*, fundo la chovyo.
KNOW, to	kuziva.	kumanya: *to be known*, *see* kuthuwukwa: *I don't know*, kaya; manyi.
KNOWLEDGE	mziviro, wa.	umanyi, wa: zeru, za.
KNUCKLE		fundo, la, gha.
KOKO (plant)		simbi, la, gha.

| KOODOO | | mperembe, ya, za. |
| KRAAL | | chivaya, cha, vya; khora, la, gha; (*goats & sheep*) chitupa, cha, vya: lukutu, lwa, gha. |

L

LABIA MAJORA (fem. genitals)		mphuti, za; maleve, gha.
LABOUR, to	kutata nchito.	kuteveta.
LACK, to		kusauka; kukavuka; (kuura; kwambura).
LACK	usiwa, wa.	usauchi, wa; ukavu, wa: chandisova, *I haven't got it.*
LAGOON		tavali, la, gha.
LAIR		mpanji, ya, za; mchembo, wa, ya.
LAKE		nyanja, ya, za.
LAME, to		kupundula: *to be lame*, kupundukwa kukhara chiti: *a lame person*, mkwakwa, wa, ya.
LAMENT, to		kutengera.
LAMP		nyali, ya, za; lumuli, lwa, gha.
LAND		charu, cha, vya; mtunda, wa, ya.
LANDING-PLACE	vu, la.	dowoko, la, gha; chirowoko, cha, vya.
LANDING-NET	ngwando, ya, za.	
LANDSLIDE		seme, ya, za: (*see* chimpungo *and* kugumura).
LANGUID, to be		kulolotera.
LAP, to		(*water—as a dog*) kukapa.
LARGE		—kuru: *at large*, chisanisani.
LARVAE		(*of mosquito*) toverove, va.
LASCIVIOUSNESS	ulankasi, wa.	ukwakwa, wa.
LAST		pa kumarira; ku- *or* pa-nyuma.
LATE, to be	kubwanjuwa.	kuchedwa; kuziulika.
the late...	chipondi cha...; wenga...	mlingi-David, valingi—David na Yobe.
LATRINE		chimbuzi, cha, vya.
LAUGH, to		kuseka; kuseka pwiripitu! (*heartily*).
LAUNCH, to	kusoro.	(*canoe*) kugurura.
LAW		dango, la, gha; *plur.* marango.
LAY DOWN, to	kurarika.	kugoneka: (*as rain lays grass*) kuwowota.
LAY up (store)	kulimbika.	kuronga.

English	Tonga	Tumbuka
LAY eggs, to		kutayira: (of a fowl wishing to lay) yikupenja chizizi.
LAZY	—lesi;	—kata: a lazy person, mkata, wa.
LAZINESS	ulesi, wa.	ukata wa.
LEAD		mtovu, wa, ya.
LEAD, to		kurongozga: a leader, chirongozgi, wa, ʋa; ndongozi, ya, za.
—(by hand)		kuteteska; kunyanyaska.
—(astray)	kurandiska.	kupuruska.
—(singing)		kutora (sumu).
LEAF	jani, la, mani, gha.	hamba, la, gha.
LEAK, to	kuchucha; kupompa.	kusurura.
LEAN, to be		kughanda: leanness, ughavu, wa.
LEAN, to	kuganuka.	kurandara; kusendama; kubwantuka.
—to make to	kuganuska.	kurandalika; kusendeka; kubwantuska.
—on, to	kuyegeme.	kweghamira, kutamira; see kunyekezga and kukokomera.
LEAP, to		kuduka; kuwuruka: (af flames of fire) kulipuka.
LEARN, to		kusambira.
LEAVE, to	kusiya.	kusida: see kupunta.
LEAVE OFF, to		kureka.
LEAVEN		chimera, cha; chirungo, cha; ndungu, ya.
LEFT side		mazere, gha: left arm, woko la mazere.
LEG		rundi, la, gha: fore-leg, mkono, wa, ya; hind-leg, mlezi, wa, ya.
LEMON		mandima, gha; zobara, ya, za.
LEND, to		kubwereka; kuteuliska; kudirizga; kopeza.
LENGTH		utari, wa.
LEOPARD		nyalubwe, wa, ʋa; ntoromi, ya, za,
LEPROSY	makhati, gha.	vyoni, vya: lepers, ʋa vyoni.
LESS		—choko: to be too little, kuchepa.
LESSEN, to		kuchefya; kuchepeska; kuwutura.
LESSON		chisambizgo, cha, vya.
LEST		mzire; chizire.
LETHAL drug		munkwara wa chifweni.
LETTER		karata, wa, ʋa; (also ya, za).

224

ENGLISH	TONGA	TUMBUKA
LEVEL with, to be		kutyana na: *a level place*, chidika, cha.
LEVER up, to		kupikura.
LIAR		mtesi, wa, ʋa.
LICE		*see louse.*
LICK, to		kumyanga; kufyonta; kukatura.
LID		chibenekerero, cha, vya.
LIE	boza, la, gha.	utesi, wa, gha.
LIE, to	kunama.	(*untruth*) kuteta; kugulizga; kumyatika.
LIE down, to	kura.	kugona.
LIFE		umoyo, wa, miyoyo, ya; uzima, wa, gha.
LIFT, to	kuyuska; kunyamuwa.	kuwuska: *see* kuweska.
LIGHT		—yuyu; —pepu: *to make light of,* kuyeya; kuchita phompha.
LIGHT		ukweru, wa; kungweruka; kuʋala; ngwe!
—(lamp)		muliko, wa, ya; lumuli, lwa, gha; lumbuni, lwa, gha; njasko, ya, za.
—to		kukozga; kukunga: *to light up a place,* kumulika.
—to bring to		kuchonjora.
LIGHTNING	limpezi, la.	leza, wa, ʋa; huʋa, ya, za: (*the noise of lightning*) chikhayo-khayo, cha.
LIKE (conj.)		nga; nga ndi: (*see as*).
LIKE, to be		kukozgana na; kulingana na; kuyana na; kufwana na.
LIKENESS		chikozgo, cha, vya.
LIMB		chiʋaro, cha, vya.
LIMP, to		kugonta; kubanta.
LINE		mzere, wa, ya.
LINGER, to		kulinda; kutandara; kuziulika; kudonda; kukhara waka.
LION		nkaramo, ya, za.
LIP		mlomo, wa, ya; (*hole in upper lip*) nthona, ya, za; *lip ornament,* mpete, ya, za: (*lip of pot*) kaʋende.
LISTEN, to		kupulika; kupulikiska; kutegherezga makutu.
LISTLESS, to be		kugongowa.

ENGLISH	TONGA	TUMBUKA
LITTLE	—mana	—choko; —ntini: *a little*, kachoko; kantini waka; (kadonodono): *also expressed by suffix*—ko *to verb*: *little by little*, wengu-wengu; pachoko-pachoko.
LIVE, to		kuva moyo; kuwuma; kughuma.
LIVER		chivindi, cha, vya; mpafwa, ya, za.
LIZARD	mtondoni, wa.	mtondori, wa, ya;
—small	chimwamafuta, cha.	
—tree		gunkwe, wa, va; bulumuti, wa, va.
—iguana		kavava, wa, va.
LOAD		katundu, wa, va; nthndu, ya, za; mphingu, ya, za: *to burden with a load*, kutwika; *to unload*, kuthura.
LOAD a gun, to		kusopera futi.
LOCHIA	(women) ntete, ya, za.	
LOCUST		zombe, wa, va; mpazi, ya, za; *hoppers*, mandova; gha.
LOG (of wood)	nkunguru, ya, za.	nkungura, ya, za; mkoko, wa, ya.
LOINS	chiwunu, cha.	luwunda, lwa, gha.
LOIN-CLOTH	tevera, la, gha. (see chingara)	mgonda, wa, ya; mtemwende, wa, ya: (*see* mwere, *and* denga).
LONELINESS		phukwa, la.
LONG		—tari.
LONGSUFFERING	unkuntiya, wa.	
—to be		kukuntirapo; kuzizipizgira.
LONG AGO		kale; mwaka; liromwaka.
LONG FOR, to	kumiziriya.	kunweka; kumiririra mata.
LOOFAH	buwa, la, gha.	
LOOK, to	kulereska.	kulaviska: *look!* hena! *look here*, razga kuno: *to gaze at*, kuthalika, kulavirira.
LOOK for, to	kulembe.	kupenja. (*see* kutava-tava).
LOOKING-GLASS		karirori, wa, va; chiwoni-woni, cha, vya.
LOOP		nkowezi, ya, za.
—for carrying	mpingwa, ya, za.	
LOOSE, to be	kufwarapuka.	kugwedera; kuserevenda; kuporowota; pokopoko! kugowoka.
—of earth	kuyoyoka.	
LOOSEN, to	kudeweyezga.	kusutula; kugowozga.
LORD	mbuya, wa, va.	fumu, ya, gha.
LOSE, to	*see* kuwara.	kutaya: *see* kusova *and* kuzgeva.
LOST, to be		kuzgeva; kusova; kutayika.

English	Tonga	Tumbuka
LOTS, to draw		kupenduzga; kudula makungwa.
LOUSE	sabwe, ya, za.	nyinda, ya, za.
LOURIE		nduvaruva, ya, za.
LOVE	chanju, cha.	chintemwa, cha; wezi, wa: *loving-kindness*, chifundu, cha.
LOVE, to	kwanja.	kutemwa.
LOW, to (oxen)		kubama.
LOWER, to	kusiska; kukizga.	kwikiska; kubwantula.
LUCK		(*good*) mwavi, wa, ya: (*bad*) soka, la, gha.
LUCKY, to be		kuskuka: *to be unlucky, see* kusikura. *as luck would have it*, nga ndi mwavi.
LULLABY		*see* kupembuzga.
LUMP		burunga, la, gha: *see* mburuma.
—of sima	dozi, la, gha.	tozi, la, gha; mphiri, ya, za.
—in sima	torong'ondo, la.	mburu, la, gha; mbinti, la, gha.
LUNGS		mapapu, gha; mpwafwa, ya, za.
LUST, to	kuwunukiya.	kulaka-laka.
LYING-IN after childbirth	chisachi, cha.	chikutu, cha.

M

English	Tonga	Tumbuka
MAD, to be		kufunta.
MADNESS		chifusi, cha, vya: *he is mad*, wa na vifusi.
MAGGOT	fusi, ya, za.	mporozi, ya, za; gulinga, wa, va: *the maggot-fly*, chizeti, cha, vya.
MAGIC		mayere, gha.
MAGNIFY, to		kukuzga: *see* kutundumula.
MAHOGANY tree		muvava, wa, ya; *also* mlombwa, wa, ya.
MAIDEN		mwali, wa, va.
MAIMED, to be		kupundukwa.
MAIZE		ngoma, ya, za; chingoma, cha, vya: *young plant*, chipozwa, cha, vya: *fresh stalks*, nyifi, ya, za; mjuwa, wa, ya: *single grain off cob*, mpuzi, ya, za: *cob centre without grains*, chisokwe, cha, vya: *broken maize*, mpali, ya, za: *maize boiled and stored*, muvuserera, wa.
MAJESTY		ufumunkuru, wa.
MAKE, to		(*create*) kulenga; (*mould*) kuwumba. (*see* kupanga *and* kuchita).
MALE		—rumi, *e.g.* mwanarumi.

ENGLISH	TONGA	TUMBUKA
MALICE		kutokota.
MALTREAT, to		kugoska; kunyungura.
MAMBA (black)	khako, wa, ʋa.	vuvi, wa, ʋa.
MAN	munturumi, wa.	muntu, wa, ʋa; mwanarumi, wa, ʋa.
MANGER	dghero, la, gha.	uryero, wa, gha.
MANGO		yembe, ya, za.
MANHOOD	unturumi, wa.	untu, wa; wanarumi, wa: see also uhurwa, and urara.
MANNER		see kwenda and kukhara.
MANURE		urongwe, wa; vundira, vya: ashes, see nteʋere, za.
MANY		—nandi: how many? —ringa?
MARGIN		mpepete, ya, za.
MARK (tribal)		simbo, ya, za. (also of writing).
MARK, to		kuchonga; kusimba.
—(notice)	kuthoʋa.	kuʋanika.
MARRIAGE		nthengwa, ya, za; ukwati, wa, gha; utezi, wa, gha.
MARROW (bone)		mongo, wa, ya.
—(vegetable)		uʋimbi, mauʋimbi, wa, gha.
MARRY, to		kutorana:
—man subj.	kuto.	kutora; kusompora; see kutenga.
MARRIED, to be (woman)	kuwirwa.	kutoreka; kusomporwa; kutengwa
MARVEL, to		kuzizwa.
MASKS		vinyawo, vya.
MASS		burunga, la, gha; mgwiriʋindi, wa; see mburuma.
MASTER	mbuya, wa, ʋa.	mwenecho, wa, ʋa.
MAT		mpasa, ya, za; mkeka, wa, ya; javi, la, gha.
MATERIAL things		(as opposed to spiritual) vya mʋimba.
MATRON		nyakatema, wa, ʋa.
MATTER, a		(e.g. a case in the mphara) mrandu, wa, ya.
MATURE, to		(to store or hang for maturing) kuvundika.
MAUNGOOSE	msuru, wa, ʋa.	
MAY BE, it		see kupamba.
ME		ine.
MEADOW		luhari, lwa, gha; dambo, la, gha.
MEAL	ufwa, wa.	mgayiwa, ya; ufu, wa; meal-water ntimpwa, ya.

ENGLISH	TONGA	TUMBUKA
MEANNESS		kasu, la.
MEASURE, to		kupima; *a measure*, mweso, wa.
MEAT		nyama, ya, za.
MEDICINE		munkwara, wa, ya; mkota, wa, ya: *see* kuvinda; chiroporo *and* seketera.
MEDITATE, to	kurunguruka.	kuranguruka.
MEDIUM		(*communicating with spirits*) nchimi, ya, za.
MEEKNESS		kuzika, kwa.
MEET, to		kukumana; kubwanyana maso ku maso; *to go to meet*, kutemerera: *to join* (*to make broken ends meet*), kukumanya; kurunga: *to meet together*, kuwungana.
MEETING, a		wungano, wa, gha.
MELANCHOLIA	sira, ya.	
—medicine for		muvavani, wa.
MELT, to	kunyakata.	kwenga: *to be melted, to dissolve*, kunyeketuka.
MEMBER		chivaro, cha, vya.
MEND, to		(*nets*) kutanda: *to patch cloth*, kuriva.
MENSTRUATE, to	kutore dondo.	kusamba; kuwamo mu masambi.
MENSES	dondo, la, gha; machika, gha.	nkwendi, ya, za;
—to miss		kusayika.
MENTION, to		kuzunula.
MERCY		lusungu, lwa, gha; *to have mercy on*, kulengera lusungu pa: *tender-mercy*, chiuravi, cha.
MESSAGE		utenga, wa, gha; nduvyo, ya, za.
MESSENGER		tenga, la, gha; ntumi, ya, za; nkaramba, ya, za.
MICTURATE, to	kukoza.	kutunda.
MIDDAY, at	msana pakati.	na muhanya pakati.
MIDDLE, in the		pakati; mukati.
MIDWIFE	mpungu, wa, va.	muzamba, wa, va.
MIGHT		mpavu, ya, za; nkongono, ya, za: *to work with all one's might* kuchita chijirijiri.
MILK		mkaka, wa; suru, la; lukama, lwa; luvisi, lwa: *to milk*, kusenga; kukama.
MILKY WAY, the	mlambagombe, wa.	
MILLET (large)		mapira, gha.
—(small)	mave, gha.	lupoko, lwa; ulezi, wa; wurumano, wa; kanchevere. wa.

229

English	Tonga	Tumbuka
MIND		mano, gha: *to set one's mind to,* kukangalizga.
MINE		mugodi, wa, ya; chikulukutu, cha, vya.
MISCARRY, to		kusoposka.
MISCHIEF		ulankasi, wa.
MISFORTUNE		soka, la, gha; kasamwa, ka, twa.
MISLEAD, to		kupuvya.
MISS, to	kumbwita.	kuwinda.
—(be late)	kubwanjuwa.	
MIST		tutwe, la; nyatutwe, wa; nyanku- vinda, wa. *see* kuchucha.
MISTAKE		ubudi, wa, gha.
MISUNDERSTAND, to		kupulika mpuvya.
MIX, to		kusazga; kutimbanya: (*with water*) kukasa; kukonka: (dendi) ku- runga.
MOAN, to	kutamanta; kubuwura.	kudagha.
MOANING	mbuwuru, wa.	
MOCK, to	kuwera.	kwerura; kuhoyera.
MODEL		mwanchi, wa, va.
MOHAMMEDANS		vamuhammadi.
MOIST, to be		kuzumbwa; kunyewa: *to moisten,* kuzumbwiska; kunyevya: konka.
MOISTURE		mtika, wa, ya; mzizi, wa, ya.
MOLE		mzumi, wa, va.
MONEY		ndrama, ya, za.
MONKEY		mkweri, wa, va; pusi, wa, va; nchima, ya, za; ndacha, ya, za.
MONTH		mwezi, wa, ya.
MOON		mwezi, wa, ya.
MOREOVER		na kwenenako.
MORE		—nyake; kukuskirako: ' *no more,* ndipera.
MORNING	mlenji, wa, ya.	machero, gha; *in the morning,* na machero.
—star, the	thondo, la; thondwe, la.	nthanda, ya.
MORTAL	*see* chifweni.	
MOSQUITO	uzuzu, wa.	nyimbo, ya, za: *larvae,* toverove, wa, va.
MOSS (in water)	kovyo, wa, va.	(*hanging from trees*) manyerenyeza, gha.

English	Tonga	Tumbuka
MOTH		burawura, wa, ʋa.
MOTHER	ama, ʋa (my).	(my, our) mama, wa, ʋa; (thy) nyoko, wa, ʋa; (your) nyinamwe, wa, ʋa; (his) nyina, wa, ʋa; (their) nyinaʋo, wa, ʋa.
MOTHER-IN-LAW		mpongozi, wa, ʋa; mamavyara, wa, ʋa; nyinavyara, wa, ʋa.
MOULD		(on damp walls &c.) chuku, cha, vya.
MOULD, to		kuwumba: brick-mould, chikomboli, cha, vya.
MOULT, to	kukuchuka.	(fowl) kutotoka; (dog &c.) kuphata.
MOUND (in garden)	tusi, la, gha.	tumba, la, gha.
MOUNTAIN		phiri, la, mapiri, gha; lupiri, lwa, gha.
MOURN, to	kutenje.	kulira; kutengera. (see also chingwazi, zintambo; and ʋachimbwe).
MOUSE		mbeʋa, ya, za.
MOUTH		mlomo, wa, ya: (of stream) zaro, la, gha.
MOVE, to		kwenda: kusama: to move along, kunderera.
	see kutongatonga, and gwi.	to move under covering, kutukuruka.
MUCH (adj.)		—nandi.
—(adv.)	ukongwa.	chomene.
MUD		tipa, la, gha; matakalimbwa, gha; matakalambwe, gha.
MULTIPARA		nchembere, ya, za; ndi nchembere kanayi, she has had four children.
MULTIPLY, to		(family &c.) kwandana: (sum) kwandaniska.
MULTITUDE	urapasi, wa.	chiwuru, cha, vya; mzinda, wa, ya.
MUMPS		katukutu, wa, ʋa.
MURDER, to	kubaya.	kukoma: (noun) uchikozi, wa, gha.
MURDERER		mbanda, wa, ʋa; chikozi, cha, vya.
MUSCLE	msipi, wa, ya.	mnofu, wa, ya; msipa, wa, ya.
MUSHROOM		wowa, wa, gha.
—(kinds of)	ndezu; gonase; madali; mpofwa; manyani.	manda; utari; karunkurwe.
MUSICAL INSTRUMENTS		kaligu, wa, ʋa; kalimba, wa, ʋa; zeze, wa, ʋa; mangorongondo, gha. &c.
MY, MINE	—ngu.	—ne: (woko lane, my hand).

231

English	Tonga	Tumbuka
MYRIAPOD		bongororo, wa, ʋa.
MYSTERY		chindindi, cha, vya.

N

English	Tonga	Tumbuka
NAGGING		kontoro, la.
NAIL		mzumali, wa, ya: (*finger-nail*) njo--ʋe, ya, za.
NAKEDNESS	malisechi, gha.	nkhuli, ya: (*I am naked*) ndiri nkhuli.
NAME		zina, la, gha: *surname*, chiwongo, cha, vya.
NAME, to		kutya.
NARROW		—finyi: *see* fyakanya.
NATION		fuko, la, gha; mtundu, wa, ya.
NATURE		kaʋiro, ka, kawiro, ka; nkharo, ya, za.
NAUGHTINESS		ulankasi, wa, gha.
NAUSEA		museru, wa, ya; *to feel nausea*, kuseruka.
NAVEL		mbwera, wa, ya. (*plur.* mimbwera).
NEAR		pafupi: *to come near*, kuneng'enera; kutegherera; kusenderera; kunderera.
NECK		mkosi, wa, ya: *back of neck*, nkonyoro, ya, za.
NECKLACE		chipoti, cha, vya: (*large stones*) peska, la, gha.
NEED, to		kusauka; kusokwa; kukavuka.
NEED		usauchi, wa; ukavu, wa; usokwano, wa.
NEEDLE	katimo, wa, ʋa.	zingano, ya, za; chitungu, cha, vya.
NEGLECT	kujowo.	kuzina-zina.
NEGLIGENT, to be		kudonda; kufwa daka.
NEIGHBOUR		mzengezgani, wa, ʋa; mwanase, wa, ʋa: *to be neighbours*, kupakana.
NEITHER...NOR		*see* nanga *and* nesi.
NEPHEW		mupwa, wa, ʋa.
NEST	(*for fowl to lay*) likanja, la.	chivimbo, cha, vya; (*bees'*) chisa, cha, vya: (*spider's*) nemba-nemba, ya, za.
NET	chirepa, cha; dangara, wa, ʋa; ntambura, ya, za.	mkwawo, wa, ya; ukonde, wa, gha.
—(landing)	ngwando, ya, za; chiwo, cha, vya.	
—(to make)		kutaʋa; kuruka; kutanda.

ENGLISH	TONGA	TUMBUKA
NEVERTHELESS	ndikweni.	ndipo uli; ndipo kweni.
NEW	—fya.	—pya.
NEWS		makani, gha.
NICE	—mampha.	—weme.
—to be	kusamuka.	kunozga: kunowa.
NIECE		mupwa, wa, va.
NIGHT		usiku, wa, gha.
NINE		nkonde na vinayi.
NIP, to	kuvana.	kusina.
NIPPLE	monkero, wa, ya.	ndomo, ya, za.
NITS (of lice)		miyi ya nyinda.
NO	awa; cha.	chara; iai.
NOBLEMAN		see chiroro, wa, va.
NOD, to		kukovama.
NOISE		chiwawa, cha; kuwawata (e.g. a crowd); mpomo, ya, za (e.g. of a waterfall).
NONPLUSSED, to be		kupukuruka.
NOON	msana, wa.	muhanya, wa.
NOOSE	nkandamo, ya.	chovyo, cha, vya.
NOR		nesi; panji nesi.
NORTH (wind)	nkonde, wa; mpungu, wa.	mpoto, ya.
NOSE		mpuno, ya, za; nose ornament, chipini, cha, vya.
—to pick	kulikinya.	to blow the nose, kupenka mpuno.
NOSTRIL		mphenkero, ya, za.
NOT	awa; cha; ng'o.	iai; chara; nta; kuti...chara; -ve, -vya, -je suffixed to verb : not even a little, na kantini kose: no water, maji na ghamo.
NOTCH		fyakanya, ya, za: to stick in a notch, kufyatika.
NOTHING		waka: kukhara waka, to sit idle.
NOTICE, to	kuthova.	kuvanika.
NOURISH, to		kulera; kuhiwa.
NOW		sono.
NURSE, to		(sick) kurwazga: (child) kulera: a nurse, mlezi, wa, va.
NUT (monkey)	mbarara, za.	skava, ya, za.
NUZZLE, to		kubunyura.

O

ENGLISH	TONGA	TUMBUKA
OATH, to take		kurapa: *an oath*, chirapo, cha, vya.
OBEISANCE, to make		kulamba; kulambira.
OBEY, to	kuvwiya.	kupulikira.
OBJECTION		kakwiya, ka.
OBSERVE, to	kuthova.	kuvanika.
OBSOLETE		—korowere.
OBSTACLE	mpindamsoro, ya.	
OBSTINATE		*an obstinate person*, kajilangi, wa, va.
OCCUPIED, to be		kusuvirira; kutangwanika.
OCEAN		mbwani, za.
ODOUR		chema, cha; fungu, la; sungu, la.
OFFERING		chisopo, cha, vya; sembe, ya, za.
OFFSPRING		mwana, wa, va; mpapu, ya, za.
OFTEN		kaviri-kaviri; lusi-lusi; ruta-ruta: *how often?* karinga?
OIL		mafuta, gha.
OLD		(*things*) —rara, —korovere; ncha kale.
OLD PERSON	kongwe, la, gha.	*old man*, doda, la, gha; *matron*, nchembere, ya, za;
OLD, to grow		kuchekura: (*of cloth*) kuvukupara: *to grow old together*, kuchembererana.
OMEN, to see		kutondwa: *an omen*, mavika, gha.
OMIT, to		kutantanya.
ON		pa.
ONCE		kamoza.
ONE		—mo; —moza: *a certain one*, ngana. *to be at one*, kurungana pamoza.
ONLY		pera; ndipera; —eka (*I only*, ine ndeka).
OPEN		mwazi: *open space*, lwarara, la, gha.
OPEN, to (intr.)		(*mushroom*) kuparara: (*flower*) kukongora.
—(trans.)		kujura; kubanula.
—bundle		kufwatura; kufwantura; *to break open*, kubaula.
—soil		(*for garden*) kugampura.
—mouth	kwasama; kutandauliya mlomo.	kusama.
—a channel		(*e.g. for water*) kupongolera.
—eye		kukwendula.
—belly		kutumbura.

234

ENGLISH	TONGA	TUMBUKA
OPENLY		pa kweru; pa lwarara; pa mtanda-sanya.
OPINION		fundo, ya, za; *to stick to one's opinion*, kulema.
OPPOSITE		pantazi; *to be opposite*, kutyana na.
OPPOSITION		*see* nkwikwi.
OPPRESS, to	kugorole.	kusuzga; kuyuzga; kugorolera; ku-zotofya; *to be oppressed*, kuzuka.
OR	pamwenga.	panji; pakunji.
ORANGE colour	—yera (uli ndi zira).	
ORANGE (Kaffir)		zayi, la, gha.
ORDAIN, to		kwimika; kulangula.
ORDEAL	kupekesa.	mwavi, wa, ya: *see* kuchinga.
ORDER		chilayizgo, cha, vya.
—to set in	kurulika.	(*to tell in order*) kukonkhoma; kukonkoska.
ORIGIN		*see* chitopoko, cha, vya.
ORION	chiuta, wa.	
ORNAMENT		*see* mphandi; *and lip, nose, &c.*
—to		kutozga; kutoweska.
ORPHAN		mranda, wa, ʋa.
OTHER	—mwenga.	—nyake; —nji: *one......another*, uyu......munyake.
OTTER	katumbwe, wa; karabwe, wa.	katubwe, wa, ʋa.
OUGHT		kwenera; *see* kuti, *and* mphanyi.
OUR	—idu.	—itu.
OUTSIDE		pawaro, kuwaro.
OVER		pachanya pa; kuchanya ku; kune-na.
OVERCOME, to		kuruska; kutonda; kugoda; kugo-rolera; kukurura.
OVERDO, to		kufuchizga.
OVERFLOW, to		kufuruka; kuzurafura; kuthura; kusapalira.
OVERHANG	*see* ndoʋa.	
OVERGROWN		(*the path is overgrown*) ntowa yakhora.
OVERSEER		kapitao, wa ʋa.
OVERSHADOW, to		kusikizga.
OVERSHOOT, to		kupurungizga.
OVERSTATE, to		kupurungizga.
OVERTHROW, to		kubwangandula.

235

ENGLISH	TONGA	TUMBUKA
OVERTURN, to		kugadabula; kugudubura.
OWE, to		kuteura; kudirira.
OWL		pururu, wa, ʋa.
OWN, to		kuʋeta.
OWNER		mwenecho, wa, ʋa.
OX		ng'ombe, ya, za.

P

ENGLISH	TONGA	TUMBUKA
PACIFY, to		kutuniska; kupembuzga.
PACK, to		kupaka; kurongezga.
PAD (for carrying a load)	nkata, ya, za.	
PAIN		nyamakazi, ya, za; (*stabbing*) chiraso, cha; (*shooting*) urwirwi, wa; sasira, za: *see* kupintuka.
PAIN, to	kuʋaʋa.	kuʋinya; kupweteka; kumwanta; kupiringizga.
PALATABLE, to be		*see* kunozga.
PALAVER		makani, gha; mrandu, wa, ya: *place for talking*, mphara, ya, za.
PALM	gwarangwa, la.	chiʋali, cha, vya; mkama, wa, ya;
—of hand		chikufi, cha, vya; lupi, la, gha.
PALSY		vimbwambwa, vya.
PANCREAS	kapamba, ka.	
PANT, to		kuʋeʋefuka.
PAPULAR ERUPTION		kauzi, wa.
PARABLE		chiyeruzgo, cha, vya; ntharika, ya, za; chintanguni, cha, vya.
PARASITE		(*on tree*) kachere, wa, ʋa.
PARCEL		chimbumbuli, cha, vya.
PARDON, to		*see* kupepa: "*I beg your pardon*," "pepani".
PARE, to		(*e.g. finger-nails, or edge of thatch*) kucheketa.
PARENT		mupapi, wa, ʋa; mubabi, wa, ʋa
PARENT-IN-LAW		muyemba, wa, ʋa; *see* —vyara.
PART		pande, la, gha; chipanduko, cha, vya: *on my* (*your &c.*) *part—see* mkara.
PARTAKE, to		kusangana.
PARTED, to be		kutagharara.
PARTING (of paths)		ndekano, ya, za.
PASS, to		kujumpa; (*time*) kutandara: *to pass through a district*, kusorota.
—(a shower of rain)	kuwazga.	

English	Tonga	Tumbuka
PASTOR		mliska, wa, ʋa.
PASTURE		luhari, lwa, gha.
PATCH		chigamba, cha, vya; chibatiko, cha, vya.
PATELLA		(knee-cap) mphandi, ya, za.
PATH		ntowa, ya, za; (well-beaten) gurwe, wa, ʋa; to wear a path smooth, kutibula.
PATIENCE	unkuntiya, wa.	chizizipizgo, cha.
PATIENT, to be		kuzika; kukuntirapo; kuzizipizga.
PATTERN		chirongolero, cha, vya; (to work a pattern in beads) kusanda.
PAY		njombe, ya, za; malipiro, gha: mpoto, ya.
PAY, to	kulambura.	kulipa; kulipira; (debt &c.) kufuta; kufutira.
PAYMENT, a		chimbondo, cha, vya.
PEAS		ndozi, ya, za.
PEACE	mlere, wa.	chimango, cha, vya; mutende, wa, ya; mtembwere, wa: (see kuzika and kutuna).
PECK, to		kugonka.
PEEL, to		kusuwa: to be peeled, kususuwuka; kutemuka.
PEEP, to		kulingizga.
PEER, to		kulingulira.
PEG		chikhomo, cha, vya.
PELICAN		tofu, wa, ʋa.
PELVIS		nyonga, ya, za; ching'a, cha, vya.
PEN (fold)		lukutu, lwa, gha; chitupa, cha, vya; chiʋaya, cha, vya.
PENIS	uka, wa; mboro, ya, za.	
PEOPLE		ʋantu, ʋa; mafuko, gha; the people of...ʋina...; a people, mtundu, wa, ʋa.
PERCEIVE, to	kuvwa.	kupulika.
PERFECT, to		kufiska. to be perfect, kukongora.
PERFORATE, to		kudorora; kuporoska.
PERHAPS	pamwenga; akumba.	kware; panji; pakunji; manyi.
PERMANENT	cha muyaya.	kwa muyira-yira; kwa ndanda; see chikhazi.
PERMIT, to		kuzomerezga.
PERPLEXED, to be		kupukuruka; kuyangazuka.

ENGLISH	TONGA	TUMBUKA
PERSECUTE, to		kuzikizga.
PERSEVERANCE	liwuma, la.	chitatata, cha; luntata, lwa; chikosa, cha.
PERSEVERE, to		kukoserezga.
PERSISTENCE		chikosa, cha: *to persist*, kukosa; kutuntika; kukangalizga; kukondovezga.
PERSON		muntu, wa, va.
PERSPIRATION	dukutira, la; chitungu, cha.	tukutira, la; "samba tukuta"— *bathe in sweat: to perspire*, kufoma.
PERSUADE, to		kupemberezga; kukopa-kopa; kusongerezga.
PESTER, to		kwavya; kusuzga.
PHILTRE	chirudu, wa.	
PICK up, to		kusora; kutora: (*out*) kupokozora.
PICTURE		chituzi-tuzi, cha, vya.
PIECE		chipanduko, cha, vya.
PIERCE, to	kutoro.	kurasa; kuchonta; kudorora; kuporota; kuporoska; kuporonkanya.
PIG		nkumba, ya, za; (*bush*) nguruve, ya, za.
PIGEON		nkhunda, ya, za: *young pigeon*, chiwunda, cha, vya: *pigeon loft*, chikunda, cha, vya.
PILES	chinyapombo chatuwa.	
PILLAGE, to		kuskogha (*also* kuskowa): *spoils*, mskowo, wa, ya.
PILLAR		mzati, wa, ya.
PILLOW		chikunku, cha, vya; msamilo, wa, ya; *see* kusaghamila.
PIMPLES	denku, la, gha.	(*on face*) ntenku, ya, za.
PINCH, to		kusina.
PINE away, to		kughanda.
PINK, to be	kufyuwira.	*see* kutuwuruka.
PIPE		(*water*) mpopi, wa, ya;
—(tobacco)	mtete, wa, ya.	chikororo, cha, vya; (*moisture in pipe*) nkumbi, za: (*hookah*) chombo, cha, vya.
PIT	zenje, la, gha.	(*small*) kululu, la, gha; (*large*) zongwe, la, gha; (*game-pit*) mbuna, ya, za; mchembo, wa, ya; (*for stamping clay*) nkando, ya, za;

ENGLISH	TONGA	TUMBUKA
PITY		lusungu, lwa, gha.
—to		kulengera lusungu.
PLACE		malo, gha: *out of place*, kupangandira.
PLACE, to		kuvika.
PLACENTA	chibali, cha.	chibaliro, cha, vya.
PLAIN		dambo, la, gha: (marambo, *the country of plains*).
PLAIT, to		kuwomba; kuruka (*e.g. basket*).
PLANE, to		(*wood*) kupara; kuvaja.
PLANK		tabwa, la, gha.
PLANT		mbuto, ya, za; mbeu, ya, za.
—to		kupanda; (*maize*) kugoma.
PLANTAIN		ndoki, ya, za.
PLASTER, to		(*wall*) kumata; (*all over*) kubulumutizga; kumbontya.
PLATE		mbali, ya, za; ngwembe, ya, za.
PLATFORM	chiguwa, cha.	chitantali, cha, vya.
PLAY, to	kuseve; kusove.	kusovera; *playing pranks*, ulankasi wa.
PLEADER,		nkoswe, ya, za.
PLEASANT, to be		kunozga.
PLEASE, to		kukondweska; kusekerereska; kuyinika.
PLEASED, to be	kukankhaviya.	kukondwa; kumwemwetera; kucha.
PLEASURE		(*to take pleasure in*) kudemwera na.
PLEDGE	ndindira, ya, za.	chikoli, cha, vya.
PLEIADES, the	sangu, za.	
PLENTY		fumpha, ya, za; kuzara, kwa; uzari, wa.
PLIABLE, to be		kulipwitika; kutepa.
PLOT	chipango, cha.	chivwamba, cha, vya; chivembu, cha, vya.
PLUCK, to	(*off*) kutoto;	(*out*) kupokozora; kutopora;
—fruit	kuponto.	kutotora; kubontora; kupontora;
—flowers		kusepa; (*to pluck a fowl*) kukunta; kukunyura.
PLUG	chizighiri, cha.	nguli, ya, za; chirozgo, cha, vya.
PLUM, wild, green		chifuwu, cha, vya.
PLUNDER, to		kuskowa; kuskogha.
POINT		songo, la, gha; (*in sermon*) fundo, ya, za.
POINT out, to		kurongora: *to point at*, kurata munwe ku.

ENGLISH	TONGA	TUMBUKA
POISON		wanga, wa, gha: (*for arrow*) ulembi, wa: (*to poison meat*) kwambizga nyama: (*to administer the poison ordeal*) kuchinga mwavi.
POLICEMAN		msirikari, wa, ʋa.
POLYGAMY		mitara, ya.
POND		taʋali, la, gha; chiziʋa, cha, vya.
POOL		chiziʋa, cha, vya; taʋali, la, gha.
POOL, to		kusangana.
POOR		—kavu: *to be poor*, kukavuka; kusauka; kusokwa.
PORCUPINE		chinungu, wa, ʋa.
PORRIDGE		sima, ya, za.
PORTENT		muntondwe, wa, ya: uzuzundi, wa.
PORTION		chigaʋa, cha, vya: (*of land hoed*) ndimi, ya, za:
—of sima		mtanda, wa, ya:
—child's	kasinaʋana, ka;	
—bolus	dozi, la, gha;	tozi, la, gha; mphiri, ya, za:
—left over	mphoro, ya, za;	chimbara, cha (*may be kept for morning feed*) :
	mkuti, wa, ya.	(*for children or servants*) makombo, gha.
POSSESS, to		kuʋeta.
POSSESSIONS		chuma, cha, vya; mpango, ya, za; viʋeto, vya.
POST		mzati, wa, ya.
—(house wall)	chiruwu, cha;	
—(verandah)	nchindamiro, ya.	
POT		chiʋiya, cha, vya; mphika, wa, ya;
—(large)		nkali, ya, za; msuku, wa, ya; chimpuli, cha, vya; lwangavya, lwa, gha; chimpani, cha, vya; mrundo, wa, ya; chivuwo, cha, vya.
—(small)		dira, wa, ʋa; kangoti, wa, ʋa; mukhati, wa, ya.
POT-STAND (at fire)		figha, la, gha.
—(not at fire)	chiguwa, cha.	chikongera, cha, vya.
POTSHERD	zinga, la, gha.	dengere, la, gha.
POTTER	muwumbi, wa, ʋa.	muwuvi, wa ʋa.
POTATO		mboholi, ya, za; mbatata, ya, za.
—(relish of leaves)	chibwaka, cha.	
POUNCE, to		kunyuntuka.

240

ENGLISH	TONGA	TUMBUKA
POUND (money)		mbondo, ya, za (*probably from English*).
POUND, to	kupuwa.	kupura: kubwanya.
POUNDING-STICK		musi, wa, ya.
POUR, to	kuda; kudiya.	kupungura; kutira; kupompa: *to pour away*, kwita.
POUT, to		kusepetura mlomo.
POVERTY	usiwa, wa; umphavi, wa.	ukavu, wa, gha; usauchi, wa.
POWER	ntazi, ya, za.	nkongono, ya, za; mazaza, gha.
PRAISE, to	kutamika; kutamanda; kululutiya.	kurumba; kutumbika; kuchindika: *see* kuthokoza.
PRAISE	tamu, la, gha. chitamiko, cha.	rumbo, la, gha; nchindi, ya, za.
PRANKS		ulankasi, wa, gha.
PRAY, to		kuromba.
PRAYER	pempo, la, gha.	(lu)rombo, la, gha; sopero, la, gha.
PREACH, to	kutaula.	kuphara; kupharazga; kuwuzga.
PRECEDE, to		kudangira; kutendeka: *see* kujandizga.
PRECIOUS, to be		kuzirwa: *preciousness*, kazirwiro, ka.
PREGNANT, to be		(*animal*) kumita; kutumbara: (*of woman*) kuva pachanya; kuva na nthumbo; kuva muntu muheni; kukumana na Chiuta.
PREOCCUPIED, to be		kusuvirira.
PREPARE, to		kurongosora; kunozga; kunozgera.
PRESENT		chawanangwa, cha, vya.
PRESENT, to be		kuvapo.
PRESENT TIME		lero; makono ghano.
PRESERVE, to		kusunga.
PRESS, to		kufyenya; kutofya; kufinyiska; kufinyirizga; kudidimizga; kusindikizga; kunyekezga; di! (*see* kupapatizga *and* kunyenkama):
—down		kudikizga; kutindivizga; kufyadulira (pasi).
—(bowels)	kukakamuka.	
—on (hurry)		kutuntira.
—gifts upon		kufuchizga.
PRETEND, to		kutezga; kudimba.
PREVENT, to		kukana; kukanizga: *see* kupuvya; kufuvya; *and* kujandizga.
PREVIOUS, to be		kutendeka; kudanga; kujandizga.
PRICE		mtengo, wa, ya: *what price?* mtengo uli? *high price*, mtengo wa patali.

241

Q

ENGLISH	TONGA	TUMBUKA
PRICK, to		kuchonta; kupintuka.
PRIDE		see proud.
PRIEST		msofi, wa, ʋa.
PRINT, to		kusindikizga.
PRISON		kayidi, la; nyumba ya magori; see magwedi.
PRISONER		mkoli, wa, ʋa; mkayidi, wa, ʋa; wa vikondo.
PRIVATE, in		ku udesi; ku ubende; ku jowa: see kudekana and kugweʋera.
PRIVATE PARTS, the		mavwaro, gha.
PRIVILEGE		see kwenera.
PROBABLE		see kupamba.
PROBE, to		kuchokonya.
PRODUCE, to		(fruit, &c.) kupasa; kupambika: (noun) vipasi, vya; vipambi, vya.
PROFESSION		chizomerezgo, cha.
PROFIT, to	kwanduwa.	kwandula: (noun) chandulo, cha, vya.
PROHIBITION		lusingo, lwa, gha; lujaro, lwa, gha.
PROCRASTINATE, to		kudalika.
PROMISE, to		kupangana; kulayizgana na.
PROMISE, a		pangano, la, gha; chipangano, cha, vya.
PROMONTORY		ndomo, ya, za.
PROMOTE, to		kukwezga.
PROMPT, to be		kutendekera: promptness, mwampu, wa.
PRONE, to lie		kuvunama.
PRONOUNCE, to		kuzunula.
PROP	nchindamiro, ya.	
PROP, to		kuchirikizga; kufighirira.
PROPERLY		makora; uruso; kwenecho.
PROPERTY		chuma, cha, vya; mpango, yạ, za.
PROPHESY, to		kuloska; kùchima; kusura.
PROPHECY		losko, la, gha.
PROPHET		nchimi, ya, za; muwukwi, wa, ʋa.
PROPITIATE, to		kupepeska: propitiation, mpepeska ya, za.
PROSPER, to		kusakata.
PROSTRATE, to fall		kuwa kavunama.
PROSTRATION		kudengenduka.

ENGLISH	TONGA	TUMBUKA
PROTECT, to		kuvikirira; kusungirira: (*garden by 'medicine'*) kwambura lwambo.
PROUD, to be		kujikuzga; kujivikamo; kujitamira; kuthumbwa; kujituntira.
PROVERB		ntharika, ya, za; chintanguni, cha, vya.
PROVISION (for journey)		mpako, ya, za: thumba la kamba.
PROVOKE, to		kusosomora: *to be provoked*, kutopoka moyo.
PUBERTY		(*male*) uhurwa, wa; (*fem.*) umwali, wa.
—	see kuchayiwa.	(*see* msindo).
PUBES, the		chinena, cha: mavwaro, gha.
PUBLICAN		(*biblical*) wamsonko, wa, va.
PUBLISH abroad, to		kuthuwuska.
PUERPERAL FEVER	mwasere ntema.	
PUFF, to		kuputa.
PUFF ADDER	chipi, wa, va.	chipiri, wa, va.
PUFFED UP, to be	kuyuyunduka.	kutukumuka; kutundumuka.
PUFFY, to be		kuwofoka.
PULL, to		kuguza;
—out	kusoro;	(*uproot*) kuzgura; kujintura;
—tooth	kusotopo.	kukhura.
—down		(*house*) kupasula.
PULLET		msoti, wa, ya.
PULPY, to be		kupweka.
PULSATE, to		kututa; kufuta.
PUMPKIN		tanje, la, gha; jungu, la, gha; uvimbi, wa, gha.
PUNISH, to		kulanga.
PUPIL (eye)		mboni, ya, za.
PURCHASE, to		kugula.
PURE		—khovu.
PURLINS	ntanta, ya, za.	sito, ya, za.
PURPLE	ropa, wa.	
—cloth	bukuwa, wa.	
PURPOSE	matunta, gha.	dazgo, la, gha: *on purpose*, nchene: *purposelessly*, waka; bweka; dara.
PURSE		chibeta, cha, vya.
PURSUE, to		kudikiska.
PUS		mafira, gha; (*from eyes*) mponke, ya, za; vimbokori, vya.
PUSH, to		kututuzga; kukanchizga: (*aside*) kusezga.

ENGLISH	TONGA	TUMBUKA
PUT, to		kuvika: *to put in,* kunjizga; (panjira mbavi (jembe) mu chaka—*put the axe (hoe) in its handle*): *to put out,* kufumya; kufumiska; (*lamp or fire*) kuzimya.
PUZZLE, to		kuzizika; *to be puzzled,* kutindikika.
PYROSIS	kuti vya ku singo.	dungulira, la.
PYTHON		sato, ya, za.

Q

QUARREL, to	kwambana; kuba-yana; kuchita mwano; kungwazurana.	kupindikana; kukomana; kuwuki-rana: *quarrels,* zawe, la, gha.
QUARTZ ROCK		sangarawe, la, gha.
QUEEN		fumukazi, ya, za; *queen bee, or ant,* chinyina, cha,
QUENCH, to		(*fire &c.*) kuzimya.
QUESTION		fumbo, la, gha: *interrogatives introducing question,* ani? asi? kasi? nesi?
QUICKEN, to		kusisipuska.
QUICKENING (in pregnancy)	kuzanta.	kubwarantika.
QUICKLY	luvi.	luviro, mata pa jani; *see* kuphinda *and* ndavara.
QUICKNESS		luviro, lwa, gha; mwampu, wa, ya.
QUIET, to be		kuchetama; *to quieten,* kuchetami-ska: *to be at peace,* kuzika; kufwasa; kudeka.
QUIETNESS	mlere, wa.	chisisi, cha.
QUIVER (for arrows)		mchenje, wa, ya; phodo, la, gha.

R

RABBIT		kalulu, wa, va.
RACE (of men)		mtundu, wa, ya.
RACE (contest)		kupharana; kupharazgana; kupharizgana.
RAFTER		pasu, la, gha.
RAGE		mbembe, ya, za; *to boil with rage,* kuvira na mbembe; kucheruka.
RAGS		viswaswa, vya; madenga, gha.
RAID, to		kupuma nkondo.
RAIL AT, to		kuhoyera; kutuka: (*in chorus*) Here! Here!
RAIN, to	kunya.	kurokwa.

ENGLISH	TONGA	TUMBUKA
RAIN	vuwa, ya, za.	vula, ya, za: *early rains*, chakuzimya marupya; chakukura nyune; chizumbwa matoli.
RAINY SEASON		chifuku, cha, vya.
—dry day in	barawara, la.	
RAINBOW		chivingavula, cha, vya.
RAISE, to	kuyuska; kunyamuwa.	kuwuska; kutumpuska: *to raise head*, kwinuka; kusaghamila.
RANSOM		thumba, la, gha; chiwomborero cha, vya; *see* chituntulu.
RARELY		kamo-kamo.
RASH (on skin)		vivawo, vya (kuvawura).
RASHNESS		mawara, gha.
RAT		mbeva, ya, za:
—kinds of	kasekesera, va.	jancha, la, gha; tondo, wa, va; todwe, wa, va; kapuku, wa, va.
RATTLE		chiyekweti, cha.
RATIONS		poso, la; mpako, wa, ya.
RAVEN	chahori, cha.	chihovi, cha, vya.
RAVINE		mpata, wa, ya; mwanya, wa, ya.
RAW, to be	kuropwa.	
RAY (light)		sanya, ya, za; lirazi, la, gha.
RAZOR	chimeta, cha.	lwembe, lwa, gha.
REACH, to		kufika; kuthurwa (*see* kuthura): *to be beyond reach*, kutagharara.
READ, to		kusambira; kuvazga.
READY, to be	(*food*) kufya.	kuva muchanya: (*food*) kupya; ulendo wapya—*ready to start*.
REAL	—eneko.	—enecho: *see* chijiti *and* di!
REAP, to	(*rice*) kuvuna.	(*millet*) kuvuna; (*maize*) kukhata *and* kukorora.
REAPING-HOOK	chikwanju, cha.	
REAR, to		(*children*) kulera.
REASON		chifukwa, cha, vya.
REBEL, to	kutwanga.	kuzgoka; kugaruka.
REBUKE, to		kulanga.
RECEIVE, to	kuronde.	kupoka; kupokera.
RECENT		*see* mayiro.
RECOIL, to		kuchizuka.
RECOMPENSE, to		kunana.
RECONCILED, to be	kusopana *see* kuwoja.	kupemana; kukong'onterana mpamba.
RECOUNT, to		kupataula.

ENGLISH	TONGA	TUMBUKA
RECOVER, to		(*from illness*) kuchira.
RECRIMINATION		chituku, cha, vya.
RECTUM		(*prolapse of*) chinyapombo chafuma.
RED	*see* —yera.	—swesi: *to be red*, kuchesama.
RED pigment for pots	nkhama, ya.	
REDEEM, to		kuwombora.
REED	dete, la, gha.	thete, matete, la, gha.
REFRAIN, to		(*from food &c.*) kuzivizga.
REFRESH, to	kusisipuwa.	kukomarira.
REFUGE		linga, la, gha.
REFUSE		viswaswa, vya; vya nthonto, vya; bibi, la, gha.
REFUSE, to		kukana; kunora; kwima.
REGARD, to		(*look at*) kulaviska; (*care for*) kupwerera.
REGRET		zgoranya, la.
REIGN, to		kuvusa.
REIMS		lukuzi, la, gha.
REINFORCED, to be		kututika.
REJECT, to	kuziriya.	kupata; kuzirira; kuduva; *see* kusavasava.
REJOICE, to		kukondwa; kusekerera; kusangwa; kuhenerera.
RELATIVES		va mbumba; va ndopa zimoza.
RELAX, to		kulipwitiska.
RELEASE, to		kusutura; kusuzura.
RELENT, to		kutuna.
RELISH (for sima)		dendi, la, gha.
—to prepare		kurunga dendi, kutendera ntendero; &c.
—kinds of		nyama; somba; skava; mpangwe; chibwaka; munkhwani; kwanya; mbidu; mtambi; &c.
RELUCTANT, to be		kudonda.
RELY on, to		kutamira.
REMAIN, to		kukharirira; kuchona.
REMEMBER, to		kukumbuka.
REMIND, to		kukumbuska; kukontora.
REMOVE, to		kusezga; kuwuskapo; (*village*) kusama; kututa; (*to wipe away*) kutatura.
REPAIR, to		(*basket*) kuzinda; (*see also mend*).
REPAY, to		kuwezga; kunana.

ENGLISH	TONGA	TUMBUKA
REPEAT, to		kuwerezga; kuwerenkhanya.
REPENT, to		kuzgoka; kung'anamuka m'mtima; kupera.
REPENTANCE	chipe, cha.	ching'anamuka, cha.
REPLY, to		kuzgora; kung'anamula.
REPORT	tente, la, gha.	lumbiri, lwa, gha; nduvyo, ya, za.
REPROACH	tozu, la;	ntombozgo, ya, za.
—to	kutoza.	kutombozga; kukontora.
REPROVE, to		kuchenya.
REPUTATION		lumbiri, lwa, gha.
REQUEST	pempo, la, gha.	rombo, la, gha.
REQUITE, to		kunana.
RESCUE, to	kutaska.	kupoka; kuponoska.
RESEMBLE, to		kukozgana.
RESENTMENT		kwiya, la; ndundumbi, ya, za; kubidwa.
RESOLUTE, to be		kukhwima.
RESOLVED, to be		kungangamika.
RESPECT, to		kutumbika; kopa.
RESPECTABLE, to be		see kunozga.
RESPOND, to		kuchemeka; kuthika.
—in song	kukovera.	kupokera.
REST, to		kupumula; kuvukuka: to rest on (trust) kutamira.
RESTLESS, to be	kutongatonga.	kutunatuna waka: restlessness, mfundukutu, wa.
RESTORE, to		kuwezga.
RESTRAINT		(self-restraint) kujikora.
RESURRECTION		kuzguka. The Resurrection, chiwuka, cha.
RETCH, to	kuvinduka; kukakamuka.	
RETRACT, to (the foreskin)	kufyono.	kukonora; kufyonora.
RETREAT, to		(backwards) kuwera chifutanyuma.
RETURN, to		(from a place) kuwera ku; (to a place) kuwerera ku: (same day) kupapikamo; kuwerenkhanya.
REVEAL, to		kuvumbula; kuchonjora; kuchombola; see kuwukwa.
REVENGE	thayu, la.	nduzga, ya, za.
REWARD		njombe, ya, za.
RHEUMATISM		nyamakazi, ya, za.
RHINOCEROS		chipembere, cha, vya.

247

English	Tonga	Tumbuka
RIB	mbaghara, ya, za.	mbambo, ya, za; mbavu, ya, za; mbambavu, ya, za.
RICE		mpunga, wa.
RICH	—sambasi;	—sambazi: *a rich man*, musambazi, va:
—to make	kusambasiska;	kusambazga.
RICHES	usambasi, wa; uromba, wa.	usambazi, wa; chuma, cha, vya.
RIDE, to		kugara.
RIDGE		mung'ong'o, wa, ya; mngongonda wa, ya.
RIGHT, to be		kurunjika; kunozga; *to make right*, kurunjiska; kunyoroska.
RIGHTEOUS, to be		kunyoroka; kurunjika.
RIGHTEOUSNESS		urunji, wa; utozi, wa: *a righteous person*, murunji, wa, va; mkongorekwa, wa, va.
RIGHT SIDE, the	marghe, gha.	maryero, gha: *right hand*, woko la maryero.
RIGHT SIDE UP, to turn		kubenekura.
RIM		mpepete, ya, za.
RING		mpete, ya, za; lundandati, lwa, gha.
RINSE, to		kusinga; (*mouth*) kusukumura (kuvuwata).
RIOT		chivulupi, cha, vya.
RIPE, to be		kupya; kucha; *see* kurozga.
RISE, to	kuyuka.	kuwuka; gharaghandu! (*from the dead*) kuzguka.
RIVER	msinji, wa, ya.	mronga, wa, ya.
ROAD		(*hoed*) mseu, wa, ya; (*path*) ntowa ya, za.
ROAM, to		kuvenka-venka.
ROAN ANTELOPE		chirembwe, wa, va.
ROAR, to		kubangura; (*waterfall*) kupopoma.
ROAST, to		kocha; kukazinga; kuvumbika (*i.e. to cover over in the fire*).
ROB, to	kuba.	kwiba; *robber*, munkungu, wa, va.
ROBE		munjirira, wa, ya; (*long*) kanjo, la, gha.
ROBUST		*a robust man*, chinkhara, cha, vya.
ROCK		libwe, la, gha; jarawe, la, gha.
ROCK, to		(*to soothe a child*) kususutizga.
ROD		ntonga, ya, za.

248

ENGLISH	TONGA	TUMBUKA
ROLL, to		kugadabura; kukunkura; kukunkuzga.
—away (clouds)	kukungunuka.	
—up		kuzinga; (mat) kutandura; (sleeves or cloth) kukwiza.
ROLLERS		nkunguru, ya, za. (on land or sea).
ROOF	bagha, la, gha.	mtenje, wa, ya: (for nkokwe) kavale, wa, va.
ROOF, to		kupasa; kwegha: see kukupika.
ROOM, a		chipinda, cha, vya; chipija, cha, vya.
ROOT	nkorozo, ya, za.	msisi, wa, ya; nkorozi, ya, za; see msuli.
ROPE	mkowa, wa, ya; luzi, la, gha; mtawo, wa, ya.	mkusa, wa, ya; chingwe, cha, vya.
ROT, to	kuwo.	kuvunda.
ROUND		(to round off) kuwurunga.
ROUSE, to	kuyuska.	kuwuska; (to stir up a crowd) kutimula; to be roused, kutirimuka.
ROW	mvizi, wa, ya.	panda, la, gha; to form a row, kundanda; to hang up in a row (fish) kupamba: see mingunguma.
RUB, to		kutukutizga; (with oil) kuphaka; (to rub grain in hands) kupikisa; (branches rubbing on each other; kukwentana.
—polish pots	kukurungiya	
RUBBER		mpira, wa, ya; (Ceara rubber), kapanti.
RUBBISH		viswaswa, vya; chichwapi, cha) vya: rubbish-heap, chizara, cha, vya: see kusosontera and chisosonyo.
RUDDER	sigiru, ya, za.	sigilo, ya, za.
RUDENESS		msunjiro, wa, ya; chikanga, cha; pampu, la.
RUFFLED		(fowl with ruffled feathers) nkuku ya sakarare.
RUINS	makuntu, gha.	mahami, gha.
RULE OVER, to		kuwusa; (noun) ufumu, wa, gha.
RULER		fumu, ya, gha; chiroro, wa, va; mrara, wa, va.
RUMINATE, to		(oxen) kusumbira.
RUMOUR	tente, la, gha; mpemere, ya, za.	mbiri, ya, za; lumbiri, lwa, gha.

ENGLISH	TONGA	TUMBUKA
RUN, to	kuthava.	kumbombonta; kusesema; (to flee) kuchimbira: to run down, kuparamura.
RUSH (es)		rukwa, la, gha.
RUSH, to		kurotoka; kuduma: see kukwata, kwata.
RUST	mbiri, ya, za; biriviri, la.	mlosko, wa, ya.
RUSTLE, to		kupakaraska.

S

SACKING		chigudulu, cha, vya.
SACRIFICE		sembe, ya, za; chisopo, cha, vya.
SAD, to be		kufipa mtima; kujungata; kuzimbwa.
SADNESS		chitima, cha, vya.
SAFE		see makora and waka.
SAFETY		mphokwa, wa; usenguli, wa.
SAIL		tanga, la, gha.
SALAMANDER		katukuvala, wa; va.
SALIVA		mata, gha: (infant's dribbles) dozo la.
SALT		mchere, wa.
—ashes from	kabu; ururu; mzuwura; mancheza.	
SALT, to		(the dendi) kuchereka; kurunga.
SALUTE, to		kutauzga.
SALVATION	utaski, wa; chipozomosko, cha.	chiponosko, cha.
SAME		—mozi-mozi: —ene (e.g. mweneuyo).
SAND		mchenga, wa, ya; sandy soil, dongo lakufukutuka.
SANDAL		skapato, za; virato, vya; chikwakwata, cha, vya.
SANITARY pad (women's)	chinga, cha, vya.	chingara, cha, vya; mwere, wa, ya; (Henga) denga, la, gha.
SAP	mambiza, gha.	(e.g. from stems of rubber, cassava, &c.) mampizira, gha.
SATAN		nyarurya, wa, va.
SATIATED, to be		kukoroka.
SATISFIED, to be	kuguta; kuvwema.	kukhuta; kukhorwa; kukondomwa.
SATISFACTION	mguto, wa.	mkhuto, wa.

ENGLISH	TONGA	TUMBUKA
SATISFACTORY, to be		kukonda.
SATURDAY		chisulo, cha, vya; chakuʋeruka, cha, vya.
SAUCE		msuni, wa, ya; dendi, la, gha.
SAUSAGE TREE	mvunguti, wa, ya.	
SAVE, to	kupozomoska; kuropo.	kuponoska; kutaska; kupoka: *to be saved,* kupona; kuphokwa.
SAVIOUR		mtaski, wa, ʋa; mponoski, wa, ʋa.
SAVOUR		kunowa: *to be savourless,* kusukuruka.
SAW, to		kucheka.
SAWDUST	utuchi, wa.	
SAY, to	kukamba.	kuti; kunena.
SCALES (fish)		mamba, gha.
SCAPULA		phampa, la, gha.
SCARS		viburubuntu, vya: (bamba *commonly used*).
SCARE, to		(*birds from garden*) kuʋinga.
SCARLET FEVER		kauzi, wa.
SCARLET, to be		kuchesama.
SCATTER, to		kuparanya; kuchupura; kuchunka.
SCATTERED, to be	kumbininika.	kumwararikika.
SCAVENGER BEETLE	fingiza, wa, ʋa.	
SCHOLAR		msambiri, wa, ʋa.
SCHOOL		skulu, ya, za.
SCOLD, to		kutombozga; *see* kukontora.
SCOOP out, to		kukatura.
SCORCHED, to be		kunyeka; kudokotara; kuʋawura.
SCORN, to		kuchonjora; kuseka; kuyuyura.
SCORPION		chipiriri, cha, vya; kalizga, wa, ʋa.
SCOURGE, to		kunyapula; kudupula.
SCOUR, to		kusukiska; kuphotora.
SCOWL, to		kusizibukira; mankwinya ghaza.
SCRAPE, to	.	kupara; kuparapata; kukwenta; *see* kufura.
—out		(*e.g. remains of food from a vessel*) kukomba; kupokozora; kukorokota; kukotora.
SCRATCH, to	kukwazuwa; kukwaramuwa.	(*body*) kukwanta; (*earth, as fowl*) kupara; (*as thorn*) kugwarambura; kufwambura.
SCRIBE		mlembi, wa, ʋa.
SCRIPTURES, the		malembo, gha; mwambi, wa, ya (Nyanja).

ENGLISH	TONGA	TUMBUKA
SCROTUM		tongo, la, gha.
SCRUB, to		kusukiska; kuphotora.
SCYBALA	mavi gha mporokoto; mavi gha mapiringindi.	
SEA, the		nyanja, ya, za; mbwani, ya, za.
SEAL, to		*see* kudidimizga.
SEASON		(*rainy*) chifuku, cha, vya; (*dry*) chihanya, cha, vya; (*harvest*) masika, gha.
SEASON, to		kurunga (*e.g.* dendi).
SEAT		chitengo, cha, vya; mpando, wa, ya.
SECLUSION	chisachi, cha.	(*after childbirth*) *see* chikutu.
SECRET		chindindi, cha, vya; ungari, wa. gha: (*in secret*) ku ubende; ku udesi; mu uzgevu; kachibisibisi:
—to tell		kudizgirana; (kusuza; kusesa).
SEDIMENT (e.g. in water)	mfumbi, wa, ya.	ntimbu, ya, za.
SEE, to	kulereska.	kuwona; kulaviska.
SEED	nje, ya, za;	njere, ya, za; (*seedlings*) mbeu, ya, za; mbuto, ya, za; (*grass seed*) nyune, ya, za; (*sexual—male*) untu, wa.
—red & black	kanderere, ka.	
—(offspring)		mpapu, ya, za.
SEEK, to	kulembe.	kupenja.
SEIZE, to		kupoka; kukora; kuvwandamira; the!
SELDOM		kamo-kamo.
SELECT, to	kutondo.	kutondora; kudova.
SELF	—ija.	(*alone*)—eka; (*very self*)—ene; (*reflex.*) medial -ji-, *e.g.* ndajipweteka.
SELFISHNESS	ususi, wa;	kasu, la; wimi, wa; uzukusi, wa; lwizga, lwa; *a selfish person*, wa chigoro.
SELFISH, to be	kusuka.	kwima.
SELF-SOWN mapira		gugu, la, gha.
SELF-WILLED, to be		kujendera; *a self-willed person*, kajilangi, wa, va.
SELL, to		kugula; kusaska.
SEMEN		untu, wa.
SEND, to		kutuma; kutumizga.
SENSE		mahara, gha; zeru, ya, za; vinjeru, vya; mano, gha.

ENGLISH	TONGA	TUMBUKA
SEPARATE, to (tr.)	kugawuwa.	kupatula; kupatuska; kupatulanya; kusankura; kudamula.
—(intr.)		kupatuka; kupatukana.
—(the legs)		kutangarara.
SERPENT		njoka, ya, za.
SERVANT	muʋanda, wa, ʋa.	mteʋeti, wa, ʋa; msepuka, wa, ʋa.
SERVE, to		kuteʋeta; kufuka-fuka.
SET, to		kuʋika; *to be set* (*resolved*) kungangamika.
—up		kwimika; kujinta:
—down		kukharika; kukhazika:
—in order		kusara; kwandulira:
—upon		kucherukira.
SETTLE down, to		kudeka; kufwasa: *settled, see* chikhazi: *at Harali &c.,* kuchona.
SETTLE a mrandu, to	kupunga.	kudumula.
SEVEN		nkonde na viʋiri.
SEVERITY		nkaza, ya, za.
SEW, to		kusona; kutunga: *sewing-machine,* makina, gha.
SHADE		mufwiri, wa, ya.
SHADE, to		(*the eyes with the hand*) kuchinga.
SHADOW		(*of person*) muzgezge, wa, ya; chizgezge, cha, vya; chituzituzi, cha, vya: (chinyawo, cha, vya).
SHAFT (of spear)	ruti, la, gha.	
SHAKE, to (intr.)	kusukunika;	(*intr.*) kusunkunika: *see* kuyaghayagha:
(tr.)	kusukuniska;	(*tr.*) kusunkunya; *to shake off dust,* kukung'unta; *to shake the head,* kupukunya; *to shake up cushion,* kutukumula; *to shake together,* kusindira; *to shake down* (*leaves &c.*) kurakaska.
SHAKE eggs, to (hen sitting)	kusukusa.	
SHAKY		pokopoko.
SHALLOW, to be		(*of stream or lake*) kupaʋama.
SHAME		soni, ya, za; lulengo, lwa, gha.
SHAME, to		kulengera soni; kulengeska; kukhozga soni: *see* kuchonjora.
SHARE, to		kugaʋana; kusangana: *a share,* pande, la, gha.
SHARP, to be		kutwa: (*in speech*) kuʋeʋera mlomo.

ENGLISH	TONGA	TUMBUKA
SHARPEN, to		kunora; (*teeth*) kusonga; (*pencil*) kusongora.
SHARPNESS	uyi, wa.	
SHAVE, to		kumeta.
SHE, HER		iye; iyo.
SHEATH (for knife)		chibazi, cha, vya.
SHED, to be (as water from roof)	kupompa.	
SHED, to be		(*as feathers from fowl*) kutotoka.
SHEEP		mberere, ya, za.
SHELL, to		(*maize*) kuwukuska; kugumuza.
SHELL (of egg)		chikonkonimbwa, cha, vya: (*of snail*) nkorombe, ya, za.
SHEPHERD		mliska, wa, va.
SHEW		see show. "*The shew*" *in obstetrics*, ntundoropa, za.
SHIELD		nguru, ya, za.
SHIFT, to (pots &c. from hut)	kututuwa.	
SHIN	msolonti, wa.	munkoza, wa, ya.
SHINE, to	kugabuka.	(*glitter*) kugadima; kung'anima; kung'azima; (*lamp when flame catches*) kugolera; kumulika; (*sun*) kungweruka; (*light*) kuvala.
SHIP		ngarava, ya, za; chombo, cha, vya.
SHIVER, to	kunjenjeme.	kupima; kutentema; kumbwambwanta.
SHOAL (fish)		panda, la, gha.
SHOE		skapato, ya, za; (*laces*) nkowezi, ya, za.
SHOOT, to		(*arrow or bullet*) kuponya: *to shoot in flight*, kutimba maruzu.
SHOOT (plant)	mtombo, wa, ya.	msonga, wa, ya: see liwondwe.
SHORE (of lake or bank of river)	vu, la.	dowoko, la; mlima, wa, ya; mtunda, wa, ya; mpepete, ya, za.
SHORE up, to		(*e.g. wall of house*) kuchindikura.
SHORT		—fupi: *to come short*, kuperewera; kuchepa: *to shorten*, kugwinda.
SHORTAGE		kugwitika.
SHOULD		*expressed by* mphanyi *or* kwenera: vantu nga vakumusopa, *men should fear him.*
SHOULDER	pewa, la, gha.	chivegha, cha, vya; see phampa.

254

ENGLISH	TONGA	TUMBUKA
SHOUT, to	kubongo.	kukuta; kugong'a; kupoma; kubangura.
SHOW, to		kurongora; kurongozga; kusonyeza; *see* kupharazgana.
SHRINE		kavuʋa, wa, ʋa; kazumbi, wa, ʋa.
SHRINK, to		(*person—from fear*) kuchizuka: (*cloth &c.*) kukwinyana; kufinyinkirira; kugwinda.
SHRIVEL, to		kufinyinkirira.
SHRUB		chivwati, cha, vya.
SHUT, to		kujara; kuvimba: (*the mouth*) kusunama; (*the eyes*) kusizimira.
SHY, to be		kupotoka.
SICK, to be	kutama.	kurwara; (*to vomit*) kuwukura.
SIDE		sirya, la, (*which see for this side, that side &c.; also* dera; chiri, rwande).
—other, beyond	pa rwegha pa.	pa sere pa.
—of chest		mbambavu, ya, za: gona pa jeka, *lie on your side.*
SIEVE	guntu, la, gha.	kuntu, la, gha.
SIFT, to		kupeta; kuseʋa.
SIFTINGS (of grain)	lisika, la.	senga, za.
SIGH, to		kukizga mtima: *sighing respiration*, tuti tuti (kututa).
SIGN		chimanyikwiro, cha, vya; chiwonesko, cha, vya.
—to	kukonozga.	kukopezga, kusinizga. (*see beckon*).
SILENT, to be		kuchetama: *a silent person*, khutupulika.
SILENCE		chisisi, cha.
—(medicine to ensure)	msisiko, wa, ya.	
SILLY, to be		kuzerezeka; kuberezuka.
SIMPLETON		mzereza, wa, ʋa.
SIN	ulakwi, wa;	uheni, wa, gha; ubudi, wa, gha; kwananga, kwa; kupuruka, kwa.
SIN, to	kulakwa.	kunanga; kuchimwa; kubuda; kutokota.
SINCE		(*because*) pakuti; mwakuti; chifukwa; mumo.
SINEW	msipi, wa, ya.	msipa, wa, ya; msempa, wa, ya.
SING, to	kumba.	kwimba; kupinga; kugong'a.
SINGE, to		kuʋawura.
SINK, to		(*intr.*) kubira; (*tr.*) kubizga.
—(in mud)	kuzoroke.	

English	Tonga	Tumbuka
SISAL (hemp)		vikorokoto, vya.
SISTER (of boy)	mzichi, wa, ʋa;	mdumbu, wa, ʋa;
—(of girl)	mbali, wa, ʋa;	mbali, wa, ʋa; mwana munyake;
—(elder)	mku, wa, ʋa;	mukuru, wa, ʋa;
—(younger)	mvurwa, wa, ʋa;	munung'una, wa, ʋa;
—(in law)		mlamu, wa, ʋa; mvyara, wa, ʋa.
SIT, to	kuja;	kukhara;
—up	kuja songa.	kukhara ukharo: *to sit on the haunches*, kutongomara.
—(on eggs)		(*hen*) kuramira.
SITE		(*deserted site of village*) chihami, cha, vya; mahami, gha.
SIX		nkonde na chimoza.
SKID, to		kuvyanta.
SKILL	njeza, ya, za.	
SKIM, to		kwengura; kuwungurura.
SKIN		chikumba, cha, vya; chipapa, cha, vya; (*of fruits &c.*) kanta, la, gha: "*goose-skin*", wundi, wa.
SKIN, to		kufuwa; *see* kufyopora.
SKULL		bwaza, la, gha; *see* luʋara.
SKUNK		kanyimbi, ka, twa.
SKY		mtambo, wa, ya.
SLACKEN, to		kusutula; kusoya-soya.
SLACKNESS		mphwayi, ya, za.
SLAG		(*from smelting furnace*) makarang'a-njo, gha.
SLANDER, to		kusesa; kusuza; kunyoza: (*noun*) matusi, gha.
SLAP, to		kupamanta.
SLASH, to		kulepura; kuheta.
SLAVE	muʋanda, wa, ʋa.	muzga, wa, ʋa; kapolo, wa, ʋa; *see* chitutulu, cha, vya.
SLAVERY		uzga, wa.
SLAVE-STICK		goriwori, la, gha.
SLEEP		tulo, twa.
SLEEP, to	kura tulo.	kugona tulo; *to sleep in*, kugonere-zga; *to be sleepy*, kusiʋa; kugo-mpora; maso ghazotopa; tulo twakora: *to be sleepless*, tulo twazgeʋa.
SLEIGHT OF HAND		vibizi, vya; mayere, gha.
SLENDER PERSON	mcheya, wa, ʋa.	munyenyembe, wa, ʋa.
SLICE, to		kuʋarura: *to slice off*, kuwunguzura; kuheta.

English	Tonga	Tumbuka
SLIGHT, to		kuparamura; kusunjizga.
SLINK away, to		kunyeta.
SLIP, to		kuteremuka: *to slip away*, kunyere-muka: *to slip out of one's grasp*, kufwantamuka; *see* kufotopoka.
SLIPPERINESS		uterezi, wa.
SLOPE, to		*see* kuskereuka.
SLOW, to be		kukava.
SLOWLY	kamana-kamana.	kachoko-kachoko; makora.
SLUGGISH, to be		kudonda.
SLY, to be		kufyafyara.
SMALL	—mana.	—choko; —ntini; —doko; —dono: *to be small*, kutina; *to make small (lessen)*, kuchepeska.
SMALL-POX		nthomba, ya, za; nduve, ya, za.
SMASH, to	kupwanyuwa.	kutekenyura: pwanku!
SMEAR, to		(*floor with cow-dung*) kusinda.
SMELL	fungu, la.	sungu, ya; chema, cha; vumba, la.
SMELL, to		(*intr.*) kununka; (*tr.*) kunuska.
SMELT, to		kwenga: *smelting-furnace*, ng'anjo, ya, za.
SMILE, to		kumwemwetera.
SMITE, to	kukoso.	kupuzura.
SMITH	msuzi, wa, va.	mfuzi, wa, va: *smithy*, luvumbu, lwa, gha.
SMOKE	usi, wa, gha.	josi, la, gha: (*of fire*) josi likusunka.
SMOKE, to		(*tobacco*) kukweva.
SMOOTH, to be		kuskesketeka; ske!
—(of clay)	kung'ata.	(*sima without lumps*) kung'atuka; *see* kurunga; rungi-rungi.
SMOOTHE, to		kuskesketeska; kupara: (*mud plaster on wall*) kukuruwa; (*floor*) kusinda.
SNAIL		nkonye, ya, za.
SNAKE		njoka, ya, za.
—kinds of	nkweza; khako; chipi.	chiko; vuvi; nkomi; mpetamani; msalali; chipiri; sato.
SNAP, to	kudomo; kutwamuwa.	kupwatura.
SNARE		chipingo, cha, vya. (*see trap*).
SNATCH, to	kufwatapuwa.	kukwapura; the! kuvwetepura.
SNEER at, to		kunyoza; kutombozga.
SNEEZE, to		kuyetchemura.

SNORE, to	kukonona;	
SNORING	chinkonono, cha.	
SNUFF	fodia, wa or li.	hona, la, gha; foro, la, gha: snuff-box, fuko, la, gha: to take snuff, kukweʋa; kubema; to give snuff, kubemisa.
SO	viyo.	nteura; see reka.
SO & SO	wamwenga.	(person) ngana.
SOAKING WET	ghara-ghara-ghara!	
SOB, to		kufwifwinta.
SOBER, to be		kuziza.
SOFT		—techi; —teta.
—to be	korowa; kuwomba.	kuwofoka; kutepa; kutapata; kulipwitika; kupwafuka.
—to become		kunyeketuka; kupweketuka.
SOFTEN, to	korovya; kuwombeska.	kutefya; (skin) kunyuka.
SOIL		dongo, la, gha; nyata, ya, za: hard red soil, dongo la katondo: deep alluvial soil, dongo la nkandasi.
SOLDIER		musirikari, wa, ʋa; wa nkondo; mukharizgi, wa, ʋa.
SOLID, to be		kukhoma.
SOME		—nji; —nyake: some of you, imwe mwaʋanyake: give me some, ndipeniko.
SON	mwana-munturumi.	mwana-msepuka.
SON-IN-LAW	mkosano, wa, ʋa.	mukweni, wa, ʋa.
SONG		sumu, ya, za; see kuʋerenga.
SOON		luʋiro.
SOOT		mwayi, wa.
SOOTHE, to		(child) kupembuzga.
SOPORIFIC drug		mgoneko, wa, ya.
SORCERY		ula, wa, gha; uchanusi, wa, gha.
—to practise		kuwukwa; kuwombeza ula.
SORE		chironda, cha, vya; bamba, la, gha; nthonto, ya, za; manyenyenko, gha.
SORROW		chitima, cha, vya; (bereavement) uranda, wa: to cause sorrow, kulengeska chitima.
SORROWFUL, to be		kurwita; kukumbata.
SOUR, to be		kunchanchamira; to turn sour, kusasa.

ENGLISH	TONGA	TUMBUKA
SOURCE (of stream)		funda, ya, za.
SOURNESS		(e.g. of green fruit) nkhanya, ya.
SOUTH	maravi, gha.	
SOW, to		(by casting seed) kumija; kuseva: (maize) kugoma.
SPACE apart, to	kutagharika.	kutaghariska.
SPARKLE, to		kunyetuka.
SPARKS		sasira, za.
SPARROW	pwitu, wa, va.	kwerenje, wa, va; kampeta, ka, twa.
SPATE, to be in	kutora.	(stream) kuthura.
SPEAK, to	kurongoro; kukamba.	kuti: kuyowoya; kunena; kudumba to be clever in speaking, kusalala lulimi: to speak softly, kudizga.
SPEAR		mkondo, wa, ya.
—butt-end	lisiza, la.	
SPECKLED fowl	nyoli yakuvaravata.	nkuku ya mavarasasa.
SPECTACLES	mbera za m'maso.	
SPEED	luvi, la.	luviro, la, gha.
SPELL, to cast		kusikura: to be under a spell, kusi-kurwa.
SPEND, to		(money &c.) kusakaza: (to spend a day at a place) kutandara.
SPIDER (also its web)	tandaudi, wa, va.	rutatavi, la, gha; duviyuvi, la, gha.
SPILL, to	kukhabwiya.	kutika; kukumpira.
SPIN, to		(top) kuvina:
SPINNING-TOY	bwangati, la.	bwanguru, la, gha.
SPINDLE (for cotton)		njinga, ya, za.
SPINE	msana, wa, ya.	muwongo, wa, ya.
SPIRIT		mzimu, wa, ya: (high spirits) nkumbi zakwera: (unclean spirit) mzimu wa unyakasi: (spirits of the dead) vivanda.
	see maskavi.	see virombo, vimbuza, umphanda, vinyawo.
SPIRITLESS, to be		kugongowa.
SPIRTLE	mdiko, wa, ya.	(for stirring sima) mtiko, wa, ya.
SPIT, to	kupemere mata.	kufunyira mata; kufunya; kutunya.
SPITTLE		mata, gha.
SPLEEN		chibambara, cha, vya.
SPLENDOUR	manyanda, gha.	
SPLINTER, to		kuswanura: (noun) kaswanyu, ka, twa.

259

ENGLISH	TONGA	TUMBUKA
SPLIT, to		(*wood*) (*tr.*) kuʋarura; kuparura; kupandura; (*intr.*) kulanga—*wood split by sun.*
SPOIL, to		(*damage*) kwananga.
SPOILS (of war)		mskowo, wa, ya; *to take*, kuskowa.
SPONGE	buwa, la, gha.	
SPOON	likezo, la, gha.	chandi, cha, vya; (*calabash or wood*).
SPOOR		bondo, la, gha.
SPORTS		*see* chaka.
SPOT		(*on skin or cloth*) banga, la, gha; (*on skin*) chiʋawo, cha, vya; (*on leopard or cloth*) doʋa, la, gha; *to be spotted*, kudoʋa: *a spotted fowl*, nkuku ya maʋarasasa.
SPREAD out, to	kukanga; kutengenduka.	kutanda; kuthaza; kwanika; kuparara.
—abroad, to be		(*information*) kuthuwukwa.
SPRING (well)		chisimi, cha, vya; mbwiwi, ya, za: *to well up as a spring*, kubwibwituka.
SPRING, to	kuzanta.	(*as a leopard*) kunyuntuka: ngwi!
—up, to		kujuruka.
SPRUNG, to be		(*of a trap*) kukwarapuka.
SPRINKLE, to	kupemere; kuwazga.	kumija; kutonyezga; kupementera; (*powder*) kunyunya.
SPROUT, to		kumera; *the early shoots*, mumera, wa, ya: *see* kubanta.
SPUR (of hill)		ndomo, ya, za.
SPUTUM	mankoro, gha.	mankanana, gha; mankananimbwa gha.
SPY		mpachi, ya, za.
SPY, to		kupachira; kuzonda.
SQUANDER, to		kusakaza.
SQUAT, to		kutongomara.
SQUEAK, to		(*of branches of trees rubbing together*) kukwikwina: (*noun*) chikwikwi, cha.
SQUEEZE, to		kufinya; kufyenya; *see* kuʋana.
SQUINT, to		jiso likuʋeʋera.
SQUIRREL		benga, wa, ʋa.
STAB, to		kugwaza; kurasa; kuchonta; *see* kupintuka.
STACK		(*of maize on stalk in garden*) mkukwe, wa, ya.
STAFF		ndodo, ya, za; muchiza, wa, ya.

260

ENGLISH	TONGA	TUMBUKA
STAKE	musu, wa, ya.	(*sharpened for digging*) msonga, wa, ya.
STALK		(*of maize, millet &c.*) pesi, la, gha; pekesi, la, gha: (*of* lupoko) mbuva, ya, za: (*broken stalks of maize &c., left in gardens for cattle food*) viswaulira, vya.
STALK, to		(*game*) kuvenda; kuvezga.
STAMMER	chimama, cha.	
STAMP, to		(*foot*) kudyaka-dyaka; kupondaponda.
STAND, to		kwima; *to stand up*, kwimirira; *to stand firm*, kuchinta; (*caus.*) kuchintiska.
STAR		nyenyezi, ya, za.
STARE, to		kudodoliska; kulaviska dodoli.
START, to	kusoka.	(*set out*) kuwuka; (kudanga, kwamba).
—(in fear)	kulipuka.	kuchiruka; kuchirifuka; kuvwetepuka.
STARTLE, to		kuchiruska; *to be startled*, kuzezeruka.
STARVE, to		kufwa njara.
STATURE		musinku, wa, ya.
STAY, to	kuja; kura.	kukhara; kugova; (*a day*) kutandara.
STEADFAST, to be		kukhwima.
STEAL, to	kuba.	kwiba; kubana.
STEEP, to		(*e.g.* mkusa *in water*) kutupika.
STEERING OAR	sigiru, ya, za.	sigilo, ya, za.
STEP, to		kukanda; kudyaka: *to step up*, kujuruka.
STEPS (walk)	mchapu, wa, ya.	
STERN (of boat)		matambi, gha.
STICK		ndodo, ya, za; muchiza, wa, ya.
—(for digging)	musu, wa, ya.	
STICK INSECT		zombwe, la, gha.
STICK, to		kudemerera; kukanirira; kubata: (*to cling to*) kubatika pa *or* ku; *to stick together*, kubampikana; kukwapatirana: *to stick in a narrow space*, kuphatira: *see* kuweska.
STICKY, to be		kunata; kulenda.
STILL	we che waka.	(*he is still alive*) wachali waka.
STILL, to be		kuzika; kufwasa: *see* kudama and yii!

261

English	Tonga	Tumbuka
STING, to		kuwozga: (noun) luwozga, lwa, gha.
STINGINESS		kasu, la; chigwinini, cha; lwizga, lwa; lukori, lwa; wimi, wa.
STIR, to		(fluid) kuvundura; kutimbula; kuvuwa; kuvindula: (to rouse) kuwuska; kutitimura; kusongerezga; kusampuka.
STOAT		likoti, wa, va.
STOCKADE		linga, la, gha.
STOEP (verandah)		lukoro, lwa, gha.
STOMACH		chifu, cha, vya; (also rufu, la, gha.).
STONE		libwe, la, mawe, gha; (quarry) mwala, wa, miala, ya (Nyanja).
STONE, to		kudina na mawe.
STOOP, to		kubwantuka.
STOP, to		(to stop doing something) kureka; (caus.) kurekeska: (to stop walking or running) kwima; jo! (to come to an end) kugota: (the rain has stopped) vula yakata.
STORE		(for grain) ntamba, ya, za; nkokwe, ya, za.
—(laid up)	mbiku, ya, za.	
STORE, to		kuronga; kurongezga.
STORK	komakachoka, wa.	konongo, la, gha: (hammer-headed stork) katawa, wa, va.
STORM	lirondo, la, gha; chimphunga, cha.	chimtunga, cha vya; chimpupuru, cha, vya.
STORY		makani, gha; ntanti, ya, za; mrandu, wa, ya.
STRADDLE, to		kutangarara.
STRAIGHT, to be		kunyoroka; kurunjika; (tidy) kunozga.
STRAIN, to	kumimita.	kukung'unta.
STRAINER	guntu, la, gha;	kuntu, la, gha.
—(for salt)	chizumbi, cha.	
STRANGE		—yeni: stranger, muyeni, wa, va; mulendo, wa, va.
STREAM	msinji, wa, ya.	mronga, wa, ya.
STRENGTH	ntazi, ya, za.	nkongono, ya, za; lusoko, lwa, gha; mpavu, ya, za; mankharo, gha; unkhara, wa, gha.
STRENGTHEN, to		kukhozga; kukhomeska.
STRETCH, to (as elastic)	kudoromo;	
—(oneself)	kunyururuka;	kubinyuka;
—(legs)	kutambazuwa;	kutambarara;
—(hands)		(to receive a gift) kuthanda.
—(bark cloth)	kunyutuwa;	
—(bow-string)	kupinda.	kutweva.

ENGLISH	TONGA	TUMBUKA
STRETCHER		kasarasara, wa, ʋa.
STRIAE GRAVIDARUM		makanta nchembere, gha.
STRIFE	mlimbano, wa.	mpindano, ya, za; zawe, la, gha.
STRIKE, to	kuchaya; kupuma; kung'anuwa.	kutimba; (on cheek) kupamanta.
STRING	chopwa, la, gha.	chingwe, cha, vya; chigwe, cha, vya; mkusa, wa, ya; nyozi, ya, za.
STRING BEADS, to		kutunga.
STRIP, to		(bark of tree, skin of fruit &c.) kusuʋa: (skin of animal) kufuʋa: (leaves from stem) kuphata; kuswaswata; kupurura.
STRIP (of meat)	muzingu, wa, ya.	
STRIPED, to be		(as zebra) kubyururika.
STRIPES		mbyururu, ya, za; dyeka, la gha.
—(of beating)	mbumu, za.	lukwepo, lwa, gha.
STRIVE, to	kuʋanga.	kulimba-limba; kupiripita; (contest) kulimbana; kupindikana.
STROLL, to		kutambura; kutonya; kunyadira: to go for a stroll, kutembeya: to stroll to and fro in a crowd, kuyingisuka; kupiringuka.
STRONG, to be	kulimba, kurama.	(man) kukhoma: (thing) kukhora.
—man		chinkhara, cha, vya.
STRUGGLE, to		kupiripita.
STUBBORNNESS	liwuma, la.	
STULTIFY, to		kupuvya.
STUMBLE, to		kukhuʋara.
STUMP	chipando, cha; chisina, cha.	chisinga, cha, vya.
—of hoe		chisuka, cha, vya.
STUPIDITY		uzereza, wa.
STUTTER	chikwikwi, cha.	
STYE (on eye)		kasungupoti, ka, twa.
SUBDUE, to		kugoda; kutereska.
SUCK, to		(breast) konka; (sweet) kunyung'umira; (pipe) kukweʋa.
SUCKLE, to		konkeska: to wean (stop suckling) kurumura.
SUDDEN, to be		(of a surprising act) kuchirukizga: suddenly, mabuchibuchi.
SUE, to	kupana.	
SUFFER, to		kukomwa; kusuzgika.

263

English	Tonga	Tumbuka
SUFFERINGS		visuzgo, vya; vipyo, vya.
SUFFICIENT	mbweno.	ndipera: *to be sufficient*, kukwana.
SUGAR-CANE		mujuwa, wa, ya; nyifi, ya, za.
SUGGEST, to		kusachizga; kusayika.
SUGGESTION		fundo, ya, za.
SUIT, to		kuyamo; kwenera.
SULK, to		kukwinyirira.
SUMMARY		(*of a statement*) chipimphia, cha, vya.
SUMMER		chihanya, cha, vya.
SUN	zuʋa, la.	dazi, la.
SUNBEAM		lirazi, la, gha.
SUNRISE		kufuma kwa dazi; kwacha; chimphara, cha.
SUNSET	kusere kwa zuʋa.	kunjira kwa dazi: *see* kupendama.
SUNSHINE	kuʋala.	muhanya, wa: (*cold season*) zuʋa lero chipita mbali, *the sun's course is low in the sky.*
SUPERIOR, to be		kutana.
SUPERSTITION		dongololo, la, gha.
SUPPLE, to be	kulita.	kutepa.
SUPPLIES		(*to draw from store*) kutapa.
SUPPORT		(*forked post*) mpanda, ya, za.
SUPPORT, to		kufighirira.
SURE, to be		kufikapo: kugomekezga.
—to make	kuteska.	kupanikizga.
SURELY		nadi.
SURFEITED, to be		kudindiʋara.
SURPASS, to		kuruska.
SURRENDER, to		kutera.
SURROUND, to	kuzunguriya; kukuka.	kuzingirira: *to be surrounded* (*by trouble*) kuzingwa.
SURPRISED, to be		kuzizwa; kuzukuma.
SUSPEND, to		(*from Church membership*) kusezga: (*see* hang).
SWALLOW, to	kumeza.	kumira.
SWALLOWS		kaʋeru-ʋeru, ka, twa.
SWAMP		chisapa, cha, vya: vwa—vwa!
SWARM (of bees)		mlembwera, wa, ya.
SWAY, to	kundenga-ndenga.	
SWEAR, to		kurapa.

264

English	Tonga	Tumbuka
SWEAT	dukutira, la.	tukutira, la: *to sweat*, kufoma; 'samba tukuta'—*bathe in sweat*.
SWEEP, to	kupeya.	kupyera (*thoroughly*—mpyempyemu): *to sweep away*, kukukura; kuparasura.
SWEET, to be		kunowa; kunong'omera.
SWEETBREAD		kapamba, ka.
SWEETHEART		mubwezi, wa, ʋa: (*also* chibwezi).
SWEET-SOP	mnthopa, wa, ya.	
SWELL, to	kutumbiriya; kututuka.	kutupa: (*grain in water*) kutumpa. *see* kuthumbwa.
SWIM, to		kusambira.
SWING, to	kundengandenga.	kuzung'unya; kudewera; (*noun*) kandewa, ka.
SWITCH		(*for flies*) chowa, la, gha.
SWORD		lupanga, lwa, gha.
SYCOPHANT, to be		kuʋeteka.
SYMBOL		chimanyikwiro, cha, vya.
SYMPATHY		chisungu-sungu, cha, vya.
SYPHILIS	kaswendi, wa.	chindoko, cha.

T

English	Tonga	Tumbuka
TABOO	kwanguzga mwanguzgu.	kuziʋizga; dongololo, li, ma: *it is taboo*, ndi mziro; ndi mwiko.
TACKY, to be		kunata.
TAIL	mchiya, wa, ya;	mchira, wa, ya; chowa, cha, vya:
—(fish)	chifyefye, cha.	(*fish*) chipyepye, cha, vya;
—(fowl)		chisukupiko, cha, vya.
TAKE, to	kutenga;	kutora; kupoka; kuyegha; kusenya;
—(away from)	kutoko;	kutorako; kuwuskapo; kukwakwarizga;
—(off cloth)		kuvura;
—(from fire)	kubuwa;	kupura;
—(out)	kutuzga.	kufumya; kufumiska; kukhutura; (*tooth*) kukhura.
TALE		chirapi, cha, vya; chisiriri, cha, vya.
TALK, to	kurongoro; kukamba.	kuyowoya; kunena.
TALON		njoʋe, ya, za.
TALL		—tari: *taller*, kuʋenuka.
TAMARIND	unyemba, wa.	
TAME, to	kuziʋirizga.	kuzgoʋezga; kuzikiska.
TANGLE, to unravel	kudadauwa.	kutataura.

English	Tonga	Tumbuka
TARRY, to		kudonda; kutandara; kulinda; kuziulika.
TASSELS		(on cloth) mponje, ya, za.
TASTE, to	kulava.	kuyezga; kucheta: to taste nice, kunowa.
TASTELESS, to be	kuropwa.	kuzizima; to eat sima without relish, kusoza.
TATTERS (of mat)	viteketi, vya.	(to be tattered, e.g. book) kupapanyuka.
TATTOO MARKS		mpololo, ya, za.
TAUNT, to		kutombozga.
TAX		msonko, wa, ya; mthulo, wa, ya: to pay tax, kusonka: tax-gatherer, wamsonko, wa.
TEACH, to	kurunguchizga.	kusambizga; teacher, msambizgi, wa, va.
TEAR, to		kuparura; to tear apart, kupwatura;
—(body, as a crocodile)	kufwefwembuwa.	(as thorns) kuzwazwandula: (as wild beast) kutwazura.
TEARS	masozo, gha.	masozi, gha.
TEASE, to		kutombozga.
—out, to		kuswazura; kupapanyura.
TELEGRAM		lamya, la, gha.
TELL, to	kutaula.	kuphalira; kunenera; kuwuzga: (in detail), kukonkoska.
TEMPER IRON, to	kochere maji.	
TEMPEST	chimphunga, cha; lirondo, la, gha.	
TEMPORAL THINGS		vya mvimba.
TEMPT, to	kwesa.	kuyezga; temptations, viyezgo, vya.
TEN	chumi, la, gha.	khumi, la, makumi, gha.
TEND, to		(flocks) kuliska; (the sick) kurwazga.
TENDER		—teta: tender mercy, chiuravi, cha, vya.
—to be	korowa.	
TENDON		msempa, wa, ya.
TENT		hema, la, gha.
TEST, to	kuteska.	kusanda; kwavya; kurozga; kusunta.
TESTICLE		tongo, la, gha.
TESTIFY, to		kupanikizga; kusimikizga.
TESTIMONY	chisimisimi, cha.	ukaboni, wa; chipanikizgo, cha.
THANK, to		kuwonga.
THAT		(pron.) uyo, icho, ilo, &c. (conj.) kuti: in that, mwene, mwakuti.

ENGLISH	TONGA	TUMBUKA
THATCH		uteka, wa, gha.
—to		kwegha; *first row*, kukunga: *to unroof*, kweghula (kweura).
THEE		iwe: (*medial*) -ku-
THEFT		unkhungu, wa, gha.
THEIR		—aʋo.
THEN		ipo; ndipo.
THERE		uko; apo; papo; para.
THEREFORE		ipo; nteura; pa chifukwa icho; (*see* reka).
THESE		aʋa; izi; ivi; agha; &c.
THEY, THEM		iʋo: (*medial*) -ʋa-: (*so for all concords*).
THICKET	lusuwa, la, gha.	matundu, gha; lusukuti, lwa.
THIEF		munkhungu, wa, ʋa; *see* kwiba.
THIGH		chigha, cha, vya; mlezi, wa, ya.
THIN, to be	kuveruka;	(*paper &c.*) kupapatara;
—(person)	konda.	kughanda; kutina; (*caus.*) kutifya;
—to become		kuphapa.
THING		chintu, cha, vya.
THINK, to	kurunguruka; kupima.	kughanaghana; kuranguruka; kuti: *to take thought for*, kwenjerwera.
THIRD		chachitatu, &c.
THIRST		nyota, ya, za.
THIRSTY, to be		komirwa; kufwa chiparanta.
THIS		uyu, uwu, ichi &c. (*all concords*) *also* yuno, chino &c.
THORN		munga, wa, ya; mkwakwazu, wa, ya.
THOROUGHLY		(*e.g. cleaning*) mpyempyemu.
THOSE		aʋo, iyo, ivyo, izo, agho, &c.
THOU, thee		iwe; (*medial*) -ku-.
THOUGH	chingana.	nanga.
THOUGHT		ghano-ghano, la, gha.
THOUSAND		chikwi, cha, vya.
THRASH, to	kutyapa; kukwechuwa.	kunyapula; kudupula; kulikita; kukhwema.
THREAD		uzi, wa, gha (wazi); uzu, wa, gha; *see* lumburwe *and* chopwa.
THREATEN, to		kufinga; kusoka.

English	Tonga	Tumbuka
THREE		—tatu.
THRICE		katatu.
THRILLED, to be		*see* kusampuka.
THRIVE, to	kutipitiya.	kutikita; kudimba.
THROAT		singo, ya, za; chigoromiro, cha, vya:
—to clear the	kukaratuwa.	
THROB, to		kumwetuka.
THRONE		chitengo, cha, vya; chizumbe, cha, vya.
THRONG, to		kutirimuka.
THROUGH		*to pierce,* kuporota mukati: *to pass through a place,* kusorota.
THROW, to		kuponya;
—(away)	kujowo.	kutaya; kujowora; kuparasura; (*water*) kutira; kwita;
—(down)		kutenyura.
THUMB		chigunwe, cha, vya.
THUNDER		chindindindi, cha; kugunda; kudumira: vula yikududumizga, *it is thundering.*
THUS	viyo.	nteura.
THY, THINE		—ako.
TICK		karani, la, gha; nkufu, ya, za; (*on fowls' eyes*) chimpumba, cha, vya.
TICKLE, to	kuchirikita.	kunyenyenka.
TIE, to	kumanga.	kukaka; kutaʋa: *to tie (one's cloth) firmly,* kuchinya; kuʋwara vikwezga.
TILL		mpaka; kufikira ku; *see* kusuka.
TILT, to		kurandalika; kugodobola.
TIMBER (kinds)		mlombwa, mbawa, muwura, &c.
TIME		nyengo, ya, za; *former times* nyengo za kale; *present time,* nyengo za makono: *what time is it?* dazi liri uli?
TINKLE, to		(*ankle bells*) yikulira were-were-were.
TIP UP, to		kupizgura.
TIRED, to be		kuvuka; kulema; vyalema! marundi yii! marundi pori!
TO		ku; kwa.
TOAD	chuwa, wa, ʋa.	chuli, wa, ʋa; tuʋi, wa, ʋa.
TOAST, to		kunyaska.
TOBACCO	fodia, wa.	hona, la, gha; foro, la, gha.

ENGLISH	TONGA	TUMBUKA
TO-DAY	msana wa le.	lero; muhanya uno.
TOE		munwe, wa, ya: *the great toe*, chigunwe, cha. vya.
TOGETHER		pamoza (pamo).
TOILET (leaves for cleaning child)	chikata, cha.	
TOKEN		chimanyikwiro, cha, vya.
TOMATO		pwetekiri, wa, ʋa; mate-mate, gha.
TOMB		dindi, la, gha; mararo, gha: *see* mpungo.
TO-MORROW	mawa.	namachero.
TONGS		mbano, ya, za.
TONGUE	lilimi, la, gha.	lulimi, lwa, gha.
TO-NIGHT		usiku uno.
TOOTH		jino, la, mino, gha; *see* songambwa *and* chibwanyu: *tooth-brush (twig)* mswaju, wa, ya.
TOP (spinning)		nguli, ya, za: (*to whip*, kuchaya).
—(calabash)	mbera, ya, za.	sikwa, ya, za. (kuponya, *to spin to goals*).
TOP of a roof	chikungu, cha.	chikurupati, cha, vya.
TORCH		chenje, cha, vya; lumbuni, lwa, gha.
—(trees for making)	chisarayi, cha; mlemba, wa, ya.	
TORMENT, to		kutombozga.
TORTOISE	fuwu, wa, ʋa.	furu, wa, ʋa.
TORTUOUS, to be		kuzweta.
TORTURE, to		kutombozga; kuʋana; kunyungura.
TOTTER, to		(*as an infant*) kunyanyata.
TOUCH, to		kukwaska: *don't touch*, reka kukasa-kasa.
TOUGH, to be	kurama.	kukhora.
TOW (for wick)	chisunda, cha.	makochi, gha.
TOWER		(*e.g. of church*) musonji, wa, ya.
TOWN		muzi, wa, ya; msumba, wa, ya.
TRACHEA		chigoromiro, cha, vya.
TRACK	mphindu, ya, za.	ntowa, ya, za; mkwevu, wa, ya; (*of game*) mukwara, wa, ya; (*of cattle*) muzira, wa, ya.
TRADE, to		kugulana: *see* maronda.
TRADITION		mdauko, wa, ya.
TRAIL		(*e.g. of snake*) mukwevu, wa, ya.
TRAIN		njanji, ya, za.

English	Tonga	Tumbuka
TRANSGRESS, to		(*the law*) kujumpa; kujuvya. *transgressions*, majuvyo, gha.
TRANSLUCENT, to be	kuveruka.	
TRANSPARENT, to be		kulangara.
TRANSPLANT, to	kuwoka	kutopora.
TRAP (kinds of)	chipinga, cha; chivana, cha; diva, la.	chipingo, cha, vya; nkoka, ya, za; msampa, wa, ya; chisali, cha, vya; chipanga, cha, vya; chivwamba, cha, vya; mbuna, ya, za; khono, la, gha.
TRAP, to		kutya: *see* konja *and* kuwonja.
TRAVEL		ulendo, wa, gha:
TRAVEL, to		kwenda; kuya; kupita: *to travel about*, kuyinga-yinga.
TRAVELLER		mulendo, wa, va.
TREAD upon, to		kukanda; kudyaka; kufyadulira pasi.
TREASURE	mbiku, ya, za.	chuma, cha, vya; ukwewu, wa, gha.
TREE	muti, wa, ya.	kuni, la, gha.
TREMBLE, to	kunjenjeme.	kutentema; kumbwambwanta: *tremor (of illness)* dumbi, la, gha.
TRENCH		ngarandi, ya, za.
TRIALS		malwavyo, gha.
TRIBE		fuko, la, gha; mtundu, wa, ya: *tribal marks*, simbo, ya, za.
TRIBUTARY		(*to river*) mpalika, ya, za.
TRIBUTE		zitero, za; mithulo, ya: *to pay tribute*, kuthura mithulo.
TRICKS		mayere, gha.
TRIFLE, to		kutonyora; kuchita phompha.
TRIGGER (of trap)	mtazi, wa, ya.	
TRIUMPH over, to		kugorolera.
TROT, to		kuchapula.
—(of donkey)	chitipi-chitipi.	
TROUBLE		suzgo, ya, za; malwavyo, gha; vipakarara, vya.
TROUBLE, to		kusuzga; kuzigha; kuzotofya: *to be troubled (in spirit)* kukweveka.
TRUANT, to play		kugwenta.
TRULY		nadi.
TRUMPET		(*horn*) mbata, ya, za; (*bugle*) lipenga, la.
TRUNK (tree)	chisina, cha.	chisinko, cha, vya; (*elephants*) mulembi, wa, ya; (*body*) chiviriviri, cha, vya.

ENGLISH	TONGA	TUMBUKA
TRUSS (calico)	mtumba, wa, ya.	mlimba, wa, ya.
TRUST, to		kugomezga; kutamira; *see* kudinganya, *and* kunyenkama.
TRUTH		unenesko, wa: *to tell the truth,* kuneneska.
TRY, to	kwesa.	kuyezga; *to try hard,* kulimba-limba; kuzukika.
TSETSE FLY		kaskembe, wa, ʋa;
TUFT (of grass)		chiputu, cha, vya.
TUMULT		chiwawa, cha, vya; mfundukutu, wa, ya.
TURN, to		kuzgora; kung'anamula: *to turn oneself,* kuzgoka: *to turn over,* kugadabura; kugadamiska; kuvunamiska: *to turn one's back on,* kurata nkonto ku, *or* kugata nkonto ku.
TURN (boat), to	kupepetuwa.	
TURTLE	nkhasi, ya, za.	
TWENTY	machumi ghaʋi.	makumi ghaʋiri.
TWICE		kaʋiri.
TWILIGHT	.	*see* marazi.
TWINS		ʋana ʋa mleza; *or* ʋana ʋa muwoli *the first* (*if male*) fumu, ya; *or* mwiza, wa; (*if female*) kamuwoli, ka: *the second,* sinya, wa; *or* nyuma, wa.
TWIST, to		kunyongorora; (*in making string*) kuposa;
—off		kuwunguzura; kunyunkutura.
TWITCHING		(*of animal after death*) *see* marunga.
TWITTER, to		(*birds*) kuchweta.
TWO	—ʋi.	—ʋiri: *second,* wa chiʋiri (*as concords*).

U

UDDER	be, la, gha.	bere, la gha; chimizi, cha, vya. (kumita).
ULCER		chironda, cha, vya.
ULULATION	kululutiya.	kampundu, ka.
UNBROKEN	cha mphumpu.	cha mburuma.
UNCLE		(*father's side*) dada, wa, ʋa; (*mother's side*) nyinarumi, wa, ʋa; msibweni, wa, ʋa.
UNCLEANNESS		unyakasi, wa, gha; uzaghali, wa, gha.
UNCOVER, to		kubenekura.

ENGLISH	TONGA	TUMBUKA
UNDER		musi; kusi; (pasi).
UNDERSTAND, to	kuwamo; kuziviska.	kumanyiska; kupulikiska: *the understanding*, mano, gha.
UNDRESS, to	kuzuuwa.	(*self*) kuvura; (*another*) kuvuriska.
UNFOLD, to		kutambazura.
UNITE, to		kurunga; kubampikana.
UNLESS		kwambura kuti.
UNLUCKY, to be		kusikurwa.
UNRAVEL, to	kudadauwa.	kutataura; kusasatura.
UNROLL, to		kuzingura; kutandika.
UNROOF, to	kuchinduwa.	kupasula.
UNTIL		mpaka; kufikira ku; *see* kusuka.
UNWILLING, to be		kudonda.
UNWILLINGNESS		mphwayi, ya, za; chigwinini, cha, vya: (*reluctance to part with things*) kasu, la.
UNWIND, to		kupomborora.
UNYIELDING, to be		kungangamika—nga-nga-nga!
UPBRAID, to		kutombozga.
UPLIFTED, to be		kukwezgeka nkumbi.
UPON		pa.
UPRIGHT, to be		kunyoroka; kurunjika.
UPROAR		chiwawa, cha: kuwawata.
UPROOT, to		kutopora; kupikura; kunyimpura.
UPSET, to		kugadabura.
UPSIDE-down,	kuvunika;	kubenekera; kuvunamiska; kung'anamula;
—to turn	kusulika.	kugadamiska.
URETHRA	kantorozi, ka.	
URGE, to		kuchiska; kuchichizga.
URINE	makozo, gha.	matuzi, gha.
—to pass	kukoza.	kutunda.
URTICARIA		manyaviri, gha.
US	ifwe.	ise: (*medial*) -ti-.
USEFUL, to be		kuva na kalimo.
USELESSLY		waka; dara.
UVULA		kabantira, ka, twa.

V

VAGINA	msome, wa; nthowa, ya;	chori, cha, vya.
—(occlusion)	we ndi jarawe; we ndi mwa; we ndi nguli.	

ENGLISH	TONGA	TUMBUKA
VAIN, to be		kujiʋikamo.
VALLEY		dambo, la, gha; mpata, wa, ya; mwanya, wa, ya.
VALUE		kazirwiro, ka; mtengo, wa, ya; *see* kufwa.
—thing of		chi ɖimo; ukwewu, wa.
———of no v.		chi..ɯu cha waka; chichwapi, cha, vya; chintu chambura kalimo kene-kene.
VALUABLE, to be		kuzirwa; kukweuka.
VANITY (worthless)	umbuuya, wa.	
VARY, to	kusaʋasaʋa.	kusarasata.
VEINS		mikoli, ya.
VENGEANCE	thayu, la.	nduzga, ya.
VENUS (planet)		chipurausiku, wa.
VERANDAH		konde, la, gha; lukoro, lwa, gha; lufuka, lwa, gha: (wandulo).
VERDIGRIS	biriʋiri, la.	
VERY	ukongwa.	chomene; -vi (kachokovi, *very small*); *very well*, makora ghene: *see* maʋika.
VESSEL		(*sailing*) chombo, cha, vya; ngaraʋa, ya, za; (*utensil*) chiyaʋiro, cha, vya.
VEX, to		kusuzga.
VICINITY, to be in the		kutyana na.
VIEW, to		kutaʋa-taʋa; kutambwa.
VIGOUR		mankharo, gha.
VILE THINGS	utokosi, wa.	ukazuzi, wa.
VILLAGE		muzi, wa, ya; kaya, la, vikaya, vya.
VINE	mphereska, ya.	mupeska, wa, ya.
VIOLIN		*see* kaligu.
VIRGIN		mwali, wa, ʋa; msungwana waku-langwa.
VISCOUS, to be		kulenda.
VISIBLE things		*see* kuvimba.
VISION		mboniwoni, ya, za.
VISIT, to		kuchezga; kupempura; kwende-rana.
VOICE		mazgu, gha.
VOMIT, to		kuwukura.
VOW, to		kurapa.

S

English	Tonga	Tumbuka
WAGES		njombe, ya, za; mpoto, ya, za; malipiro, gha.
WAGTAIL		kavizu-vizu, ka, twa; katye-tye, ka, twa.
WAIT, to		kulinda; kutandara; kusimpa.
WAKEN, to	kuyuka.	kuwuka (tr. kuwuska); kupampuka (tr. kupampuska).
WALK, to		kwenda; to walk in line, kundonda; to walk sedately, kutonya; to walk unsteadily (as a drunk man) kwenda pentya-pentya: to teach (e.g. a child) to walk, kunyanyaska, kuteteska.
WALL		(of house) chimati, cha, vya; chiliva, cha, vya: (round village) linga, la, gha; boma, la.
WALLOW, to		(on ground) kujivivika pasi.
WANDER, to	kulankasa.	kuranda.
WANT	usiwa, wa.	ukavu, wa; msara, wa; usauchi, wa.
WANT, to		kukhumba; kusauka; kukavuka; kusokwa.
WANTING, to be		kulije; kulive; kulivye: kwambura.
WAR		nkondo, ya, za; warrior, wankondo, wa, va: an overwhelming attack, nkondo ya kamrupuri.
WARD off, to		(danger) kupháska; kuphasizga.
WARM, to be	kufunda.	kutukira.
WARMTH	chifundizi, cha.	chithukivu, cha.
WARN, to	kucheweska.	kuchenjezga: (rebuke) kulanga; kusoka.
WART		susuva, ya, za.
WASH, to (dish)		kusuka; kusinga; kusukuruzga:
—(clothes)		kuchapa:
—(hands)		kugeza; kukarava:
—(own body)	kowa;	kusamba;
—(another)	koweska;	kusavya; kukaravya; kugurumura:
—(hands of an affair)	kusasa manja; kusasamo.	
WASHED away, to be		(gully) kugumuka.
—out, to be		(colour of cloth) kusayuka; kuvuvutuka.
WASTE, to		kusakaza; kutaya waka.
WATCH, to		kulinda; kukhazga; kulavira: to be sleepless, kucherezga.

ENGLISH	TONGA	TUMBUKA
WATCH-HUT		(*in garden*) chilindo, cha, vya; ndinda, ya, za.
WATCHMAN		mlinda, wa, va. (Nyanja, mlonda).
WATER		maji, gha: *cool water from spring*, maji gha mbwiwi.
WATER-BRASH		dungulira, la.
WATER-BUCK		chuzu, wa, va.
WATERSPOUT	kanthenga, wa.	kavuru-vuru, wa, va.
WATTLE WALL		chiliva, cha, vya.
WAVE		jigha, la, gha.
—to	*see* kukhabwiya.	(*flag*) kukupura.
WAY	nthowa, ya, za.	ntowa, ya, za.
WAY, in this	viyo.	nteura.
WAX		(*bees'*) pura, la, gha.
—(in ear)	mbowuwowo, za.	
WE, US	ifwe.	ise: *with verb*, ti-, *and medial* -ti-.
WEAK		—techi.
—to be	kuropwa.	kutomboroka; kuworofoka; kutempenta; *see* kutepeta: *to weaken*, kutifya.
WEAKLY PERSON		chifwafwa, cha, vya.
WEAKNESS		utechitechi, wa, gha; untomboro, wa, gha.
WEALTH	usambasi, wa; uromba, wa.	usambazi, wa, gha; chuma, cha, vya.
WEAN, to		kurumura; kutumbirizga.
WEAPONS	vidya, vya.	mahomwa, gha.
WEAR, to		(*clothes*) kuvwara: *to wear out* (*old clothes*) kusukuruzga; *to wear off*, *see* kurakata: *to be worn away*, kuskengeka.
WEARY, to be		kuvuka; kulema (vyalema).
WEASEL		likoti, wa, va.
WEAVE, to		kuruka; *see* kusanda.
WEB (spider's)	tandaudi, wa, va.	rutatavi, la, gha.
WEDGE		chirozgo, cha, vya.
WEED		nchesa, ya, za; thondo, la.
WEED, to		kuchesa; kutipa; kuharura.
WEEP, to	kuliya.	kulira masozi.
WEEVIL		fufuzi, ya, za.
WEIGH, to	kutompo.	kupima; *to weigh down*, kunyekezga; kuponderezga.
WELCOME, to		kupokerera; kuhenera; kwankira.

ENGLISH	TONGA	TUMBUKA
WELL		chisimi, cha, vya.
WELL UP, to		(*spring of water*) kubwibwituka: *see* kufunka.
WELL (adv.)		makora.
WELL, to look		(*face*) kuphotoka; *to be well* (*well-being*) kuchenjereketa.
WERSH, to be	kuropwa.	kuzizima. (*as* dendi *without salt*).
WEST		ku manjiriro gha dazi; ku zambwe.
WET, to be		kuzumbwa; kunyewa.
WHACK, to		*see* kukwapa.
WHAT?		nchichi? uli? mbu? *what does he say?* wakuti mbu? *what about it?* ndiko nkwachi? ndivyo nvyachi? kunachipo?
WHEAL	buli, la, gha; chikukusa, cha.	(*of chikoti*) mingunguma, ya; mitupi, ya: mvimbi, wa, ya.
WHEAT		trigu, wa, ʋa.
WHEEL		njinga, ya, za.
WHEN		(*relative*) apo; para; penepapo; mwene: *when he had done*, wakati wachita.
WHEN?		pauli? pa mbu? zuʋachi? dazichi? pa dazi ndi?
WHERE		(*relative*) apo; uko; umo:
WHERE?		nku? mpa? *whereabouts?* ku dera nku?
WHEREFORE		(*relative*) ipo; nteura; chifukwa icho.
WHEREFORE?	chifukwa chine?	chifukwa nchichi?
WHETHER...OR	chingana...... chingana.	panji... panji; nanga...pakunji; chankuru......chankuru.
WHEY		mraza, wa.
WHICH		(*relative*) uyo, ilo, icho (*as concord*).
WHICH?	—ne?	nju? ngu? nchi? nji? &c. (*as concord*).
WHINE, to		*see* kuninizika.
WHIP		chikoti, cha, vya; (*birch*) luswazu, lwa, gha.
WHIP, to		kutyapula.
WHIRLWIND		kavuru-vuru, wa, ʋa.
WHISPER, to	kutokotezga.	kutokotoska; kupwepwa.
WHISTLE, to		kulizga kaluvi.
WHISTLE, a	kawuzi, ka.	pito, la, gha.
WHITE		—tuʋa: *a white man*, mzungu, wa ʋa.

English	Tonga	Tumbuka
WHITLOW		kasuli, ka; katungu, wa; (*blistering the skin*) kafurifuri, wa: *medicine for whitlow*, sakazinje, wa, va.
WHO		(*relative—as corresponding demonstrative*).
WHO?	ndi yani?	njani? vakudanga ndi mba? *who are the first?*
WHOLE	—mphumpu.	—ose; —mburuma; —zirima.
WHOLENESS		(*health*) *see* msuma.
WHOOPING-COUGH		chikoso-koso, cha, vya.
WHY	chifukwa chine?	chifukwa nchichi?
WICK (of lamp)		chisunda, cha, vya; nkorezezgo, ya, za.
WIDE		—sani: *widespread*, chisani-sani.
WIDOW	choko, cha, vya.	chokoro, cha, vya.
WIDOW'S CAP	mraza, wa, ya.	chingwazi, cha, vya: (*strings on chest*) zintambo, za.
WIFE		muwoli, wa, va: *second wife of same family*, mbirigha, wa, va (*or* ya, za).
WILD BEAST		chikoko, cha, vya.
WILDERNESS		chiparamba, cha, vya; malo gha mapopa.
WILFULLY		nchene.
WILL		khumbo, la, gha: *to be willing*, mtima uli mchanya kale kuchita.
WILL (testament)	marayi, gha.	*see* kulayira.
WIND		mpepo, ya, za; *south-east wind*, mwela, wa: (*of game, see* mtunga).
WIND, to	kuzingizga; kupaka.	kuzinga; kupomba; kukurunga.
WINDOW		dangazi, la, gha.
WINE		vinyo, la.
WING	papiko, la, gha.	papindo, la, gha; papa, la, gha.
WINK, to	kukupiya.	kupayira; kuphinya.
WINNOW, to		kwera; kupeta.
WINTER		chipwe-pwe, cha, vya; chifuku, cha, vya.
WIPE, to	kuleska.	kufyura: (*water off anything*) kukurumura: (*sima off fingers*) kukatura.
—an infant	kupipa.	
WISDOM		mahara, gha; zeru, za; vinjeru, vya; mano, gha.
WISE		—chenjezi: *in no wise*, na pantini pose chara.

English	Tonga	Tumbuka
WISH, to	kulembe.	kukhumba; kupenja.
WITCHCRAFT		ufwiti, wa; uhavi, wa; maula, gha; seketera, la.
WITCH-DOCTORS		vafwiti, va; vahavi, va; vachanusi, va.
WITH	ndi.	na; pamoza na.
WITHER, to		(plant) kufota: (withered arm) woko lakuphapa, or lakukwinyata.
WITHHOLD, to		kunora.
WITHIN	mu; mo; mwenimo.	mu; umo; mukati; mwenemuno.
WITHOUT (lack)		—amzira; —ambura: to be without, kwambura; kwamzira; kuwura: see kusova.
WITNESS, a		kaboni, wa, va.
—to		kupanikizga; kusimikizga.
WOE TO YOU!		soka kwaku imwe! timukawone!
WOMAN	muntukazi, wa.	mwanakazi, wa, va. (see chijiti and nchembere).
WOMB	nyalibaza, ya.	nthumbo, ya, za; chibabiro, cha, vya.
WONDER		muntondwe, wa, ya.
—to		kuzizwa; kuzukuma; kutondwa.
WOOD (material)		kuni, la, gha; tabwa, la, gha: firewood, nkhuni, ya, za.
—(forest)	lusuwa, la.	nkorongo, ya za; thengere, la, gha.
WOODPECKER		gong'onta, wa, va.
WOOL		(sheep's) weya, wa, gha; (for knitting) uzi, wa, gha; uzu, wa, gha: (cottonwool) tonje, la, gha.
WONT, to be	kuziviriya.	kuzgovera.
WORD	mazu, gha	mazgu, gha: (liu and lizgu also heard).
WORK		nchito, ya, za; mlimo, wa, ya.
—to	kutata nchito.	kuchita; kukora nchito; kulima: to work without mid-day rest, kuchezera.
WORK HARD, to	kutakataka; kufyapuwa.	kutuntika: (see chowa lakwera.)
WORLD		charu, cha, vya.
WORM		mnyororo, wa, ya; msundu, wa, ya; (blind worm) mlinga, wa, ya; (maggot) mporozi, ya, za; (thread-worm) nthabani, za.
WORM-EATEN, to be		kufutwa; kufufurwa.

ENGLISH	TONGA	TUMBUKA
WORN away, to be		kuskengeka; kusoya.
WORRY, to		kukweveka.
WORSHIP, to		kusopa.
WORTHY of, to be		kwenera.
WORTHLESSNESS	umbuuya, wa.	upwafu, wa: *worthless people*, vauli-uli.
WOULD		(*would that I might help you*) ndakhumba kuti nga ndingakovwira).
WOUND		bamba, la, gha: *to wound*, kurasa; kupweteka.
WRAP, to		kufuka; kuvungira; kuzinga: *self*) *in blanket*) kudika; (*another*) kudikiska.
WRATH	kandundu, ka.	mbembe, ya, za; ukali, wa, gha; kukaripa.
WRECK, to		kubudubura.
WRESTLE, to		kulimbana; (met. *against evil*) kulimba-limba.
WRING, to		(*e.g. wet cloth*) kukama.
WRINKLES		(*on face*) mankwinya, gha; (*on body, or cloth*) mankwanda, gha.
WRITE, to		kulemba; kusimba: *writing*, lembo, la, gha.
WRITHE, to		kuvivira.
WRONG		(*adj.*) —heni: *to do wrong*, kubuda; kuchimwa; kusovya.

X

XYLOPHONE	mangurongondo, gha.	

Y

YAM		linyanya, la, gha; chiyao, cha, vya.
YARD (of house)		chipanga, cha, vya; luvaza, lwa, gha: boma, la, gha.
YAWN		mwawu, wa, ya; *to yawn*, kwaura mwawu.
YAWS	magava-gava, gha.	
YEAR		chirimika, cha, vya; mwaka, wa, ya; chaka, cha, vya.
YEARN OVER, to	kumiziriya.	kumiririra (mata).
YEAST		chirungo, cha; chimera, cha; ndungu, ya.
YELLOW	kufyuvara; —fyu.	—swesi; —pyu. (kupyururukira).

ENGLISH	TONGA	TUMBUKA
YES		inya; (*emphatic*) inya cha; yevo.
YESTERDAY	zana.	mayiro: *the day before yesterday*, juzl.
—day before	ku tangi.	
YET		(*but*) kweni; ndipo uli: (*we have not yet done it*) tindachite.
YIELD, to	korowa.	kutera: *see* kupyorera msoro.
YOKE		goriwori, la, gha.
YONDER		uko; kura.
YOU		imwe; (*with verb*) mu-; (*medial*) -mu-: *you boy*! wa mwana! *you deceiver*! wa mpusikizgi!
YOUNG	—mana.	—choko.
YOUR		—inu.
YOUTH	wana, wa.	wanichi, wa.
—a	mvurwa, wa, va.	pungwe, wa, va.

Z

ZEAL		pampu, la, gha; mwampu, wa; pyumpyu, la.
ZEBRA		bori, wa, va.

APPENDIX

LIST OF NAMES OF BIRDS KINDLY SUPPLIED BY REV. W. P. YOUNG

HENGA	CONCORD	ENGLISH
Baka (ma)	ili	Duck
Bwabwarara	uyo	Nightjar—cf. Linkuwi
Byambyali	uyo	Gray headed Sparrow—cf. Khwerenje
Chibave	uyo	Osprey
Chabwerekera	uyo	Black cap Bulbul—cf. Matotero
Chagaga	uyo	Robin Chat ("Heuglins")
Chihovi	(wa)	Crow or Raven
Chakupompa	uyo	Red-chested Cuckoo
Chakupusa	uyo	Pale Flycatcher
Chibuntu	uyo	Crombee (Tail-less Warbler)
Chibwitinkanga	ichi	Pytelia (Finch)
Chigoga	ichi	Giant Heron or Stork—cf. Khonongo
Chikweyukweyu	ichi	Francolin ("Partridge")
Chimbuvi	ichi	Quail—cf. Zwili
Chimpanga	ichi	Black Harrier—Hawk
Chimphungu	ichi	Bateleur (Tail-less Eagle)
Chiruma	ichi	Black-collared Barbet
Chohelo	uyo	Scimitar-billed Hoopoe
Dunduru	uyo	Ruddy Waxbill
Fefe	uyo	Mosilikatze Roller
Fulumbe	uyo	Black Widow-bird
Fyongo	uyo	Sunbird—cf. Jongwe, Songwe
Fyukuku	iyi	Mouse-bird—cf. Sghazi
Gong'onta	uyo	Woodpecker
Hekeya	(ma)	Kirk's Babbler
Horo	uyo	Button Quail
Jongwe	uyo	Sunbirds
Kaba	uyo	Blue Spotted Wood Dove
Kabave	uyo	Yellow-billed Kite—cf. Nyalweve
Kachikonkoro	uyo	Black and white Flycatcher

281

APPENDIX

HENGA	CONCORD	ENGLISH
Kakarundundu	uyo	Little Sandpiper
Kakova	uyo	White Egret—cf. Nyanginyangi
Kalikorombe	uyo	Kingfishers (Lake Shore)
Kamkuvezi	uyo	Black Shouldered Kite
Kamkwichi	uyo	Pin-tailed Widow Bird
Kamzengamuzi	uyo	Pied Wagtail—cf. *Katyetye*
Kapurumpembe	uyo	Little Owls
Kasaranyanda	uyo	Tinker Bird
Kasekerezgani	aka	Seed Eaters
Kasisisi	aka	Blue Waxbill
Katava	uyo	Hammerhead Stork
Katimbiri	uyo	Long-tailed ("Namaqua") Dove
Katumbura Mbeva	uyo	Long-tailed black and white Shrike ("Fiscal")
Katyetye	aka	Pied Wagtail
Kavandwe	uyo	Lizard-Buzzard
Kaverovero	uyo	Swallows, Swifts, Martins
Kayewere	aka	Common Waxbill
Kayuwuru	aka	Hooded Finch
Khupe	uyo	Larger Red-eyed Dove
Khuvi	(ma)	Vulture
Khwerenje	uyo	Larger (Brown-headed) Parrot (but used for Gray headed Sparrow in Ekwendeni)
Khwiriri	uyo	Larger Red Wing Starling
Khwita	(wa)	Owl—cf. Phururu
Konongo	ili	White Stork (Migrant)
Lohera	uyo	cf. Kavandwe
Lukoma	uyo	Crowned Hornbill
Lunkhuwi	uyo	Standard Wing Nightjar
Luvi	uyo	Paradise Flycatcher—cf. *Tyeda*
Masokoyezi	ili	cf. Viyowoyero
Matovero	uyo	cf. Chabwerekera
Mazere	uyo	Meyer's Parrot
Mbuyi	iyi	Sea-gull
Mchakahuve	uyo	Black and White Bush Shrike
Mfuko	uwo	Coucal
Mperempi	iyi	Nyika Francolin
Mphembya	iyi	Tern
Mpheta	iyi	Bishop-birds and Weaver birds
Msuko	uyo	White-eye

APPENDIX

HENGA	CONCORD	ENGLISH
Msuwi	uyo	Gray Lourie ("Go-away" bird)
Mgubani	uwo	Senegal Bush Shrike
Mukwevavyamba	uyo	Bee Eaters
Mukokafodya	uyo	Bee Eaters
Mulititi	uyo (uwo)	Ground Hornbill
Mung'ombwa	uwo	Ground Hornbill
Muntyengo	uyo	Drongo and Black Flycatcher
Mwanawawa	uyo	Glossy Ibis—cf. Vihaha
Mwilo	uyo	Puff-Back Shrike
Nchekenene	iyi	Golden breasted Bunting
Nchepe	iyi	Nyika Warbler
Ndhlurudhluru (Hluruhluru)	iyi	Livingstone's Lourie and purple Lourie (Turaco)
Nduvaruva	iyi	do do do
Ng'onga	iyi	Grey Hornbill (South African)
Ng'wali	iyi	Crested Crane
Njiva	iyi	Common Dove
Njoyo	iyi	Cormorant
Nombo	iyi	Martial Eagle
Nyangi-nyangi	iyi	Paddy bird ("Egret")
Nyalweve	uyo	Yellow billed Kite—cf. Kabave
Nkarimbo	aka	Lesser Red Wing Starling
Nkolikoli	iyi	Plover
Nkombokombo	iyi	Green Pigeon
Nkukuruji	iyi	Black Crake or Reed Hen
Nkuruwara	iyi	Crested Hoopoe ("South African")
Nkwali	iyi	Common Francolin ("Partridge")
Nkwazi	iyi	Sea-Eagle
Nkwazi-Nyika	iyi	Vulturine Sea-Eagle
Phururu	uyo	Owl
Pipiyo	uyo	Common Thrush ("Kurrichaine")
Pyogo	uyo	Black-headed Oriole
Sekwa	(vi)	Goose
Sghazi	iyi	cf. Fyukuku—Mouse birds
Solo	iyi	Honey-Guides
Songwe	uyo	cf. Jongwe—Sunbirds

APPENDIX

HENGA	CONCORD	ENGLISH
Titi	uyo	Wren-Warblers
Tyeda	uyo	cf. Luvi—Paradise Flycatcher
Tyeme	uyo	Golden Weaver birds
Vihaha	ichi	Ibis cf. Mwanawawa
Viyowoyero	ivi	Wood-Hoopoes cf. Masokoyezi
Wakharapochi	uyo	Black Cuckoo
Wando	uyo	Gray Helmet Shrike
Zwili	uyo	Quail cf. Chimbuvi

Lightning Source UK Ltd.
Milton Keynes UK
18 September 2010

159925UK00001B/18/A

9 789990 814149